Beginning
to See
the Light

Ellen Willis

Beginning
to See
the Light

Pieces of a Decade

Alfred A. Knopf   New York   1981

THIS IS A BORZOI BOOK
PUBLISHED BY ALFRED A. KNOPF, INC.

Library of Congress Cataloging in Publication Data
Willis, Ellen.
Beginning to see the light.
I. Title.
AC8.W66   081   80-22890
ISBN 0-394-51137-9

Manufactured in the United States of America
First Edition

For Karen, M, and the Sex Fools

Contents

Contents

Acknowledgments

I want first of all to thank my close friends, feminist co-conspirators, and colleagues at the *Village Voice*, Karen Durbin and M. Mark. They have officially or informally edited many of the pieces in this book, as well as freely shared their insights into politics, music, sex, love, friendship, my virtues and faults. Next, I owe an enormous intellectual debt to the women's liberation movement. A comprehensive list of feminists who have influenced my ideas on sexual politics would have to include all present and past members of the unnamed women's liberation group I've belonged to for five years, my former associates in New York Radical Women and the original Redstockings, and dozens of other women. But I am especially grateful to Rosalyn Baxandall, Bonnie Bellow, Cindy Carr, Judy Coburn, Deirdre English, Shulamith Firestone, Brett Harvey, Susan Lee, Irene Peslikis, Kathie Sarachild, Alix Kates Shulman, Ann Snitow, and Katy Taylor.

My writing on rock-and-roll and popular culture reflects the pervasive influence of Bob Christgau and Greil Marcus. Bob convinced me, back in 1966, that journalism was a plausible way to make a living, and wangled me assignments to get me started.

Acknowledgments

William Shawn, who brought me to *The New Yorker* and edited my column, *Rock, Etc.*, gave me the space and encouragement to develop my central ideas about the music and its social context. My article on Janis Joplin owes a good deal to discussions with Susan Lydon and to her review, written with David Getz, of two Joplin biographies.

Mike Willis, Denah and Noach Weinberg, and the Orthodox Jewish community of Jerusalem shared with me their knowledge of Judaism and their spiritual insights, and relentlessly challenged all my secular assumptions. My encounter with them not only became the material of "Next Year in Jerusalem" but permanently affected my sense of myself as a Jew and a woman—though not in the way they would have liked. Elsworth Baker has helped me to confront my emotional conflicts, a process that has also changed my perception of myself and the world, and therefore the way I write.

As my editor at *Rolling Stone*, Marianne Partridge always pushed me to do my best work; I am particularly indebted to her for persuading me to undertake "Next Year in Jerusalem" and for making suggestions that immeasurably improved "The Trial of Arline Hunt." Jann Wenner of *Rolling Stone* is the only magazine editor I know who would have paid for me to go to Israel to investigate Orthodox Judaism, then given me 20,000 words' worth of space to describe a failed conversion experience. David Schneiderman's respect for writers and commitment to free discussion have made the *Voice* a happy and exciting place to work. After a year of telling myself I would write about anti-Semitism someday when I had the time, I wrote "The Myth of the Powerful Jew" because David asked me to comment on the Andrew Young affair and have it in, please, by the end of the week. I am also grateful to my editor at Knopf, Victoria Wilson, for her encouragement and editorial suggestions; to Ruth Peltason for technical assistance; and to my agent, Betty Anne Clarke, for her business advice and personal support.

Finally, I would like to acknowledge the Greenwich Village

Acknowledgments

restaurants at which large chunks of this book were written—
Elephant & Castle, the Salaam Restaurant, and the Peacock Caffè.

———————

Since I believe that journalism exists in and draws much of its
meaning from a specific historical context, I have done a minimum
of editing on these articles. In some pieces I have made minor
stylistic changes; in others I felt that improvements would falsify
the spirit of the writing. In a few articles I have added, expanded,
condensed, or clarified ideas, but I have made no changes inspired
by political or intellectual hindsight; rather, where I've felt the
need, I've quarreled with myself in footnotes. The date at the end
of each piece indicates when it was written, not when it was
published, though in most cases there was no significant gap between the two.

E.W.

Introduction

Until I started putting this collection together, I did not realize how consistently I've been obsessed with the idea of freedom. In one way or another, my pieces on such apparently diverse subjects as rock-and-roll and feminism, radical politics and religion reflect my belief in the possibility of a genuinely democratic culture—a community based on the voluntary cooperation of equals. If this book can be said to make one central assumption, it is that there really is such a thing as liberation, however hard it may be to define or describe, let alone attain.

My definition is political; it assumes the need for organized opposition to the present social system. But it is also psychological; it has to do with self-knowledge, with the ability to make conscious choices and take responsibility for them rather than act compulsively from unconscious (that is, unadmitted) motives. Since on some level we never really believe the illusions and rationalizations we insist on porting around like boulders from some totemic mountain, it is a relief to drop the burden—or so I've always found. Still, I never feel quite comfortable talking about choice and responsibility. Those words usually imply an antimaterialist moral and religious outlook—a fact that, to my mind, reveals the limitations of both materialist and moral/religious vocabularies. I don't believe in "free will," if by that one means choice unconditioned by its material context, but I do regard the idea of freedom as inseparable from the idea of the individual self, the subject who chooses. We are shaped by history and culture, by our economic and social situations, yet we are not just passive recipients—or victims—of external pressures. It is human beings who create history and culture, who change their situation or fail to do so. I think there is an aspect of the human personality, a core of basic—if you will, biological—impulses, that transcends and resists the incursions of an oppressive culture. And I think the craving for freedom—for self-determination, in the most literal sense—is a basic impulse that can be suppressed but never eliminated.

Politically, this view of freedom aligns me with cultural radicals rather than socialists; as I see it, the enemy is not capitalism per se, but the authoritarian structure of all our institutions, including those—the family, especially—that regulate our so-called private lives. From a conventional Marxist perspective the individual is a historical artifact, invoked by the rising bourgeoisie as a rationale for capitalism; since the concept of individual freedom is a mask for the reality of class exploitation, it is illusory, or at least fundamentally suspect. I would argue rather that it was in part the impulse toward freedom that led to the bourgeois rebellion against feudalism; that the bourgeoisie did not create the individual, only the conditions for the emergence of self-conscious individuals as a powerful political force. From this standpoint capitalism is a massive paradox, particularly in its later stages. On the one hand, bourgeois democracy represents the first great phase of the cultural revolution; capitalism has instituted certain basic civil rights, supplied the libertarian ideas behind all radical movements, weakened the authority of the patriarchal family and church, allowed masses of people unparalleled personal freedom and social mobility. Yet the corporate state and its global empire are themselves authoritarian, hierarchical structures. Most Americans have little or no control over the conditions of their own working lives, let alone the overall direction of the economy, nor do our formal democratic rights give us real power to determine public policy. The colonized people who have contributed to the enrichment of the capitalist West share neither its prosperity nor its relative freedom. And the imperatives of the marketplace set people against each other; the comforts of middle-class life are bought at the expense of the poor, liberty at the expense of community. Under these conditions our emancipation from the coercive bonds of traditional societies exacts a high price—even for the privileged—in insecurity and psychic isolation.

Obviously, the next phase of the cultural revolution requires a radical alternative to capitalism. But because the socialist-minded left is inclined to focus on the second half of the capitalist paradox while ignoring or discounting the first, much of what passes for a radical critique of this society is insidiously conservative. The tendency to see capitalist individualism solely in negative terms has, for instance, led many leftists to indulge a sentimental view of the family as an oasis of human warmth in the capitalist wasteland, as if the warmth the family offers were any less contingent on conformity to a set of institutional rules than the wages our bosses dispense. At times this "haven in a heartless world" mentality verges on outright nostalgia for tradition, for the lost security of the old organic community—an emotion I find doubly difficult to share, given that women in precapitalist societies were chattel, while Jews were economic and political pariahs. The same brand of selective perception feeds leftist romanticism about Third World dictatorships, also organic communities of a sort. But collective liberation without individual autonomy is a self-contradiction. To be anticapitalist is not enough. Socialist regimes have attacked the grosser forms of economic inequality, yet in terms of the larger struggle for freedom, socialism in practice has been, if anything, a devastating counterrevolution against the liberal concept of individual rights.

Overtly or implicitly, most of the essays reprinted here carry on this quarrel with the left. The first section of the book is, among other things, an extended polemic against standard leftist notions about advanced capitalism—that the consumer economy makes us slaves to commodities, that the function of the mass media is to manipulate our fantasies so we will equate fulfillment with buying the system's products. These ideas are at most half true. Mass consumption, advertising, and mass art are a corporate Frankenstein; while they reinforce the system, they also undermine it. By continually pushing the message that we have the right to gratification *now*, consumerism at its most expansive encouraged a demand for fulfillment that could not so easily be contained by products; it had a way of spilling over into rebellion against the constricting conditions of our lives. The history of the sixties strongly suggests that the impulse to buy a new car and tool down the freeway with the radio blasting rock-and-roll is not unconnected to the impulse to fuck outside marriage, get high, stand up to men or white people or bosses, join dissident movements. In fact, the mass media helped to spread rebellion, and the system obligingly marketed products that encouraged it, for the simple reason that there was money to be made from rebels who were also consumers. On one level the sixties revolt was an impressive illustration of Lenin's remark that the capitalist will sell you the rope to hang him with.

But the subversive element in mass culture is not just a matter of content, of explicit invitations to indulge and/or rebel; it also has to do with the formal properties of mass art. Here too the left has tended to be obtuse, assuming that because mass art is a product of capitalism, it is by definition worthless—not real art at all, but merely a commodity intended to enrich its producers while indoctrinating and pacifying consumers. And again this assumption betrays a hidden conservatism. Why, after all, regard commercial art as intrinsically more compromised than art produced under the auspices of the medieval church, or aristocratic patrons? Art has always been in some sense propaganda for ruling classes and at the same time a form of struggle against them. Art that succeeds manages to evade or transcend or turn to its own purposes the strictures imposed on the artist; on the deepest level it is the enemy of authority, as Plato understood. Mass art is no exception. It is never simply imposed from above, but reflects a complicated interplay of corporate interests, the conscious or intuitive intentions of the artists and technicians who create the product, and the demands of the audience. The distinctive aesthetic of mass art, which is based on images (and sounds) designed to have an intense sensory, erotic, and emotional impact, clearly derives from the necessities of marketing—the need to distinguish one's product from its competitors, to grab and hold the largest possible audience. But the forms invented to fulfill those requirements—the bright colors, bold, linear patterns, and iconic simplicity of advertising art; the sexual rhythms, tight construction, irresistible hook lines, and insistent repetition of rock-and-roll songs—have an autonomous aesthetic existence. They convey their own message, which, like the content of advertising (or the content of pop lyrics) is essentially hedonistic.

Implicit in the formal language of mass art is the possibility that given the right sort of social conditions, it can act as a catalyst that transforms its mass audience into an oppositional community. This is precisely what rock-and-roll did for teen-agers, and rock for the counterculture, in the fifties and sixties. Logically, the prominent role of pop music in the sixties revolt should have changed the left's attitude toward mass culture. After all, most leftists were rock fans, and even the group that came to symbolize the most uncompromising hatred of America took its name from a Bob Dylan song. Instead, radicals tended to evade the issue by making distinctions between "commercial" and "serious" rock. That serious rock was as commercial as the other kind did not deter some movement folk from making extravagant claims for it as revolutionary people's music. Others, unable to avoid noticing that rock was big business, complained about its "co-optation" by the music industry, as if the two had ever been separate.

For a time the seventies seemed to vindicate the co-optation theory. A lot of things changed—the state of the economy, the structure of the record business, the mood of the audience—and rock became a conservative force, a vehicle for assimilating the trappings of the counterculture into the social mainstream while purging it of threatening content. The dropout posture that had once implied membership in a community of outsiders came to mean no more than a smug upper-middle-class solipsism. But this complacency incited its own rebellion, the rude eruption of the punk movement, which sparked the larger phenomenon of new wave rock-and-roll. Compared to the mass audience that standard rock enjoys, new wave fans are a cult (though a sizable one). Still, new wave is rock-and-roll, now self-consciously based on the same formal principles that were once a commercial necessity. And it means something that these principles remain a focus for aesthetic and social dissidence.

Of course, rebellion is not the same thing as revolution. It's not only that capitalists are experts at palming off fake rope—as the development of the rock establishment attests—but that revolt does not necessarily imply radicalism, as a long line of rock-and-rollers, from the apolitical Little Richard to the antipolitical Ramones, attests. Which is only to say that neither mass art nor any other kind is a substitute for politics. Art may express and encourage our subversive impulses, but it can't analyze or organize them. Subversion begins to be radical only when we ask what we really want or think we should have, who or what is obstructing us, and what to do about it.

The second section of this book is about politics—mostly about the politics of sex. This concern has also put me at odds with the left. The suppression of sexuality and the subjugation of women raise the question of freedom in the most direct and inescapable way. The essence of women's oppression is the denial of our autonomy, particularly in regard to our sexual and reproductive functions; though restrictions on women's access to economic resources have been a major means of keeping us in our place, the object has been less to create a class of specially exploited workers than to ensure our dependence on marriage and subordination to men. I also agree with Freud that sexual repression, transmitted from one generation to the next through the patriarchal family, is the basis of civilization and morals as we know them—that is, authoritarian culture and values. It seems to me that there is no task more radical, more in keeping with a vision of a free society, than changing sexual relations. This conviction has generated a political tradition that includes radical Freudians, cultural-revolutionary Marxists, communitarian anarchists, radical feminists, gay liberationists. But for the most part the left has refused to take sexual politics seriously. Even during the sixties, when cultural radicalism was an influential current in the new left, feminists were attacked as "bourgeois" for claiming that all women were oppressed. Leftists dismissed our criticisms of male-female relations as the petty, selfish complaints of a white middle-class elite, condemned our demands for autonomy as mere individualism, and insisted that working-class and minority women—women with *real* (i.e., economic) problems—couldn't care less about women's liberation. ("Women are starving on welfare, and you're worrying about orgasms!" men would scoff, as if it were impossible to worry about sex and poverty at the same time.) Versions of this argument continue to be a staple of leftist rhetoric, which, on matters pertaining to sex and the family, is increasingly hard to distinguish from the conservative sort.

For all the obvious sexism in such attacks, in a way it's true that feminism is bourgeois. Women's demand for self-determination is rooted in the idea of the autonomous individual, and it is the institution of wage labor that made it possible for women to conceive of independence from men. It is also a historical fact that women who are struggling for sheer survival against severe economic oppression are not, by and large, the first to begin demanding freedom from male domination. That the mainstream of both reformist and radical feminist movements has been relatively privileged cuts two ways. White middle-class feminists have too often defined the movement's priorities in ways that ignore or reinforce class and racial divisions. Yet precisely because we do not have to cope with three forms of oppression at once, we are freer to confront the sexual questions and explore their most radical implications. In that sense, the "bourgeois" impulse at the core of feminism is truly revolutionary.

There is a common theme in leftists' reductive view of bourgeois liberties, their contempt for mass culture, and their dismissal of sexual politics. I think all these antipathies reflect a puritanical discomfort with the urge—whatever form it takes—to gratification now, an assumption that social concern is synonymous with altruism and self-sacrifice. The same earnest lefty who carries on about the iniquity of Bloomingdale's is all too likely, in the next breath and in the same moralistic tone, to accuse feminists of a self-indulgent preoccupation with personal happiness. Yet it is the longing for happiness that is potentially radical, while the morality of sacrifice is an age-old weapon of rulers. I don't mean to suggest that social revolution can be painless—only that there is no reason to go through the pain if not, finally, to affirm our right to pleasure.

In the meantime we have to live our lives, which means living with the contradictions of a system built on the premise that one must continually choose—insofar as one has a choice—to be either an oppressor or a victim. So long as that system exists, our pleasures will be guilty, our suffering self-righteous, our glimpses of freedom ambiguous and elusive. Temperamentally, I'm unhappy with contradictions, especially moral ones. I want resolution, integration, synthesis. Ultimately, I believe that appearances to the contrary, the universe is orderly, and that this order is the foundation of values. This intuition is central to all religious experience, and I'm convinced that despite my secular upbringing I somehow absorbed it from Judaism. Several years ago, when my younger brother, now an Orthodox rabbi, embraced religion, I found myself caught up in an intense confrontation with my own Jewishness, an experience recorded in "Next Year in Jerusalem," the long essay that concludes this book. In the process I discovered that my utopian vision of freedom was bound up with a craving for coherence and moral certitude that could also be tempted by a vision of supernatural authority—a vision that, unlike my radicalism, was embodied in an existing social system, a, well, organic community. In the end I settled (uneasily) for the contradictions of my middle-class, female, secular, American writer's life.

If my absolutist impulses are in some sense Jewish, my pragmatic ones have something to do with class. Most contemporary radicals come from the upper middle class and tend to share its aristocratic biases; at bottom their hostility to commerce and all its works flows less from radical indignation than from old-fashioned conservative disdain. I moved up from lower-middle-class origins via an Ivy League education. As a result I have some experience of the advantages of bourgeois mobility; I'm always aware that if I'd been denied certain opportunities, I would have led a much narrower life. Though I assimilated upper-middle-class values in college, I also resisted them, and afterward I veered off the conventional class ladder into bohemia. The bohemianism of most of the sixties radicals I knew involved an explicit rejection of materialism and consumerism, an attempt to root out the bourgeois in themselves (or their families). For me bohemianism was, in part, an attempt to resolve conflicting values. It was a convoluted form of loyalty to my background as well as an implicit admission that I'd left it, a refusal to join the class I'd been educated into and yet a way of passing. But there was no question of rooting out the bourgeois in myself, because what else was I? Not an aristocrat, certainly; and, despite my modest income and slum apartment, not really proletarian, either.

Nearly two decades later my situation, though different in details, is much the same in essentials. I doubt that I'll be able to say this twenty years from now. Economic and social conditions in this country are changing with disquieting rapidity. American dominance in the world is coming to an end; American capitalism is shaky; the prosperity we have enjoyed since World War II and the political liberalism it encouraged are eroding. Whatever one thinks of consumerism, it is already obsolescent, except for the rich. Bohemianism—at least the comfortable sort my generation has known—is probably obsolescent too. The articles in this book are the product of a special time, a period that provided, for more of us than ever before, a certain freedom from the limits imposed by scarcity. This freedom—however qualified, however tenuous—enlarged our idea of what was possible. But as realities get grimmer, the possibilities tend to be forgotten. I offer my version of the sixties and seventies in the hope of resisting that amnesia—and the resignation that goes with it.

Beginning
to See
the Light

Part One

Out of the
Vinyl Deeps

Dylan

I

Nearly two years ago, Bob Dylan had a motorcycle accident. Reports of his condition were vague, and he dropped out of sight. Publication of his book, *Tarantula*, was postponed indefinitely. New records appeared, but they were from his last album, *Blonde on Blonde*. Gruesome rumors circulated: Dylan was dead; he was badly disfigured; he was paralyzed; he was insane. The cataclysm his audience was always expecting seemed to have arrived. Phil Ochs had predicted that Dylan might someday be assassinated by a fan. Pete Seeger believed Dylan could become the country's greatest troubadour, if he didn't explode. Alan Lomax had once remarked that Dylan might develop into a great poet of the times, unless he killed himself first. Now, images of James Dean filled the news vacuum. As months passed, reflex apprehension turned to suspense, then irritation: had we been put on again? We had. Friends began to admit, with smiles, that they'd seen Bobby; he was rewriting his book; he was about to sign a contract with MGM Records. The new rumor was that the accident had been a cover for retreat. After *Blonde on Blonde*, his intensive foray into the pop demimonde, Dylan needed time to replenish his

3

imagination. According to a less romantic version, he was keeping quiet till his contracts expired.

The confusion was typical. Not since Rimbaud said "*I* is another" has an artist been so obsessed with escaping identity. His masks hidden by other masks, Dylan is the celebrity stalker's ultimate antagonist. The original disparity between his public pose as rootless wanderer with southwestern drawl and the private facts of home and middle-class Jewish family and high school diploma in Hibbing, Minnesota, was a commonplace subterfuge, the kind that pays reporters' salaries. It hardly showed his talent for elusiveness; what it probably showed was naiveté. But his attitude toward himself as a public personality was always clear. On an early recording he used the eloquent pseudonym "Blind Boy Grunt." "Dylan" is itself a pseudonym, possibly inspired by Dylan Thomas (a story Dylan now denies), possibly by a real or imaginary uncle named Dillon, who might or might not be the "Las Vegas dealer" Dylan once claimed was his only living relative.

In six years Dylan's stance has evolved from proletarian assertiveness to anarchist angst to pop detachment. At each stage he has made himself harder to follow, provoked howls of execration from those left behind, and attracted an ever-larger, more demanding audience. He has reacted with growing hostility to the possessiveness of this audience and its shock troops, the journalists, the professional categorizers. His baroque press conference inventions are extensions of his work, full of imaginative truth and virtually devoid of information. The classic Dylan interview appeared in *Playboy*, where Nat Hentoff, like a housewife dusting her furniture while a tornado wrecks the house, pursued the homely fact through exchanges like: "Do you have any unfulfilled ambitions?" "Well, I guess I've always wanted to be Anthony Quinn in *La Strada*. . . . I guess I've always wanted to be Brigitte Bardot, too; but I don't really want to think about *that* too much."

Dylan's refusal to be known is not simply a celebrity's ploy, but a passion that has shaped his work. As his songs have become more introspective, the introspections have become more impersonal, the confidences of a no-man without past or future. Bob Dylan as

4

identifiable persona has been disappearing into his songs, which is what he wants. This terrifies his audiences. They could accept a consistent image—roving minstrel, poet of alienation, spokesman for youth—in lieu of the "real" Bob Dylan. But his progressive self-annihilation cannot be contained in a game of let's pretend, and it conjures up nightmares of madness, mutilation, death.

The nightmares are chimerical; there is a continuing self, the Bobby Dylan friends describe as shy and defensive, hyped up, careless of his health, a bit scared by fame, unmaterialistic but shrewd about money, a professional absorbed in his craft. Dylan's songs bear the stigmata of an authentic middle-class adolescence; his eye for detail, sense of humor, and skill at evoking the archetypal sexual skirmishes show that some part of him is of as well as in the world. As further evidence, he has a wife, son, and house in Woodstock, New York. Instead of an image, Dylan has created a magic theater in which the public gets lost willy-nilly. Yet he is more—or less—than the sum of his illusions.

Many people hate Bob Dylan because they hate being fooled. Illusion is fine, if quarantined and diagnosed as mild; otherwise it is potentially humiliating (is he laughing at me? conning me out of my money?). Some still discount Dylan as merely a popular culture hero (how can a teen-age idol be a serious artist—at most, perhaps, a serious demagogue). But the most tempting answer—forget his public presence, listen to his songs—won't do. For Dylan has exploited his image as a vehicle for artistic statement. The same is true of Andy Warhol and, to a lesser degree, of the Beatles and Allen Ginsberg. (In contrast, James Dean and Marilyn Monroe were creatures, not masters, of their images.) The tenacity of the modern publicity apparatus often makes artists' personalities more familiar than their work, while its pervasiveness obscures the work of those who can't or won't be personalities. If there is an audience for images, artists will inevitably use the image as a medium—and some images are more original, more compelling, more relevant than others. Dylan has self-consciously explored the possibilities of mass communication just as the pop artists explored the possibilities of mass production. In the same sense that pop art is about commodities, Dylan's art is about celebrity.

This is not to deny the intrinsic value of Dylan's songs. Everyone interested in folk and popular music agrees on their importance, if not their merit. As composer, interpreter, most of all as lyricist, Dylan has made a revolution. He expanded folk idiom into a rich, figurative language, grafted literary and philosophical subtleties onto the protest song, revitalized folk vision by rejecting proletarian and ethnic sentimentality, then all but destroyed pure folk as a contemporary form by merging it with pop. Since then rock-and-roll, which was already in the midst of a creative flowering dominated by British rock and Motown, has been transformed. Songwriters have raided folk music as never before for new sounds, new images, new subject matter. Dylan's innovative lyrics have been enthusiastically imitated. The folk music lovers who managed to evolve with him, the connoisseurs of pop, the bohemian fringe of the literary community, hippies, and teen-agers consider him a genius, a prophet. Folk purists and political radicals, who were inspired by his earlier material, cry betrayal with a vehemence that acknowledges his gifts.

Yet many of Dylan's fans—especially ex-fans—miss the point. Dylan is no apostle of the electronic age. Rather, he is a fifth-columnist from the past, shaped by personal and political nonconformity, by blues and modern poetry. He has imposed his commitment to individual freedom (and its obverse, isolation) on the hip passivity of pop culture, his literacy on an illiterate music. He has used the publicity machine to demonstrate his belief in privacy. His songs and public role are guides to survival in the world of the image, the cool, and the high. And in coming to terms with that world, he has forced it to come to terms with him.

II

By 1960 the folk music revival that began in the fifties had expanded into an all-inclusive smorgasbord, with kitschy imitation-folk groups at one end, resurrected cigar-box guitarists and Ozark balladeers at the other. Of music that pretended to ethnic authenticity, the most popular was folk blues—Leadbelly, Sonny Terry and Brownie McGhee, Lightnin' Hopkins. The response to blues was in part a tribute to the ascendancy of rock-and-roll—Negro rhythms had affected the consciousness of every teen-ager in the fifties. But blues, unlike rock, was free of identification with the dominant society. Its sexuality and rebelliousness were undiluted, and it was about people, not teen-agers. Besides, the Negro, always a dual symbol of suffering and life force, was gaining new political importance, and folk blues expressed the restlessness of activists, bohemians, déclassé intellectuals. Since younger Negro performers were not interested in preserving a genre they had abandoned for more distinctly urban forms, white city singers tried to fill the gap. Patronized unmercifully by blues purists, the best of them did not simply approximate Negro sounds but evoked personal pain and disenchantment with white culture.

At the same time there was a surge of folk composing. The Weavers, in the vanguard of the revival, had popularized the iconoclastic ballads and talking blues of Woody Guthrie, chronicler of the dust bowl and the Depression, the open road, the unions, the common man* as intrepid endurer. Pete Seeger, the Weavers' lead singer in the early days and the most prestigious folk musician in the country, had recorded albums of topical songs from the thirties and forties. With the emergence of the civil rights movement, freedom songs, some new, some updated spirituals and union chants, began coming out of the South. Northern musicians began to write and perform their own material, mainly variations on the hard-traveling theme and polemics against racism, the bomb and middle-class conformity. Guthrie was their godfather, Seeger their guru, California songwriter Malvina Reynolds

---

* When I wrote this piece (and a few others in the book), I had not yet stopped using "man," "he," etc., as generic terms applying to both sexes. In the interest of historical accuracy I've left these locutions intact, though they grate on me aesthetically as well as politically. For the same reason I have not changed "Negro" to "black."

their older sister. Later, they were to acquire an angel—Joan Baez, who would record their songs and sing them at racial demonstrations and peace rallies; an organ—*Broadside*, a mimeographed magazine founded in 1962; and a sachem—Bob Dylan.

Gerde's Folk City, an unassuming, unbohemian cabaret in Greenwich Village, was the folk fans' chief New York hangout. On Monday, hootenanny night, blues interpreters like Dave Van Ronk, bluegrass groups like the Greenbriar Boys, the new topical songwriters—Tom Paxton, Phil Ochs, Len Chandler—would stop in and perform. Established singers came because Gerde's was part of the scene, because they enjoyed playing to the aficionados who gathered after midnight. The young ones came for a showcase and for contact with musicians they admired.

When Bob Dylan first showed up at Gerde's in the spring of 1961, fresh-skinned and baby-faced and wearing a schoolboy's corduroy cap, the manager asked him for proof of age. He was nineteen, only recently arrived in New York. Skinny, nervous, manic, the bohemian patina of jeans and boots, scruffy hair, hip jargon and hitchhiking mileage barely settled on nice Bobby Zimmerman, he had been trying to catch on at the coffeehouses. His material and style were a cud of half-digested influences: Guthrie cum Elliott; Blind Lemon Jefferson cum Leadbelly cum Van Ronk; the hillbilly sounds of Hank Williams and Jimmie Rodgers; the rock-and-roll of Chuck Berry and Elvis Presley. He was constantly writing new songs. Onstage, he varied poignancy with clownishness. His interpretations of traditional songs—especially blues—were pretentious, and his harsh, flat voice kept slipping over the edge of plaintiveness into strident self-pity. But he shone as a comedian, charming audiences with Charlie Chaplin routines, playing with his hair and cap, burlesquing his own mannerisms, and simply enjoying himself. His specialty was composing lightly sardonic talking blues—chants to a bass-run guitar accompaniment, a favorite vehicle of Woody Guthrie's: "Them Communists were all around/ in the air and on the ground/ . . . I run down most hurriedly/ and joined the John Birch society."

Dylan

That fall, *New York Times* folk music critic Robert Shelton visited Gerde's and gave Dylan an enthusiastic review. Columbia Records signed him and released a mediocre first album in February 1962. It contained only two Dylan compositions, both nonpolitical. Dylan began publishing his topical songs in *Broadside*. Like his contemporaries, he was more propagandist than artist, his syntax often barbarous, his diction crude. Even so, his work stood out—it contained the most graphic descriptions of racial atrocities. But Dylan also had a gentler mood. Road songs like "Song to Woody" strove—not too successfully—for Guthrie's expressive understatement and simple, traditional sound.

In May 1962, *Broadside* published a new Dylan song, "Blowin' in the Wind." Set to a melody adapted from a spiritual, it combined indignation with Guthriesque simplicity and added a touch of original imagery. It received little circulation until nearly a year later, when Peter, Paul and Mary heard Dylan sing it at a coffeehouse. Their recording of the song sold a million copies, inspired more than fifty other versions, and established topical song as the most important development of the folk revival. The relative subtlety of the lyric made the topical movement aesthetically self-conscious. It did not drive out direct political statements—Dylan himself continued to write them—but it set a standard impossible to ignore, and topical songs began to show more wit, more craftsmanship, more variety.

"Blowin' in the Wind" was included in Dylan's second album, *The Freewheelin' Bob Dylan*, which appeared in May 1963. This time, nearly all the songs were his own; five had political themes. It was an extraordinary record. The influences had coalesced; the voice, unmusical as ever, had found an evocative range somewhere between abrasion and sentimentality; the lyrics (except for "Masters of War," a simplistic diatribe against munitions-makers) were vibrant and pithy. The album contained what may still be Dylan's best song—"It's A Hard Rain's a-Gonna Fall," a vivid evocation of nuclear apocalypse that owed much to Allen Ginsberg's biblical rhetoric and declamatory style. Its theme was modern, its spirit

9

ancient. At first hearing, most of the *Freewheelin'* songs sounded less revolutionary than they were: so skillfully had Dylan distilled the forms and moods of traditional music that his originality took time to register.

Freewheelin' illuminated Dylan's America—or rather, two Americas. "Hard Rain" confronted the underside, "where the executioner's face is always well-hidden," "where black is the color and none is the number," a world of deserted diamond highways, incipient tidal waves, clowns crying in alleys, children armed with guns and swords, "10,000 whisperin and nobody listenin" and occasional portents of redemption: "I met a young girl, she gave me a rainbow." The satirical "Talking World War III Blues" toured the country's surface: hot dog stands, parking meters, Cadillacs, rock-and-roll singers, telephone operators, cool females, officious doctors. Dylan's moral outrage coexisted with a grudging affection for American society and its foibles. If there was "Masters of War," there was also "I Shall Be Free": "My telephone rang, it would not stop, it was President Kennedy callin me up./ He said my friend Bob what do we need to make this country grow I said my friend John, Brigitte Bardot."

For a time the outrage predominated. Dylan's output of bitter protest increased and his humor receded. He was still learning from Woody Guthrie, but he often substituted despair for Guthrie's resilience: his finest ballads chronicled the disintegration of an unemployed miner's family; the killing of a Negro maid, punished by a six-month sentence; the extremity of a penniless farmer who shot himself, his wife, and five kids. At the same time his prophetic songs discarded the pessimism of "Hard Rain" for triumph in "The Times They Are A-Changin' " and vindictiveness in "When the Ship Comes In": "Then they'll raise their hands, say we'll meet all your demands, and we'll shout from the bow, your days are numbered."

It was Dylan's year. Stimulated by the wide acceptance of his work, inspired by his ideas and images, topical songwriters became more and more prolific. Dylan songs were recorded by dozens of folk singers, notably Joan Baez (at whom he had once sneered, "She's still singing about Mary Hamilton. Where's that at?"). No folk concert was complete without "Hard Rain," or "Don't Think Twice," or a protest song from Dylan's third album, *The Times They Are A-Changin'*. The college folk crowd imitated Dylan; civil rights workers took heart from him; masochistic journalists lionized him. And in the attenuated versions of Peter, Paul and Mary, the Chad Mitchell Trio, even Lawrence Welk, his songs reached the fraternity house and the suburb.

Then Dylan yanked the rug: he renounced political protest. He put out an album of personal songs and in one of them, "My Back Pages," scoffed at his previous moral absolutism. His refrain—"Ah, but I was so much older then, I'm younger than that now"— seemed a slap at the thirties left. And the song contained scraps of uncomfortably private imagery—hints of aesthetic escapism?

Folk devotees were shocked at Dylan's apostasy. Folk music and social protest have always fed on each other, and the current revival had been political all along. For children of Depression activists growing up in the Eisenhower slough, folk music was a way of keeping the faith. When they converged on the Weavers' Town Hall hootenannies, they came as the anti-McCarthy resistance, pilgrims to the thirties shrine. The Weavers were blacklisted for alleged Communist connections; Pete Seeger had been *there*, singing for the unions, for the Spanish Republic. It didn't matter what they sang—in the atmosphere of conspiratorial sympathy that permeated those performances, even "Greensleeves" had radical overtones. Later, as the left revived, folk singing became a badge of involvement, an expression of solidarity, and most important, a history-in-the-raw of struggle. Now, Dylan's defection threatened the last aesthetically respectable haven for believers in proletarian art.

Dylan had written personal songs before, but they were songs that accepted folk conventions. Narrative in impulse, nostalgic but restless in mood, their central image the road and its imperative, they complemented his protest songs: here was an outlaw, unable to settle for one place, one girl, a merely private life, committed to that symbolic onward journey. His new songs were more psychological, limning characters and relationships. They substituted ambition for the artless perfection of his best early songs; "It Ain't Me, Babe," a gloss on the spiritual possessiveness of woman, took three stanzas to say what "Don't Think Twice, It's All Right" had suggested in a few phrases: "I'm thinkin and wonderin, walkin down the road/ I once loved a woman, a child I'm told/ gave her my heart but she wanted my soul."* Dylan's language was opening up—doves sleeping in the sand were one thing, "crimson flames tied through my ears" quite another. And his tone was changing: in his love songs, ingenuousness began to yield to self-possession, the spontaneity of the road to the gamesmanship of the city. They were transitional songs, full of half-realized ideas; having rejected the role of people's bard, Dylan had yet to find a new niche.

I I I

In retrospect, Dylan's break with the topical song movement seemed inevitable. He had modeled himself on Woody Guthrie, whose incessant traveling was an emotional as well as economic necessity, whose commitment to radical politics was rooted in an individualism as compulsive as Dylan's own. But Guthrie had had to organize or submit; Dylan had other choices. For Guthrie, the road was habitat; for Dylan, metaphor. The closing of the iron mines had done to Hibbing what drought had done to Guthrie's

---

* Here as elsewhere in this prefeminist essay I refer with aplomb if not outright endorsement to Dylan's characteristic bohemian contempt for women (which he combined with an equally obnoxious idealization of female goddess figures). At the time I did not question the idea that women were guardians of oppressive conventional values; I only thought of myself as an exception. *I* was not possessive; I understood men's need to go on the road because I was, spiritually speaking, on the road myself. That, at least, was my fantasy; the realities of my life were somewhat more ambiguous.

Oklahoma, but while Guthrie had been a victim, Dylan was a bystander. A voluntary refugee from middle-class life, more aesthete than activist, he had less in common with the left than with literary rebels—Blake, Whitman, Rimbaud, Crane, Ginsberg.

The beauty of "Hard Rain" was that it exploited poetry while remaining a folk lyric, simple, repetitive, seemingly uncontrived. Now Dylan became self-consciously poetic, adopting a neo-beat style loaded with images. Though he had rejected the traditional political categories, his new posture was if anything more scornful of the social order than before. "It's Alright, Ma (I'm Only Bleeding)" attacked both the "human gods" who "make everything from toy guns that spark to flesh-colored Christs that glow in the dark" and their acquiescent victims. "Gates of Eden," like "Hard Rain," descended into a surreal netherworld, the menace this time a psychic bomb, the revolt of repressed instinct. As poetry these songs were overrated—*Howl* had said it all much better—and they were unmusical, near-chants declaimed to a monotonous guitar strum. Yet the perfunctory music made the bohemian commonplaces work—made them fresh. Perhaps it was the context: though few people realized it yet, the civil rights movement was losing its moral force; the Vietnam juggernaut was becoming the personal concern of every draftable man; a new generation of bohemians, more expansive and less cynical than the beats, was about to blossom. The time was right for a reaffirmation of individual revolt.

But Dylan had also been exposed to a very different vision: in May 1964, he had toured an England transformed by mod fashion and the unprecedented excitement over the Beatles and the Rolling Stones. When his new record came out the following spring, its title was *Bringing It All Back Home*. On the album jacket a chiaroscuro Dylan, bright face emerging from ominous shadows, stared accusingly at the viewer. In black suit and striped shirt, he perched on a long divan, hugging a cat, behind him a modish, blank-faced beauty in scarlet lounging pajamas. The room, wreathed in light and dominated by a baroque mantelpiece, abounded with artifacts—*Time*, a movie magazine, a fallout shelter sign, folk and pop records (including earlier Dylan), a portrait, a candlestick, a few mysterious objects obscured by the halo.

Most of side one was devoted to "Gates of Eden" and "It's Alright, Ma." But the most arresting cut on the side was "Mr. Tambourine Man," a hymn to the psychedelic quest: "take me disappearing through the smoke-rings of my mind. . . . take me on a trip upon your magic swirling ship." Drug-oriented bohemians loved it; it was another step away from the sobersided politicals. It was also more like a folk song than anything Dylan had written since giving up politics, a spiritual road song with a lilting, singable melody.

The other side was rock-and-roll, Dylan on electric guitar and piano backed by a five-man band. It was not hard rock. There was no over-dubbing, and Dylan played his amplified guitar folk-style. But the beat was there, and the sound, if not overwhelming, was big enough to muffle some of the lyrics. These dispensed a new kind of folk wisdom. Chaos had become a condition, like the weather, not to analyze or prophesy but to gripe about, cope with, dodge: "Look out, kid, it's somethin you did/ God knows when but you're doin it again." The message was pay attention to what's happening: "Don't follow leaders, watch the parkin meters."

One rock song, "Subterranean Homesick Blues," was released as a single. As Dylan's pop debut, it was a modest success, hovering halfway up the *Cash Box* and *Billboard* charts. That summer, Dylan cut "Like a Rolling Stone," the most scurrilous and—with its powerful beat—the most dramatic in a long line of non–love songs. It was a number-one hit, as "Blowin' in the Wind" had been two years before—only now it was Dylan's own expressive snarl coming over radio and jukebox.

"Like a Rolling Stone" opened Dylan's first all-rock album, *Highway 61 Revisited*. More polished but less daring than *Bringing It All Back Home*, the album reworked familiar motifs. The title song, which depicted the highway as junkyard, temple, and battlefield, was Dylan's best face-of-America commentary since "Talking World War III Blues." The witty and scarifying "Ballad of a Thin

Man," which derided the rationalist bewildered by the instinctual revolt, was an updated "Times They Are A-Changin'," with battle lines redrawn according to pop morality. Dylan did not hail the breakdown of sanity he described but merely kept his cool, mocking Mr. Jones (the pop equivalent of Mr. Charlie) for committing squareness: "The sword-swallower he comes up to you and then he kneels/ . . . and he says here is your throat back, thanks for the loan/ and something is happening but you don't know what it is, do you, Mr. Jones?" "Desolation Row" was Dylan's final tribute to the Götterdämmerung strain in modern literature—an eleven-minute freak show whose cast of losers, goons, and ghosts wandered around in a miasma of sexual repression and latent violence underscored by the electronic beat.

The violent hostility of traditionalists to Dylan's rock-and-roll made the uproar over "My Back Pages" seem mild. Not only orthodox leftists but bohemian radicals called him a sellout and a phony. At the July 1965 Newport Folk Festival he appeared with his electric guitar and was booed off the stage. Alan Lomax, America's foremost authority on folk song, felt Dylan had chucked his artistry for a big audience and forsaken a mature culture for one that was evanescent and faddish. Tom Paxton, dean of the new crop of topical songwriters, commented: " 'Where it's at' is a synonym for 'rich.' "

Defiantly, Dylan exacerbated the furor, insisting on his contempt for message songs and his indifference to causes, refusing to agonize over his wealth or his taxes ("Uncle Sam, he's my *uncle!* Can't turn your back on a member of the family!"). In one notorious interview he claimed he had written topical songs only to get published in *Broadside* and attract attention. Many former fans took the bait. Actually, Dylan's work still bristled with messages; his "opportunism" had absorbed three years of his life and produced the finest extensions of traditional music since Guthrie. But the purists believed in it because they wanted to. Their passion told less about Dylan than about their own peculiar compound of aristocratic and proletarian sensitivities.

Pure folk sound and idiom, in theory the expression of ordinary people, had become the province of middle-class dissidents who identified with the common man but whose attitude toward common men resembled that of White Russian expatriates toward the communized peasants. For them popular music—especially rock-and-roll—symbolized the displacement of the true folk by the mass. Rock was not created by the people but purveyed by the communications industry. The performer was incidental to engineer and publicity man. The beat was moronic, the lyrics banal teen-age trivia.

These were half-truths. From the beginning, there was a bottom-up as well as top-down movement in rock-and-roll: neighborhood kids formed groups and wrote songs; country singers adopted a rhythm-and-blues beat. Rock took a mechanized, acquisitive society for granted, yet in its own way it was protest music, uniting teen-agers against adults' lack of sympathy with youthful energy and love and sex. The mediocrity of most performers only made rock more "authentic"—anyone could sing it—and one of the few remaining vindications of the American dream—any kid from the slums might become a millionaire. (The best singers, of course, were fine interpreters; Elvis Presley and Chuck Berry did not have golden voices, but neither did Leadbelly or Woody Guthrie.) Rock-and-roll was further from the grass roots than traditional music, but closer than any other kind of pop. If folk fans did not recognize this, the average adult did, and condemned the music for its adolescent surliness and its sexuality, covert in the lyrics, overt in the beat and in the intense response to idols.

But it remained for the British renaissance to prove that the mainstream of mass culture could produce folk music—that is, antiestablishment music. The Beatles, commercial without apology, delighted in the Americanized decadence of their environment. Yet their enthusiasm was subversive—they endorsed the reality of the culture, not its official myths. The Rolling Stones were iconoclastic in a different way: deliberately ugly, blatantly erotic, they exuded contempt for the public while making a fortune. Their cynicism, like Leadbelly's violence or Charlie Parker's heroin, was part of their charisma. Unlike traditional folk singers, they could cheerfully censor their lyrics for Ed Sullivan without seeming domesticated—the effect was more as if they had paraded a sign saying "Blank CBS." British rock was far superior to most early rock-and-roll.* Times had changed: electronic techniques were more sophisticated, radio stations and record companies less squeamish about sexual candor, and teen culture was merging into a more mature, less superficial youth culture with semibohemian tastes. Most important, the British groups successfully assimilated Negro music, neither vitiating rhythm-and-blues nor imitating it, but refining it to reflect their own milieu—white, urban, technological, materialistic, tough-minded.

Most folk fans—even those with no intrinsic objections to rock, who had perhaps listened to it when they were teen-agers and not obliged to be serious—assumed that commercial exploitation automatically gutted music. Yet the Stones were creating blues as valid as the work of any folk singers, black or white. After *Bringing It All Back Home*, the contradiction could no longer be ignored, and those not irrevocably committed to the traditional folk ethos saw the point. Phil Ochs praised *Highway 61*; Joan Baez cut a rock-and-roll record; more and more folk singers began to use electronic instruments. Folk-rock generated an unaccustomed accord between the folk and pop worlds. In *Crawdaddy!* Richard Fariña lauded "this shift away from open-road-protest-flat-pick-style to more Nashville-Motown-Thameside, with the strong implication that some of us had been listening to the A.M. radio."

* This statement now strikes me as absurd, a confusion of aesthetic sophistication and self-consciousness with merit in some absolute sense. It makes even less sense when applied to the best mid-sixties British rock versus the best early rock-and-roll. Precisely because they had a more spontaneous, direct relation to their material and their audience, performers like Elvis Presley, Chuck Berry, Little Richard, and Jerry Lee Lewis got to places that the Beatles, the Stones, and the Who never even tried to reach. The reverse is also true, of course.

Malvina Reynolds pronounced the new rock-and-roll "a wonder and delight." By November 1966, folk-rock had received the final imprimatur—Pete Seeger recorded an album backed by three members of the Blues Project.

Folk-rock was never a form, but a simpleminded inspiration responsible for all sorts of hybrids. At first it was mostly rock versions of Dylan folk songs, social protest rock, and generational trauma rock, a weekend-hippie version of the classic formula, children against parents. Then, self-styled musical poets Simon and Garfunkel began imitating Dylan's apocalyptic songs ("The words of the prophets are written on a subway wall"), starting a trend to elaborate and, too often, sophomoric lyrics. The Lovin' Spoonful invented the "good-time sound," a varying mixture of rock, blues, jug, and old pop. Donovan wrote medieval fantasies and pop collages like "Sunshine Superman" and "Mellow Yellow." And there was acid-rock, the music of new bohemia.

Psychedelic music, like folk-rock, was a catchall label; it described a variety of products shaped by folk, British rock, Chicago blues, jazz, Indian music. Psychedelic lyrics, heavily influenced by Dylanesque imagery, used the conventions of the romantic pop song to express sexual and mystical rather than sentimental love and focused on the trip—especially the flight—the way folk music focused on the road. The Byrds, who had started folk-rock moving with their hit record of "Mr. Tambourine Man," launched the California psychedelic sound with "Eight Miles High," which picked up on the Beatles' experiments with Indian instrumentation and was ostensibly about flying over London airport (it was banned anyway by right-thinking disc jockeys). Though the Byrds were from Los Angeles, the scene soon shifted north, and a proliferation of underground rock groups—some, like Jefferson Airplane, the Grateful Dead, and Country Joe and the Fish, quickly surfaced—made San Francisco the new center of avant-garde pop, superseding Britain.

The California groups came closest to making the term folk-rock say something. For hippie culture, bastard of the beat generation out of pop, was much like a folk culture—oral, naive, communal, its aphorisms ("Make love, not war," "Turn on, tune in, drop out") intuited, not rationalized. Pop and beat, thesis and antithesis of the affluent society, contained elements of synthesis: both movements rejected intellect for sensation, politics for art, and Ginsberg and Kerouac glorified a grass-roots America that included supermarkets and cars as well as mountains and apple pie. The hippies simplified the beats' utopian anarchism and substituted psychedelic drugs for Zen and yoga; they also shared the pop enthusiasm for technology and the rainbow surface of affluence— their music was rock, their style mod. Like Dylan, they bridged old culture and new—they were still idealists—and they idolized him. But he did not consider himself their spokesman. At twenty-five, he was too old ("How can I be the voice of their generation? I'm not their generation") and, though he did not admit it publicly, too well-read. While "Mr. Tambourine Man" was becoming the hippie anthem, he was saying "LSD is for mad, hateful people" and making fun of drugs in "Memphis Blues Again." Dylan was really at cross-purposes with the hippies. They were trying to embody pop sensibility in a folk culture. He was trying to comprehend pop culture with—at bottom—a folk sensibility.

I V

It is a truism among Dylan's admirers that he is a poet using rock-and-roll to spread his art: as Jack Newfield put it in the *Village Voice*, "If Whitman were alive today, he too would be playing an electric guitar." This misrepresentation has only served to discredit Dylan among intellectuals and draw predictable sniping from con-scientious B-student poets like Louis Simpson and John Ciardi. Dylan has a lavish verbal imagination and a brilliant sense of irony, and many of his images—especially on the two *Blonde on Blonde* records—are memorable. But poetry also requires economy, co-herence, and discrimination, and Dylan has perpetrated prolix verses, horrendous grammar, tangled phrases, silly metaphors, embarrassing clichés, muddled thought; at times he seems to believe one good image deserves five others, and he relies too much on rhyme. His chief literary virtue—sensitivity to psychological nuance—belongs to fiction more than poetry. His skill at creating character has made good lyrics out of terrible poetry, as in the pre-rock "Ballad in Plain D," whose portraits of the singer, his girl, and her family redeem lines like: "With unseen consciousness I possessed in my grip/ a magnificent mantelpiece though its heart being chipped."

Dylan is not always undisciplined. As early as *Freewheelin'*, it was clear that he could control his material when he cared to. But his disciplines are songwriting and acting, not poetry; his words fit the needs of music and performance, not an intrinsic pattern. Words or rhymes that seem gratuitous in print often make good musical sense, and Dylan's voice, an extraordinary interpreter of emotion though (or more likely because) it is almost devoid of melody, makes vague lines clear. Dylan's music is not inspired. His melodies and arrangements are derivative, and his one technical accomplishment, a vivacious, evocative harmonica, does not approach the virtuosity of a Sonny Terry. His strength as a musician is his formidable eclecticism combined with a talent for choosing the right music to go with a given lyric. The result is a unity of sound and word that eludes most of his imitators.

Dylan is effective only when exploiting this unity, which is why his free-verse album notes are interesting mainly as autobiography (or mythology) and why *Tarantula* is unlikely to be a masterpiece. When critics call Dylan a poet, they really mean a visionary. Because the poet is the paradigmatic seer, it is conventional to talk about the film poet, the jazz poet. Dylan is verbal, which makes the label even more tempting. But it evades an important truth—the new visionaries are not poets. Dylan is specifically pessimistic about the future of literature. Far from Desolation Row, "The Titanic sails at dawn/ . . . Ezra Pound and T. S. Eliot fighting in the captain's towers/ while calypso singers laugh at them and fishermen hold flowers." The infamous Mr. Jones, with his pencil in his hand, his eyes in his pocket, and his nose on the ground, is a literary man. With the rock songs on *Bringing It All Back Home*, Dylan began trying to create an alternative to poetry. If Whitman were alive today, he might be playing electric guitar; then again, he might be writing advertising copy.

In May 1966, Dylan recorded *Blonde on Blonde*, a double album cut in Nashville with local musicians. Formally, it was his finest achievement since *Freewheelin'*, but while the appeal of the *Freewheelin'* songs was the illusion of spontaneous folk expression, the songs from *Blonde on Blonde* were clearly artifacts, lovingly and carefully made. The music was rock and Nashville country, with a sprinkling of blues runs and English-ballad arpeggios. Thematically, the album was a unity. It explored the subworld pop was creating, an exotic milieu of velvet doors and scorpions, cool sex ("I saw you makin love with him,/ you forgot to close the garage door"), zany fashions ("it balances on your head just like a mattress balances on a bottle of wine,/ your brand-new leopard-skin pillbox hat"), strange potions ("it strangled up my mind,/ now people just get uglier and I have no sense of time"), neurotic women ("she's like all the rest/ with her fog, her amphetamine, and her pearls").

The songs did not preach: Dylan was no longer rebel but seismograph, registering his emotions—fascination, confusion, pity, annoyance, exuberance, anguish—with sardonic lucidity. Only once, in "Just like a Woman," did his culture shock get out of control: "I can't stay in here/ ain't it clear/ that I just can't fit." Many of the songs were about child-women, bitchy, unreliable, sometimes vulnerable, usually one step ahead: "I told you as you clawed out my eyes/ I never really meant to do you any harm." But there were also goddesses like Johanna and the mercury-mouthed, silken-fleshed Sad-Eyed Lady of the Lowlands, Beatrices of pop who shed not merely light but kaleidoscopic images.

The fashionable, sybaritic denizens of *Blonde on Blonde* are the sort of people despised by radicals as apologists for the system. Yet in accepting the surface that system has produced, they subvert its assumptions. Conservative and utopian ideologues agree that man must understand and control his environment; the questions are how, and for whose benefit. But pop culture defines man as a receiver of stimuli, his environment as sensory patterns to be enjoyed, not interpreted (literature and philosophy are irrelevant) or acted upon (politics is irrelevant). "If you want to understand me, look at my surface," says Andy Warhol. And "I like my paintings because anybody can do them." The bureaucrat defends standardization because it makes a complex society manageable. Yet he thinks of himself as an individualist, and finds the idea of mass-produced, mechanized art incomprehensible, threatening—or a put-on. The pop artist looks at mass culture naively and sees beauty in its regular patterns; like an anthropologist exhibiting Indian basket-weaving, Warhol shows us our folk art—soup cans. His message—the Emperor has no clothes, but that's all right, in fact it's beautiful —takes acceptance of image for essence to its logical extreme. *Blonde on Blonde* is about this love of surface.

Dylan's sensitivity to pop comes straight out of his folk background. Both folk and pop mentalities are leery of abstractions, and Dylan's appreciation of surface detail represents Guthriesque common sense—to Dylan, a television commercial was always a television commercial as well as a symbol of alienation. From the first, a basic pragmatism tempered his commitment to the passionate excesses of the revolutionist and the *poète maudit* and set him apart from hipster heroes like James Dean. Like the beats, who admired the total revolt of the hipster from a safe distance, Dylan is essentially nonviolent. Any vengefulness in his songs is either impersonal or funny, like the threats of a little boy to beat up the bad guys; more often, he is the bemused butt of slapstick cruelty: "I've got a woman, she's so mean/ sticks my boots in the washing machine/ sticks me with buckshot when I'm nude/ puts bubble gum in my food."

Dylan's basic rapport with reality has also saved him from the excesses of pop, kept him from merging, Warhol-like, into his public surface. *John Wesley Harding*, released after twenty months of silence, shows that Dylan is still intact in spirit as well as body. The songs are more impersonal—and in a way more inscrutable—than ever, yet the human being behind them has never seemed less mysterious. For they reveal Dylan not as the protean embodiment of some collective nerve, but as an alert artist responding to challenge from his peers. If Dylan's first rock-and-roll songs were his reaction to the cultural changes the new rock represented, *John Wesley Harding* is a reaction to the music itself as it has evolved since his accident. The album is comprehensible only in this context.

As Dylan's recovery advanced, he began making the papers again. He signed a new contract with Columbia—the defection to MGM never came off—and the company announced that he was recording. Dylan was still revered, his near-mythic status only solidified by his long absence from the scene. But whether he could come back as an active performer was another question. Shortly after the appearance of *Blonde on Blonde*, three important albums—the Beatles' *Revolver*, the Stones' *Aftermath*, and the Beach Boys' *Pet Sounds*—had all set new standards of musical ambition and pretension. Ever since, the "serious" rock groups had been producing albums that said, in effect, "Can you top this?"—a competition that extended to album covers and titles. In the spring of 1967 the Beatles released *Sgt. Pepper's Lonely Hearts Club Band*, possibly the most elaborate rock album ever made and certainly the most celebrated. It was reported that Dylan had listened to the first few cuts of *Sgt. Pepper* and snapped "Turn that off!"; perhaps the new developments in rock—which he had done so much to inspire—had left him behind. On the other hand, perhaps he was leaving rock behind. Many of Dylan's associates—notably Tom Wilson, his former A&R man—had always insisted that Dylan was much more sophisticated musically than he let on. And in May a New York *Daily News* reporter quoted Dylan as saying he was at work on "two new sounds."

By Christmas the Stones were first in the pretensions sweepstakes—*Their Satanic Majesties Request*, with its 3-D cover, was almost a parody of the whole art-rock phenomenon. How was Dylan going to top *that?* Everyone waited for a revolutionary masterpiece or an extravagant flop. What we got was *John Wesley Harding* in a plain gray jacket with a polaroid snapshot of Dylan and three Indians in the country. The first sound to greet the eager listener was the strumming of an acoustic guitar. The first line of the first song was "John Wesley Harding was a friend to the poor." Dylan had done it again.

The new melodies are absurdly simple, even for Dylan; the only instruments backing his guitar, piano, and harmonica are a bass, a drum, and in two songs an extra guitar; the rock beat has faded out and the country and English ballad strains now dominate. The titles are all as straight as "John Wesley Harding": most are taken from the first lines of the songs. The lyrics are not only simple but understated in a way that shows Dylan has learned a trick or two from Lennon-McCartney, and they are folk lyrics. Or more precisely, affectionate comments on folk lyrics—the album is not a reversion to his early work but a kind of hymn to it. Nearly all the songs play with the clichés of folk music. The title song, for instance, seems at first hearing to be a second-rate "Jesse James" or "Pretty Boy Floyd." It starts out with all the catch phrases about the benevolent outlaw, then goes into the story: "It was down in Cheney County the time they talk about/ With his lady by his side he took a stand." But the next line goes right out of it again: "And soon the situation there was all but straightened out." You never learn what happened in Cheney County or why it wasn't *entirely* straightened out, and the song ends with more stock lines about the bandit's elusiveness and the helplessness of the law. It is not about John Wesley Harding, but about a familiar formula: and this, friends, is how you write the generic outlaw song.

Several of the songs are folk-style fantasies. "Frankie Lee and Judas Priest" is both a folk ballad (based on another stock situation, the gambler on the road) and one of Dylan's surrealist dream songs; "As I Walked Out One Morning" describes a run-in with an Arthurian enchantress as if she were a revenue agent or the farmer's daughter. This juxtaposition of the conventional and the

24

fantastic produces an unsettling gnomic effect, enhanced in some cases by truncated endings—in "The Drifter's Escape," the drifter's trial for some unknown offense ends abruptly when lightning strikes the courthouse and he gets away in the confusion; "All along the Watchtower" ends with a beginning, "Two riders were approaching, the wind began to howl." The aura of the uncanny that these songs create is probably what Dylan meant when he remarked, years ago, that folk songs grew out of mysteries.

But some of the album is sheer fun, especially "Down Along the Cove," a jaunty blues banged out on the piano, and "I'll Be Your Baby Tonight," a thirties-type pop tune that rhymes "moon" with "spoon" for the benefit of those pundits who are always crowing over the demise of "Tin Pan Alley pap." And "Dear Landlord," the best cut musically, is further evidence that Dylan has—well, the only word for it is mellowed: "Now each of us has his own special gift and you know this was meant to be true,/And if you don't underestimate me I won't underestimate you." In the end, what this album is about is Dylan's reconciliation with his past, with ordinary people, and even—warily, ambivalently—with his archenemies, the landlords of the world.

Of course, being Bob Dylan, he has turned this reconciliation into a rebellion. His sudden removal of the mask—see, it's me, a songwriter, I just want to write nice songs—and the apparent step backward could be as traumatic for the public as his previous metamorphoses; Dylan is still in the business of shaking us up. *John Wesley Harding* does not measure up to *Blonde on Blonde*. It is basically a tour de force. But it serves its purpose, which is to liberate Dylan—and the rest of us—from the *Sgt. Pepper* straitjacket. Dylan is free now to work on his own terms. It would be foolish to predict what he will do next. But I hope he will remain a mediator, using the language of pop to transcend it. If the gap between past and present continues to widen, such mediation may be crucial. In a communications crisis, the true prophets are the translators.

1967–1968

You Can't Go Down
Home Again

It was a hot, bright Saturday afternoon, and some nine thousand sunburned fans roamed through Newport's Festival Field sampling the folk music workshops. Although there was a semblance of a schedule (the staff had mimeographed a map of offerings ranging from Folk Dance to Banjo, from Bluegrass to Blues Jam Session Open to All), groups formed and dissolved and regrouped pretty much as they pleased. Some people tried to guess where the celebrities would go—the workshops provided informal contact with performers, and everyone wanted informal contact with B. B. King, Taj Mahal, and Janis Joplin—but most took potluck. Over at Area 17 (Contemporary), Tim Buckley sang to fifty people; down behind the food tent, Pete Seeger admired a Yugoslavian fan's homemade guitar and told someone from WBAI if he ever needed free records to write to him. The ticket-buying crowd was on the straight side. Most of the grungier types—the ones who made Newport cabdrivers slow down and say "Willyalookit that!"—were nonpaying fellow travelers who gathered in the hills behind the fairgrounds, like Hitchcock's birds, waiting for the evening concert. Inside, the norm was hair above shoulders, work shirts rather than beads, McCarthy and Peace and We Cry Harder Schlitz Beer buttons. Near the main gate, next to tents displaying guitars, Times Square psychedelic jewelry, and Joan Baez's autobiography, stood a VISTA recruiting booth emblazoned with a poster of Dustin Hoffman captioned "What'll You Do When You Graduate?"

Then into this pastoral carnival crashed the sound of—electric blues. The workshops were not supposed to use amplification, but for obvious reasons this rule could not apply to City Blues, so a minimum of sound equipment had been set up on the amphitheater stage. Behind the amps the stage filled up with kids; others gravitated to the seats below. They were hoping for B. B. King or Big Brother and the Holding Company but were happy to get Junior Wells and Buddy Guy. Wells and Guy are much closer to pop than to folk. Their blues are hard, almost r.-&-b., with drumming that could pass at Motown; their act—dancing, hugging each other, exhorting the audience, jumping off the stage—resembles a soul show. And they are loud. Within minutes they had attracted a concert-sized crowd (nearly as large, in fact, as the audience the previous night). Finally, George Wein, the festival's rotund director, clambered onstage and suggested turning down the sound a bit.

The spectators groaned.

"But it's too loud, it's interfering with the other workshops."

"Kill the others!"

"Stop the other workshops!"

Supporting shouts and applause.

"Suppose we turn these mikes off, and turn them on when somebody's singing—"

The crowd booed and hissed.

Wein capitulated, and Buddy Guy announced, "This is my first year at Newport, and now you people have to come to Chicago. We play *loud!* I'd like this mike even louder!"

Everybody cheered.

27

As soon as Wells and Guy had finished, the audience began yelling "B. B.!" and "Big Brother!" and "*Jan-niss!*"

"We had something unique set up here," Wein announced sadly. "Twenty-two workshops . . . no amplification . . . so each little group could . . ."

"BIG BROTHER!"

They settled for the Jim Kweskin Jug Band and, a little less graciously, for Doc Watson ("This was supposed to be *blues*," someone grumbled), but the excitement was gone. Watson, an excellent country guitarist, did a fine set, which got an appreciative but reserved reaction, and everyone filed out. A blond girl in a floppy hat raced backstage to join some friends. "Hello, you freaks!" she squealed. "I shook hands with Buddy Guy!"

That same afternoon, Richard Goldstein, pop music columnist for the *Village Voice*, entered the press tent to make a phone call. Goldstein, who is twenty-four but looks eighteen and has long, straggly hair, a mustache, and muttonchops, was wearing a white jacket trimmed with embroidered flowers. A festival official, Charles Bourgeois (*sic*), stopped him at the door; when he showed his press pass and stood his ground, Bourgeois called him "just another one of those young punks" and confiscated the pass, because, he said later, he assumed it was stolen.

That was the way it went at Newport this year. Perhaps it is presumptuous to call the folk festival a failure; it did draw seventy thousand people, and most of the concerts were worth hearing. But it failed as a *festival*. Instead of camaraderie, there was tension; instead of participation, consumership. All weekend, the management was busy trying to manipulate a sullen audience and a bunch of equally hostile, if more reticent, performers. As usual, the trouble can be traced less to individuals than to the system. The Newport Folk Festival and its many imitators were conceived according to a simple and (at the time) brilliant formula: popular folk stars, performing for almost no money, would attract a huge audience and subsidize the appearance of noncommercial, traditional musicians, thus exposing the kids who came to see Baez and

Dylan to authentic ethnic music. During the peak years of the folk revival the formula worked beautifully. Folk festivals were, above all, exercises in community. There was a continuity of values, style, and musical goals between urban and ethnic musicians; the former regarded the latter as their mentors and were eager to meet them. Similarly, the audience approached the traditional performers receptively and reverently, even making heroes—new stars—out of the Doc Watsons and the John Hurts. There was real respect for amateur creation; thousands of kids brought their own instruments and spent their time learning from performers and from each other. The producers, the fans, and many of the musicians shared the urban folk ethos, which combined rejection of mass culture with an amorphous, sentimental, pro–civil rights, propeace leftism. But now the folk revival has been eclipsed by the excitement over pop music, and an entirely different spirit prevails. Most pop stars, including those whose roots are in folk music, have little in common with rural, ethnic types. They are pros, very much involved in commerce, in show business, in pleasing an audience, and not at all apologetic about it; they are also personalities, incapable of effacing themselves in the we-are-all-equals-here folk manner even if they should want to. Nor is the rock audience especially interested in traditional musicians and the values they represent. As a result, the strategy that was so successful in 1963 was a fiasco in 1968. The stars brought the crowd, all right, but their glow failed to illuminate the less commercial acts, which were received with restless apathy. So were attempts to appeal to political emotions. One performer invoked Fannie Lou Hamer, another compared a Serbian peasant uprising to the Vietnamese revolution, another sang songs about burning cities and indifferent middle-class Negroes. No one seemed to hear. Only Joan Baez, reminiscing about the time she spent in jail for civil disobedience, revived some of the old feeling, but then she was Joan Baez.

Most of those seventy thousand people had apparently come not as true believers but as businesslike consumers, determined to get their money's worth. I saw few offstage guitars and banjos, or groups of kids getting together to play and sing. The audience wanted to participate in its own way—to be allowed to respond to the idols it had come to hear. But orgiastic hero worship was exactly what the festival staff was trying to avoid. The focus of the tension here was amplification. Every year since 1965, when a purist crowd booed Bob Dylan for playing his electric guitar, Wein has cautiously increased the festival's quota of electric musicians. But he can go just so far. The town, which has always been dubious about the festival and the assorted bohemians it attracts (this year Wein had to fight for a permit to put on an auxiliary concert in the local high school), will not tolerate a lot of loud music. Even more important, amplified music tends to overwhelm everything else. If the festival is to remain a *folk* festival, rock and urban-blues groups cannot be allowed to dominate it. Nevertheless, it is ridiculous to invite electric acts—especially when they are supposed to be the drawing cards—and tell them they can't make music the way they want to make it and the audience wants to hear it. For most of the weekend, amplifiers were kept at low volume. This was especially disastrous for Taj Mahal, who sounded sickly, but all the electric performers resented it; they were not willing to go along with the Newport game, which decreed that they were mere crowd-pleasers and that Libba Cotten, Henry Crowdog, and Buell Kazee were the real V.I.P.s. The staff aggravated the bad feeling by regarding the festival crowd—particularly the hangers-on camping on the hill—mainly as a nuisance and a potential threat to order. There were fences and cops all over the place; the half-empty box seats were guarded from incursions by the proles, and God help the unwary spectator who tried to buy a Coke at the performers' refreshment stand. But the weekend passed with only one serious incident: several kids went to the hospital after dropping some unidentified pills, and the rumor persisted, in spite of Wein's denial, that one girl had died. On Sunday, Yippie leader Jerry Rubin was hustled out of Festival Field for giving "pornographic literature" (a Yippie leaflet illustrated with a sketch of a copulating couple) to a nun; the nun took it in stride, but Wein was outraged. Otherwise, things were all too peaceful.

The first evening concert, on Thursday night, was a grim affair called Free Form Folk. Jim Kweskin, a member of the festival's board of directors, had instigated an experiment in spontaneity. There was to be no schedule, no program; a group of performers would get onstage, and the rest would be up to them. "In this new age of LSD, pot, macrobiotics, yoga masters, and the total involvement of psychedelic ballrooms and light shows," he explained in the festival program (why, I wondered, did he leave out scientology and glossolalia?), "people seem to be no longer satisfied with the old concept of a stage with performers and an audience with spectators." Further on, he declared, "We want to take that step into the void of the unknown." Predictably, the spontaneity that resulted was that of a bad party. ("I was told that a lot of people here don't know what's happenin'," said Kweskin, acting as nonannouncer. "Well, you're not alone, ha ha! We don't know what's happenin', either.") The two dozen or so performers remained on the stage, where they didn't quite know what to do, and the spectators remained in the audience, where they were bored. The only void in evidence was a large patch of empty seats—the weekend influx had barely begun. And new age or not, the air was permeated with the scent of moldy fig; the performer who copped my Almeda Riddle "Go Tell Aunt Rhody" Folk-Camp Award with a song about the joys of apple-picking had plenty of competition.

There were a few happy moments. Eric von Schmidt, the Henry Miller of the folk revival, sang a lusty "London Waltz" ("The Rolling Stones were there/ Strapped to the electric chair"); the Kaleidoscope, a rock band strongly influenced by Middle Eastern music, was impressive; and Sandy Bull played, much too briefly. But Taj Mahal, handicapped by a mediocre band as well as anemic amps, was a disappointment. As for the evening's star attraction, Richie Havens, he did his classic, *you*-know-the-words hummed version of "A Little Help from My Friends," mangled a couple of Dylan songs, treated us to the ultimate in folk art—the guitar-strum solo—and got a standing ovation. If he had just stood there, it would have made no difference; the crowd was hungry for someone it knew. The concert lasted much too long; since there was no program, no one knew when to stop. But I was afraid to leave, still tyrannized by stories about Bobby or Joanie dropping in after the tourists had gone and playing for the *real* fans. Finally, all the performers joined in on about ten drippy verses of "At the End of a Long, Lonely Day"—a finale if I'd ever heard one. I had gone as far as the parking lot when Joan Baez made an unscheduled appearance and sang something about lending a helping hand.

Friday night, Streets and Mountains, was better. The draggier part of the program, which included a fatter, louder version of Odetta and a superannuated mountain singer, was enlivened by Janis Joplin, who breezed through the audience wearing a flow-ered hat and carrying a champagne glass in each hand. There was a soft buzz—superstar in our midst. Happy and tough and above it all, she stopped in the middle of the aisle, looked around, and disappeared into the performers' tent. Then Arlo Guthrie came on, with his white suit, electric hair, mock-hillbilly-gangster ac-cent, and wide-eyed deadpan, and milked his one joke—the ab-surdity of the bureaucratic mind—for fifteen funny minutes of song and monologue. During the second half Joan Baez surprised me with an imaginative selection of songs, including "Gentle on My Mind" and "Suzanne"; her main faults used to be overserious-ness and lack of variety, and she seems to have conquered both. The most interesting act on the bill was the Bread and Puppet Theatre, a troupe that blends mime, dance, puppetry, and music into the most polished protest art I have ever seen. At its best the staging is so tight that you can't tell the giant papier-mâché puppets from the people. But a lot of the effect depends on lighting and on an intimate atmosphere, so in the huge amphitheater it didn't quite come off. At the end of the play, which involved a highly stylized confrontation between young people and robed figures in death masks, a confused audience waited in silence for it to continue, then clapped uncertainly. Joan Baez and the other performers, along with what looked like a large LBJ puppet, came on for a finale, "Down by the Riverside." And it wasn't even midnight.

The high point of the festival was the Saturday night concert, Country Music for City Folks. The performances were almost uniformly good, and for once the unresponsiveness of the audience annoyed me. George Hamilton IV (remember "A Rose and a Baby Ruth"?) brought his strong voice and mellow (electric) guitar to Gordon Lightfoot's "Early Morning Rain"; Roy Acuff mugged, twirled his yo-yo, and did "Wabash Cannon Ball"; Joan Baez sang—right out there onstage—one of my guilty secret loves, "The Green Green Grass of Home," which has about as much cachet as "Yummy Yummy Yummy." But everyone waited impatiently for the two big acts, which weren't country at all. B. B. King appeared just before intermission and put on his usual superlative show. I admire B. B. more than I like him. I'd rather watch Willie Mays than Joe DiMaggio, and King's music is too controlled and sophisticated for me. Still, I was a little disturbed when King—perhaps trying to emulate Otis Redding's success at the Monterey Pop Festival—ended his performance with a spiel about how the world needs love. It wasn't like him, and it didn't work. Big Brother, of course, was held till the end, while the crowd grew steadily more restless; people kept walking in and out, and bought a lot of hot dogs. Then it was time, and Janis, in one of her great sleazy outfits—a low-cut black minidress with a tinselly bodice, a Dracula cape, and rhinestone arm bracelets—launched into "Piece of My Heart." Her voice was a bit thin (paranoiacally, perhaps, I suspected skulduggery with the mike), but the group played much better than I had remembered. The amps were turned up, and it was good to hear real rock again. Afterward, there was a party in town. B. B. played, Taj Mahal thought his own thoughts, Janis danced and drank ("They don't pay you *nothin'*, man," she said. "But I had a good time tonight, that's what counts"), and the college kids with phony passes gaped. The music was very loud.

Sunday, the last day. The afternoon Fresh Faces concert was entertaining. The most exciting fresh faces belonged to the Kaleidoscope, who did a mordant contemporary version of "Oh Death" and a quasi-oriental piece, "Taxim." In the evening, it rained; Doc Watson was great; Janis Ian did her best to prove that "Society's Child" and "Janey's Blues" were happy flukes; George Wein announced that this was the best festival ever and that the crowd had behaved beautifully. The second half of the evening concert was dedicated to Woody Guthrie; the performers sang Guthrie's songs and read from his autobiography. I might have enjoyed this more if I had not seen the original Guthrie Memorial at Carnegie Hall, which was warmer and better organized and had Bob Dylan besides. Still, it was a good way to end. Guthrie represents the best of what the Newport Folk Festival has stood for; his songs transcend fashion—as all folk music is supposed to do, though little of it does. An hour of "This Train" and "Talkin' Dust Bowl" and "This Land Is Your Land" did a lot to soothe the bitterness of that uptight weekend. At the end I even wanted to linger, but my friends were anxious to get started, hoping to beat the inevitable jam at the ferry. That transportation problem won't be around much longer—a bridge and an interstate highway are in the works. Neither will Festival Field, which is in the path of the highway. Cheap irony, perhaps, but I can't help hoping that someone will take the hint. The folk festival needs more than a new home. It needs a whole new rationale.

August 1968

The Who Sell

E arly in 1966, I got hold of two 45s a tourist friend had brought
back from England—"Anyway Anyhow Anywhere" and
"Substitute," by an unknown (in the States) rock group called
the Who. The records turned out to be driving, snarling, harder-
than-Stones rock-and-roll, with tough, sophisticated lyrics. "Substitute" was—though I didn't think in such terms then—the best
rock-as-paradox song ever written. ("Street Fighting Man" is
second.) It embodied the tension between the wildness of rock
and its artificiality. Its hero remarks that he might look tall, but only
because of his high heels: "I look all white, but my dad was black."
In addition, these musicians I had never heard of were using the
feedback from their amplifiers to make unheard-of noises, adding
chaos to the steady violence of the beat. It seemed an odd case
of cultural lag that the Who hadn't caught on here. They were
obviously superstar material, they were apparently making it big
in England, and "Substitute" was a sure hit if I had ever heard
one. I went looking for more Who records. I had to look pretty
hard, but within a few weeks I had found an American version of
"Substitute," recorded on Atco (with the reference to interracial

parentage deleted), and the Who's first album, *My Generation* (on Decca), both of which I immediately bought.

As funny as the Beatles, as arrogant as the Stones, the Who specialized in an unbohemian youth-prole defiance that was much closer to the spirit of fifties rock. As Peter Townshend, the group's lead guitarist, chief songwriter, and presiding genius put it recently, "Mick Jagger was a beatnik. I only became one later." The unadorned message of the album's title song ("Why don't you all f-f-fade away?/ Don't try to dig what we all s-s-say") was familiar, though the anarchic electronic noise was new. That summer, when the Beatles amazed us with *Revolver*, I decided that the Who had missed their chance. They were wonderful, but too provincial and unpolished for the great studio-rock era then emerging. Neither Atco, which had not yet learned how to promote the new rock, nor Decca, an easy-listening, country-oriented label, had recognized the Who's potential, and now it was too late. By rights, the Who should have been up there with the Beatles and the Stones—international celebrities, cosmopolites. Instead, I figured, they would wind up in some Birmingham factory. In taking the Who's image so literally, I was badly underestimating Townshend's brilliance—but also paying it unwitting tribute.

Months later, the Who finally had their first Stateside success. "Happy Jack," a medium-sized hit, became the title song of a new album. In accordance with the times, the Who's music had grown more complex and subtle; the violence was balanced by playfulness, and the suggestion of the fifties was gone. Generational polemics had given way to narratives and character sketches, often infused with whimsy. I missed the crude energy but liked what had replaced it. The major achievement of the album was "A Quick One While He's Away," a series of brief songs about a woman, her late-arriving lover, and her temporary comforter, Ivor the Engine Driver. The mini-opera, as Townshend called it, ended with a transcendent, *Messiah*-like chorus of "You are forgiven!"—energy transformed into love and exaltation.

The Who toured the United States and established themselves as fine live performers. Roger Daltrey, the blond lead singer, made angel faces for the Who's newer, gentler songs, with their freaky characters—"Tattoo," "I'm a Boy," "Happy Jack"—but could switch to convincing j.-d. truculence for old standards like "My Generation." Keith Moon gave a nonstop, manic show on the drums. Townshend kept up and elaborated his cathartic smash-the-guitar (and sometimes the sound equipment) finale. The Who were enthusiastically received at the Monterey Pop Festival and began to gather an underground following—"underground" in that Decca wasn't pushing them. The group's managers pushed them instead and, aided by the hip community's efficient grapevine, generated another hit single, "I Can See for Miles," and made a best seller out of the Who's next L.P., *The Who Sell Out*.

The album was presented as a top-forty program, complete with commercials and disc-jockey patter, on Radio London, one of the illegal offshore radio stations that had been challenging the B.B.C.'s monopoly and, not incidentally, providing England with its first authentic rock radio. *The Who Sell Out* was not a satire—as many American bohemians, with their anticommercial reflexes, assumed —but a tribute. It was also the Who's first direct acknowledgment of the pop consciousness that had always informed their style and their music, from Townshend's British-flag jackets to footnotes on mass culture like "Substitute" to songs like "Anyway Anyhow Anywhere," which, as Townshend explains, "looked, felt, and sounded like pop records but were deliberately polished up to make them more exciting." *The Who Sell Out* emphasized the tender aspect of pop—its humanity, rather than its aggressive vulgarity. The characters portrayed in the songs were all more or less unworldly—misfits in some way—but nonetheless the kind of people who eat Heinz baked beans and sign up for instruction from Charles Atlas. In a sense the record was a protest against the idea of mass man; the characters in the beautifully crafted singing commercials (Spotted Henry, who found salvation in Medac pimple-remover, and the actress whose deodorant let her down in "Odorono") had the uniqueness and the spiritual dignity of, say,

Mary-Anne with the Shaky Hands or Silas Stingy or the religious crusader of "Rael." Townshend's message seemed to be that people's foibles made them worthy of love. As in "A Quick One," with its theme of sin and redemption, the Christian overtones were there, but deflated to the level of the ridiculously, banally human. People might be too preoccupied with acne, money, sex, or crazy religious wars on islands, but "You are forgiven!"

The fourth Who album was a debacle. Without the Who's knowledge or permission, Decca, which still hadn't caught on to what was happening—or didn't care—took their current single, "Magic Bus," threw in whatever old Who tracks were available, some of them from previous albums, and created a mediocrity called *Magic Bus: The Who on Tour*. From Decca's standpoint this was perfectly logical: when you have a hit record, you squeeze extra money out of it by putting out a padded album—right? Right—five years ago. The group was furious, and the resulting showdown apparently blew some cobwebs out of Decca's offices. In any case, the Who's new double-album rock opera, *Tommy*, has been packaged with as much care, and released with as much fanfare, as it deserves—which is plenty.

As befits an opera, *Tommy* has a highly melodramatic plot. Little Tommy Walker sees his father kill his mother's lover and goes blind, deaf, and dumb when his parents exhort him, "You didn't hear it,/ You didn't see it./ You won't say nothing to no one." He is bullied by a cousin, raped by an alcoholic uncle, and pitied by his parents, but develops a rich inner life. He takes LSD, becomes a famous pinball champion, is finally cured of his afflictions, and is hailed by thousands as a new messiah. But when he insists that his followers seek enlightenment by playing pinball with their eyes covered and their ears and mouths stopped, the people reject him, and he reverts to a solipsistic existence. *Tommy* succeeds purely as rock; like most of the Who's work, it combines maximum breakout frenzy (which they perfected long before the white blues bands came along) with maximum economy and restraint. But there is an added dimension, first hinted at in "A Quick

38

One"—a quiet, melodic lyricism that represents spirituality. The melodies in *Tommy* are the most compelling that Townshend has written, especially in the songs that go on wholly or partly inside Tommy's head—"Amazing Journey," "Sensation," "Go to the Mirror." The result is a dramatic—even operatic—tension, expressed as noise vs. music, between the outside world's destructiveness toward Tommy and his inner peace and growth.

Although Tommy is clearly sympathetic and, in fact, a hero, struggling out of a hopeless situation to attain near-divinity, Townshend is too much of a populist simply to glorify mysticism. Tommy's version of enlightenment has its ludicrous side—it's hard to blame the people for backing out. And he is ultimately a failure, a wounded ego going back into himself instead of out into the world. The people's point of view is best articulated in a song about a groupie named Sally Simpson: though she reaches out to Tommy because he serves a need, for sex or love or rebellion against her father, "She knew from the start/ Deep down in her heart/ That she and Tommy were worlds apart." Townshend's basic skepticism about transcendental solutions comes through in one of the opera's key songs, "The Acid Queen." Not only does acid fail to cure Tommy, as advertised, but there is a suggestion that the trip is a torture much like nasty Cousin Kevin's or dirty Uncle Ernie's: "He's never been more alive./ His head it shakes, his fingers clutch./ Watch his body writhe!"

Tommy works both as a long coherent piece and as a collection of songs. Although rock opera is a dangerously pretentious concept, the album is neither arty nor boring, because each cut—except for one rather monotonous instrumental—is a short, self-contained, excellent pop song. "Pin Ball Wizard" is even more than excellent—it's one of the great rock songs of the decade. With those two exceptions, the records are too uniformly good for one track or another to be singled out for mention.

So the Who have finally made it, both critically and commercially, and everyone is happy for them and especially for Townshend. Yet the years of struggle did have their positive side. For rock musicians, freedom is the recognition of commercial necessity; no one knows that better than Pete Townshend. From the beginning, the Who knew they had it ("All the groups knew they had it," says Townshend, "but we *really* knew we had it") and were determined to break through, differentiate themselves from the hundreds, maybe thousands, of British groups that had been inspired by the Beatles. Townshend created and exaggerated an image ("American bands don't understand about image; that's why you can't tell one from the other"), and the image *became* the Who and became a myth. Pete's guitar-smashing climax started as an assault on indifference: "There was magic in the group, and we weren't communicating it; I had to do something." Decca's neglect and the elusiveness of success in America forced the Who to keep honing and refining the image, the music, the act.

The group's evolution has also been a function of Townshend's personal growth: "Look, rock and roll is above all an expression of the frustrations of youth. Well, this is 1969, I'm an adult, I don't have the same frustrations anymore. My concerns now are mainly spiritual." Nevertheless, the Who remain the Who, and at the core of their music, however spiritualized, is rock-and-roll. They look all white, but their dad was black. They are no longer kids, but they have not forgotten.

July 1969

Elvis in Las Vegas

Las Vegas is more like Hollywood than Hollywood, because the money is changing hands right out front. Committed to veneer as an art form, over-thirty and relentlessly white in essence, if not always in packaging, Vegas is the antithesis of the cultural revolution. Its hopelessly reactionary nature is best exemplified not by the fountains in front of Caesars Palace, or even by the ethnic comedians, but by the existence of—yes—prominent citizens who want to Make Las Vegas Beautiful, which means toning down the neon on Fremont Street and creating vest-pocket parks. Andy Warhol, tolerant as he is, would have a hard time justifying that. Yet the metaphor of the crap game does have its application to rock: "Just give me money,/ That's what I want." The crass determination to get rich has been one of the great unsung forces behind the cultural revolution. Of course, it has also worked the other way. In the past fifteen years Hollywood and its variants have bought off plenty of rock performers: the Paul Anka types, who used rock as a detour until the nightclubs were ready for them; black people—like the Supremes—who identified success with whiteness; and, most important of all, Elvis Presley. Elvis, the very definition of rock-and-roll for its vociferous defenders and detractors, became the first rock-and-roller to switch to ballads for the whole family and a pioneer (here he had some competition from Annette Funicello and friends) of the unalienated youth movie. You couldn't blame Elvis. In those days everyone kept speculating about what would happen to punks like him when the rock-and-roll fad was over. It took the Beatles to affirm the first principle of the cultural revolution: the kids have money, and kid music equals kid capitalism. Colonel Parker, meet Brian Epstein.

When I heard that Presley had accepted an engagement at the new International Hotel in Las Vegas and was to give his first concert in nine years, I knew the confrontation had to be interesting. Elvis was at once old money and young money, sellout and folk hero. How would he play it? In his television special last winter he wore a leather jacket and wiggled his hips. But then he recorded "In the Ghetto," which was weak on beat and strong on slush. It was a number-one hit—except in the ghetto—and no doubt met with the approval of the Make Las Vegas Beautiful folks. Now Kirk Kerkorian, who owns the International and apparently wants to become Nevada's other famous tycoon, was energetically promoting Elvis's return to the stage. He invited all the New York rock writers to come out in his plane—the first privately owned DC-9, remodeled to seat twenty people and make the usual first-class accommodations look chintzy. The press releases for the hotel promised that all its features would be the largest, the newest, and the most expensive. I decided to ignore my misgivings about junkets (a traditional Hollywood institution). In a medium as sensitive to context as rock, the hype is an essential part of the message; the story, I rationalized, was not just Elvis, but Elvis and all of us in Kerkorian's womb. Along with other refugees from the cultural revolution, armed with long hair, giant sunglasses, and artificial euphoriants, I set out to dig Babylon: garish is beautiful. There was something to be said for the Las Vegas thing. At the same time I hoped Elvis would be crude and surly and stomp all over the veneer with his blue suede shoes.

Elvis in Las Vegas

The opening took place in the Showroom Internationale, a two-thousand-seat nightclub whose sublimely irrelevant decor included relief carvings of Greek temples and winged gods and goddesses, and whose menu that night consisted of such tasty items as Aloyau Rôti à l'Anglaise Périgourdine and Pointes d'Asperges au Beurre. The audience was 99.44 percent white and predominantly middle-aged and moneyed; the celebrities present ranged from Fats Domino and Phil Ochs to Pat Boone and Henry Mancini. I was surprised at how seriously people were taking the occasion. They seemed to feel that Elvis was theirs, not just a progenitor of the music their kids listened to. A woman of fifty who had come from Los Angeles whispered excitedly, "My husband thinks I'm real silly, but I always wanted to see Elvis in person." It was obviously the raunchy Elvis, not the Hollywood Elvis, that she wanted to see.

We had to sit through the Sweet Inspirations—a great black gospel-rock group that persists in wasting its talent singing "Alfie" —and one of those unmentionable comedians. Then Presley came on and immediately shook up all my expectations and preconceived categories. There was a new man out there. A grown man in black bell-bottoms, tunic, and neckerchief, devoid of pout and baby fat, skinny, sexy, totally alert, nervous but smiling easily. For some reason he had dyed his hair black. It was the same length as ever, but combed down instead of back into a ducktail. He started with "Blue Suede Shoes." He still moved around a lot, but in a much different spirit. What was once deadly serious frenzy had been infused with humor and a certain detachment: This is where it began—isn't it a good thing? Though the show was more than anything else an affirmation of Presley's sustaining love for rhythm-and-blues—we knew it all the time, Elvis—it was not burdened by an oppressive reverence for the past. He knew better than to try to be nineteen again. He had quite enough to offer at thirty-three. He sang most of his old songs, including a few of the better ballads, and a couple of new ones. When he did "In the Ghetto," his emotion was so honest it transformed the song; for the first time I

43

saw it as representing a white Southern boy's feeling for black music, with all that that implied. "Suspicious Minds," an earthy country-rock song about jealousy, which is going to be Presley's new single, was the highlight of the show. Almost as exciting was his version of "What'd I Say." The only mistake he made was to sing the coda from "Hey Jude;" once a gimmick has been picked up by Eydie Gorme on a cerebral-palsy telethon, it loses something. But the gesture was understandable. Elvis was clearly unsure of himself, worried that he wouldn't get through to people after all those years, and relieved and happy when he realized we were with him. As the evening went on, he gained in confidence, and the next night he was loose enough to fool around with the audience, accepting handkerchiefs to mop his forehead and reaching out his hands to women in the front row. During both performances there was a fair amount of sighing and screaming, but like Elvis's sexual posturing, it was more in fun than in ecstasy. It was the ritual that counted: "Of *course* I screamed. I'm not dead *yet*." At the opening-night press conference I asked Presley if he had had trouble relating to an audience of mostly older people. He shook his head and smiled. "The older people have learned, you know. They can do it, too." Yeah, yeah, yeah.

If Elvis continues to perform—he says he wants to—and "Suspicious Minds" is as big a hit as it should be, he could have a significant impact on pop music in the coming months. It remains to be seen whether he can transcend either his grand-old-man image or the Hal Wallis years, but he seems to want to try. I wonder if Colonel Parker approves. Is Parker just an ectoplasmic projection of Presley's Hollywood side? Will he now shrivel up? The night before I left Las Vegas, I saw him drop five hundred dollars at roulette. You can't win 'em all.

August 1969

44

Cultural Revolution Saved

from Drowning

You have to give the producers of the Woodstock Music and Art Fair this much credit: they are pulling off a great public relations coup. They have apparently succeeded in creating the impression that the crisis in Bethel was a capricious natural disaster rather than a product of human incompetence, that the huge turnout was completely unexpected (and in fact could not have been foreseen by reasonable men), and that they have lost more than a million dollars in the process of being good guys who did everything possible to transform an incipient fiasco into a groovy weekend. Incredibly, instead of hiding from the wrath of disappointed ticket-buyers and creditors, they are bragging that the festival was a landmark in the development of youth culture and have announced that they plan to hold it again next year. But before history is completely rewritten, a few facts, semifacts, and strong inferences are in order.

For at least a month before the festival it was obvious to everyone involved in the music scene—industry people, writers for both the straight and the underground press, radicals, and hippies—and also to the city fathers of Wallkill, New York, that the crowd was

45

going to be enormous and the facilities inadequate. The four under-thirty backers of Woodstock Ventures seemed to be motivated less by greed than by sheer hubris: the ambitiousness of the project was meant to establish them as *the* pop producers, kingpins of the youth market. Their promotion was pervasive. On July 18, a month before the festival, the *Times* reported that the management expected as many as 200,000 people and had already sold fifty thousand tickets. At that time, they were planning to hold the festival in Wallkill, on a three-hundred-acre site—half the size of the grounds in Bethel—linked to civilization by three country roads. When a Concerned Citizens Committee warned that Wallkill's water supply could not accommodate the anticipated influx and that festival officials had not made realistic plans to cope with traffic, health, or security, the producers vowed to fight the town's attempt to exclude them and implied that the opposition came from antiyouth rednecks. When the change of site was announced, just twenty-four days before the scheduled opening of the fair, there was a lot of speculation that it would never come off at all. An experienced promoter told me, "It'll happen, but only because they've got so much money tied up in it. They can't afford to back out. But they'll never finish their preparations in three weeks. Monterey took three months. It's going to be complete chaos." Al Aronowitz of the *Post*, one of the few journalists to cast a consistently cold eye on the four young entrepreneurs, wrote witty on-location reports giving them the needle and adding to the general pessimism. Meanwhile, back on St. Marks Place, Woodstock was rapidly evolving into this year's thing to do. A "Woodstock Special" issue of the underground weekly *Rat*, published the week of the festival, featured a page of survival advice that began, "The call has been put out across the country for hundreds of thousands to attend a three-day orgy of music and dope and communal experience." I left for Bethel in much the same spirit that I had gone to Chicago at the time of the Democratic Convention. I was emotionally prepared for a breakdown in services and a major riot. If I enjoyed the festival, that would be incidental to participating in a historic event. The actual number of people who showed up was a surprise. The only other real surprise was that there was no riot. The extra numbers could not excuse the flimsiness of the water pipes (they broke down almost immediately), the paucity of latrines (about eight hundred for an expected 200,000 people) and garbage cans, or the makeshift medical facilities (the press tent had to be converted into a hospital). One kid reportedly died of a burst appendix—an incident that in 1969 should at least inspire some questions.

Although it is possible that the fair lost money, many knowledgeable people are inclined to doubt that the loss was anywhere near the $1.5 million dollars Woodstock Ventures is claiming. The corporation should open its books to the public. The thousands of ticket holders who were turned away from the site because of traffic jams (while other thousands of contributors to the traffic jams got in free) deserve some consideration. So far, the management has said nothing about refunds, and there has been talk of setting up a group suit to demand the money. One complication is that since no tickets were collected, there is no way of distinguishing those who made it from those who didn't, but rumor has it that the state may sidestep this problem by suing the producers on the ground that they had no serious intention of taking tickets at the fairgrounds.

If the festival succeeded in spite of the gross ineptitude of its masterminds, it was mostly because 300,000 or more young people were determined to have a good time no matter what. The accounts of the peacefulness and generosity of the participants are all true, but they have tended to miss the point. The cooperative spirit did not stem from solidarity in an emergency—the "we all forgot our differences and helped each other" phenomenon that attends power blackouts and hurricanes—so much as from a general refusal to adopt any sort of emergency psychology. The widespread conviction that the Lord (or the Hog Farm, or the people of Monticello, or someone) would provide removed any incentive to fight or to hoard food, and the pilgrims simply proceeded to do what they had come to do: dig the music and the woods, make

47

friends, reaffirm their life style in freedom from hostile straights and cops, swim naked, and get high. Drug dealing was completely open; kids stood on Hurd Road, the main thoroughfare of the festival site, hawking mescaline and acid. But the most exhilarating intoxicants were the warmth and fellow-feeling that allowed us to abandon our chronic defenses against other people. As for the music, though rock was the only thing that could have drawn such a crowd, it was not the focal point of the festival but rather a pleasant background to the mass presence of the hip community. Few of us got close enough to see anything, and as the music continued for seventeen hours at a stretch, our adrenalin output naturally decreased. (On Sunday a boy who had driven in from California commented, "Wow, I can't believe all the groups here, and I'm not even listening to them." "It's not the music," said another. "It's—all this!") The sound system was excellent, and thousands listened from camps in the woods, dozing and waking while the music went on till dawn. Everyone was so quiet you felt almost alone in the dark, but you couldn't move very far without stepping on someone's hand or brushing against a leg.

The festival site was like the eye of a storm—virtually undisturbed by the frantic activity behind the scenes. Once the nuisance of getting there was over with (I eventually got a ride in a performers' police-escorted caravan) and the Lord had provided (I just happened to bump into some friends with a leakproof tent and plenty of food), I found the inconveniences trivial compared to the pleasures. But then I did not have to sleep out in the mud for two nights, and by Sunday I couldn't help suspecting that some of the beautiful, transcendent acceptance going around was just plain old passivity. It was a bit creepy that there was such a total lack of resentment at the fair's mismanagement, especially among those who had paid from seven to eighteen dollars. People either made excuses for Woodstock Ventures ("They couldn't help it, man; it was just too big for them") or thought of the festival as a noble social experiment to which crass concepts like responsible planning were irrelevant. For the most part they took for granted not only the discomforts but the tremendous efforts made by the state, the local communities, and unpaid volunteers to distribute cheap or free food and establish minimum standards of health and safety. No one seemed to comprehend what the tasks of mobilizing and transporting emergency food, water, and medical personnel, clearing the roads, and removing garbage meant in terms of labor and money. Ecstatic heads even proclaimed that the festival proved the viability of a new culture in which no one worked and everything was free. And in the aftermath anyone who has dared to complain has been put down as a crank. It should be possible to admit that the people created a memorable gathering without embracing promoters who did their best to make it memorable in quite another sense. (A letter writer in the *Village Voice* went as far as to say, "Woodstock Ventures should be congratulated and not chastised for giving us smiles, peace, music, and good vibrations." All those paying customers might disagree about being "given" music; personally, I don't see why Woodstock Ventures should get credit for my smiles.) But maybe it isn't. And maybe there is a lesson here about the political significance of youth culture. From the start, the cultural-revolutionary wing of the radical movement saw Woodstock as a political issue. The underground papers made a lot of noise about businessmen profiting from music that belonged to the community, and some movement people demanded and received money to bring political groups to the festival and set up an enclave called Movement City as a center for radical activity. If the festival staff had been foolish enough to try to restrict the audience to paid admissions, the movement might have had something to do. As it was, Movement City was both physically and spiritually isolated from the bulk of the crowd. It was not the activists but a hundred-odd members of the Hog Farm, a Santa Fe–based pacifistic commune, who were the most visible community presence, operating a free kitchen, helping people recover from bad acid trips, and setting up a rudimentary communication system of oral and written survival bulletins. A few radicals talked hopefully of liberating the concessions or the stage area. Abbie Hoffman interrupted the Who's set on Saturday night to berate the crowd for listening to music when John Sinclair, a Michigan activist, had just been sentenced to a long prison term for giving some marijuana to a cop. Peter Townshend hit Hoffman with his guitar, which is more of a commentary on the relation of rock to politics than all of *Rat*'s fuzzy moralizing.

What cultural revolutionaries do not seem to grasp is that, far from being a grass-roots art form that has been taken over by businessmen, rock itself comes from the commercial exploitation of blues. It is bourgeois at its core, a mass-produced commodity, dependent on advanced technology and therefore on the money controlled by those in power. Its rebelliousness does not imply specific political content; it can be—and has been—criminal, fascistic, and coolly individualistic as well as revolutionary. Nor is bohemianism inherently radical. It can simply be a more pleasurable way of surviving within the system, which is what the pop sensibility has always been about. Certainly that was what Woodstock was about: ignore the bad, groove on the good, hang loose, and let things happen. The truth is that there can't be a revolutionary culture until there is a revolution. In the meantime, we should insist that the capitalists who produce rock concerts offer reasonable service at reasonable prices.

September 1969

See America First:

Easy Rider and *Alice's Restaurant*

In 1969, the Year of the Pig, participants in what is known as (descriptively) youth culture or (smugly) hip culture or (incompletely) pop culture or (longingly) the cultural revolution are going through big changes. For choices have to be made now; they can no longer be left to a dubious mañana. After hearing Nixon's speech—"North Vietnam cannot defeat us; we can only defeat ourselves"—who can doubt that America as we have known it could completely disappear between one day and the next? Or maybe it already has, and what we are feeling now is phantom pain from an amputated limb. In this crisis our confusions and ambivalences about this country, *our* country, no matter how securely they seem to have occupied it, become more than intellectual gossip. Our lives may literally depend on how we resolve them.

The current generation of bohemians and radicals hasn't decided whether to love or hate America. On a superficial level the dominant theme has been hate—for the wealth and greed and racism and complacency, the destruction of the land, the bullshit rhetoric of democracy, and the average American's rejection of aristocratic

European standards of the good life in favor of a romance with mass-produced consumer goods. But love is there, too, perhaps all the more influential for being largely unadmitted. There is the old left strain of love for the "real" America, the Woody Guthrie–Pete Seeger America of workers-farmers-hoboes, the open road, this-land-is-your-land. And there is the newer pop strain, the consciousness—initiated by Andy Warhol and his cohorts, popularized by the Beatles and their cohorts, evangelized by Tom Wolfe, and made respectable in the bohemian ghettos by Bob Dylan and Ken Kesey—that there is something magical and vital as well as crass about America's commodity culture, that the romance with consumer goods makes perfect sense if the goods are motorcycles and stereo sets and far-out clothes and Spider Man comics and dope. How can anyone claim to hate America, deep down, and be a rock fan? Rock *is* America—the black experience, the white experience, technology, commercialism, rebellion, populism, the Hell's Angels, the horror of old age—as seen by its urban adolescents.

At this point, hate and love seem to be merging into a sense of cosmic failure, a pervasive feeling that everything is disintegrating, including the counterculture itself, and that we really have nowhere to go. The current exodus of young people to the country, while a healthy expression of people's survival instincts, is in a way an admission of failure, a retreat rather than a breakthrough. The back-to-the-land movement, insofar as it represents a serious attempt by both communes and conventional families to make a living at farming, with all the hardships that involves, is just a replay of that part of the American dream that dies the hardest. There is an obvious contradiction between the consciousness of the dissident culture, which is based on an apprehension of what it means to be human once simple survival is no longer a problem, and small-scale farming, an activity that requires almost total commitment to simple survival.

If enough people, with enough social support to make judicious, cooperative use of technology and create new forms of social organization that were more than isolated experiments, were to get involved in farming, a new synthesis might be created. But so long as the return to rural life remains an individual revolt—and in relation to the whole society a commune is a unit only slightly less parochial than a family—with no support and no guidance except for history, it would be suprising if anachronistic patterns did not assert themselves, especially since the decision to farm is so often made out of the erroneous conviction that machines and cities are causing all our problems. The new farming communities tend, for instance, to be conspicuously male supremacist, partly because of the practical problems in dividing the work (technology makes women's lesser muscular capacity irrelevant) and partly because the American farming myth is very much a scenario for the dominant male—the woman stays in the background and bakes bread while her mate chops down trees. It is as if we are all trapped in a maze; some of us who have gotten bored or horrified with the official route through the maze have found all sorts of creative ways to cut corners and wander through back alleys, but we are now ending up in pretty much the same places. It's the maze itself that needs to be opened up, rearranged, or simply destroyed.

Tom Wolfe's *The Electric Kool-Aid Acid Test* asked the pertinent questions—Is it possible to reinterpret and salvage the American trip by painting the bus with Day-glo? Is there an underground exit from the maze?—at a time when most of us were not yet especially concerned. Now two enormously popular movies, *Easy Rider* and *Alice's Restaurant*, have attempted to deal with the same theme in very different ways. Neither film is definitive, and neither goes nearly as deep as Wolfe's book—but both hit pretty close.

Easy Rider is the better and more important of the two movies.

When I first saw it, at a press screening in New York, I didn't understand why it moved me so deeply. Certainly much of it was enjoyable, even memorable. Dennis Hopper, playing Peter Fonda's egotistical, slightly paranoid friend, gave a thoroughly convincing performance, the only realistic portrayal of a head I've seen on film. Jack Nicholson was brilliant as the good-hearted, fucked-up juicer lawyer who joins the travelers and trades a slow death in a small southern town for a fast one on the road. The rock sound track was great, especially for anyone who loves the Byrds and Steppenwolf as much as I do. The dope-smoking scenes were beautifully real. Most movies that acknowledge the existence of grass (*Alice's Restaurant* included) tend to treat it with oppressive reverence; in *Easy Rider*, as in life, stoned people were, for one thing, very funny and, for another, very happy. (Just because of their lack of tendentiousness the scenes were a significant commentary —when Nicholson, turned on for the first time, went into a long, fantastic rap about extraterrestrial beings, it became poignantly clear that people who condemn marijuana as an "escape from reality" are proceeding from the same fallacy as those who think children should be reading about coal trucks instead of elves.) Finally, who could resist all those juicy shots of the road and motorcycles?

But in fact, what was *Easy Rider* but another superromantic account of individual rebellion against the straight world, depicted as every northern liberal's fantasy of the implacable South? There was Peter Fonda, the superhandsome, supercool hero with the symbolic names (Wyatt, and in case we didn't get it, Captain America, and in case we didn't get *that*, his sidekick's name is Billy), looking sexy and inscrutable. There was all that superpastorality: as a friend pointed out, the road from Los Angeles to New Orleans displayed not a single billboard. (True, the filmmakers would have had to pay to photograph billboards, but it says something if they didn't think it was worth the money.) The commune scenes—all those wholesome-looking people with gleaming white teeth, the women in the kitchen, of course, making like good pioneer wives

—and a nude swimming scene, the ultimate in idyllic purity, and a sophomoric acid sequence in a cemetery. The heroes throwing away their watches, and Fonda letting out profundities like "I'm hip about time." And the ending—oh, wow!—sheer shock-melodrama.

Yet that ending really shook me. Though I saw the shotgun blast and the flames, I couldn't quite believe it; it was too final. My mind kept coming back to it. Then I saw *Easy Rider* again, shortly after I had made my own move away from the big city. Colorado Springs, where I had gone to live, to do political organizing, and to hassle out my own response to the American condition, 1969, is an ultraconservative army town in the shadow of the Rockies that comes close to embodying the extremes of natural beauty and social horror that provide the setting for *Easy Rider*. And from that vantage, I saw why the movie affected me the way it did: beyond the melodrama of groovy kids vs. rednecks is an emotion that more and more of us, young and old alike, are experiencing, the overpowering sense of loss, the anguish of *What went wrong? We blew it—how?*

Easy Rider is about the failure of America on all levels, hip and straight. Billy and Wyatt on their bikes, riding free down the open road, are living another version of the rugged individualist frontier fantasy, and the big dope deal that made them financially independent is just hip capitalism. It won't work, and by the end of the movie Wyatt knows it. The key line of the film is his admission, "We blew it!" I have no idea if the allusion is intentional, but *The Electric Kool-Aid Acid Test* ends with the same line. There it refers to the failure of Ken Kesey's particular frontier fantasy. Kesey envisioned a psychedelic frontier that went beyond drugs, but he couldn't bring it off. "We blew it!" . . . Somehow we have to face it that the pioneer thing is over, that we have to create some new myths—or better yet, move aside and let somebody else have a chance to create them; now there would be a *real* cultural revolution. As for the violent ending, it could hardly be more appropriate. Isn't that exactly where America is heading, to some abrupt, apocalyptic explosion—even if the explosion occurs only in our heads?*

Of course there is another possibility—that we will simply withdraw, that resignation will set in. That seems to be the alternative suggested in *Alice's Restaurant*, which despite the clowning of Arlo Guthrie is one of the more depressing movies I've seen lately, much more so than *Easy Rider*, because confusion and passivity are more demoralizing than violence. *Alice's Restaurant* concentrates almost entirely on decay from within. Although much of the "plot," such as it is, pits Guthrie against the outside world—he is thrown out of a couple of schools, hassled by the cops and by people who don't like long hair, put through the whole jail-courtroom ritual for dumping garbage in the wrong place, and finally almost drafted—the villains are not taken seriously. Conflict with authority is still a game—Officer Obie is a comic figure, jail a lark, Whitehall Street an exercise in absurdity, and the worst thing that happens to Arlo is that he is pushed through a plate glass window by some toughs (this could have been pretty serious, but Hollywood being what it is, he gets up and walks away). The really important conflicts are between Arlo and his supposed friends.

* A while after this review was published, I saw *Easy Rider* again. This time I was startled and chagrined to notice a crucial detail I had twice missed: the shooting that culminates in the murder of the heroes is an accident. Two men in a car pull up alongside the motorcyclists; the passenger points his shotgun out the window at Dennis Hopper, trying to scare him; Hopper gives him the finger; the car hits a bump and the gun goes off, to its owner's evident surprise. The men then go back and finish the job, presumably because they can't afford to leave witnesses. This final irony—in which two American subcultures play out their clashing versions of the American myth to the unintended but no less horrifying death—would seem to support my sense of *Easy Rider*'s ecumenical pessimism, as opposed to the view, expressed most cogently by Diana Trilling, that the movie is a perniciously simplistic celebration of hip innocence and virtue struck down by middle-American corruption.

See America First: Easy Rider and Alice's Restaurant

It is hard to tell how much of the pessimism in *Alice's Restaurant* is deliberate and how much is simply betrayed. Unlike *Easy Rider*, which has a kind of mythic simplicity and is most striking as a parable, *Alice's Restaurant* is disjointed, episodic, and ambivalent in its relation to reality. Some of the incidents in the movie really happened, others are invented; some of the actors play themselves, others (notably Alice and Ray Brock) do not. There is plenty of room for free-floating, semidocumentary revelation, much of which is provided by Guthrie himself. Arlo is this year's Dustin Hoffman, the man of a thousand grimaces, the awkward, scrawny, waiflike antihero. I know he is supposed to be heart-tuggingly appealing and all, and in a way he is, but I would be much more receptive if he weren't so conceited about it. Although in most respects he is the antithesis of Peter Fonda, he has the same unshakable cool, sense of his own rectitude, and basic detachment from other people. In fact, if Guthrie proves anything in two hours on the screen, it is that the alleged love generation has severe hang-ups about personal relationships, particularly sexual ones.

One of the major flaws of the counterculture is that for all its concern with the dispossessed, it is as oppressive as the surrounding society toward the female half of the race. It treats women as "chicks"—nubile decorations—or mothers or goddesses or bitches, rarely as human beings. Some heroes of the cultural revolution—recently jailed Michigan activist John Sinclair is a classic example—equate rebellion with assertion of their maleness, become obnoxiously aggressive, arrogant, and violent, and espouse a version of utopia in which women are reduced to faceless instruments of their sexual fantasies. Others, more cleverly, consider themselves "liberated" from the strictures of the traditional male role—the obligation to support women financially and protect them physically, to be strong, competitive, and ambitious, to suppress their emotions and their personal vanity—and imitate women in the manner of whites imitating blacks, while nonetheless insisting that women serve them and defer to them.

Usually this second pattern goes along with a hypocritical idealization of women: "Chicks really know where it's at, man!" (said fondly, as he smells dinner chick is cooking). *Easy Rider* is an embarrassing commentary on the hip male's contempt for women. As in most Westerns, the world of our two existential cowboys is almost exclusively male; thus the issue of sex does not have to be confronted. The women who enter their domain are strictly two-dimensional figures. Women who show any sexual interest in them —one of the communards, a group of giggling teen-age girls—are portrayed as ridiculous. When they stop at a New Orleans whorehouse as a tribute to their dead friend, the lawyer, who had recommended it, only Billy, the more frivolous of the two characters, is at all eager to sleep with a woman; Captain America is far above such concerns.

In *Alice's Restaurant*, in contrast, sex is a central theme. But Guthrie's attitude toward women is not much different from Fonda's. Female sexual aggressiveness, for instance, is regarded as either a peculiarity of eccentrics or the product of an abnormal state of mind. For some reason unclear to me, women are constantly trying to seduce Arlo and being turned down. After rejecting a pathetic groupie ("I want to, you know, with you, because you're probably going to be an album"), a hard-faced older woman (a friend of his father's, who owns a folk-singing joint), and even Alice (he is a little nicer to her than to the others—she only did it because she was upset), he settles on a girl whose only definable characteristic seems to be that she waited demurely for him to choose her. To be fair, *Alice's Restaurant* does not ignore the sexual problem; Alice is sympathetically followed as she is pushed closer and closer to a breakdown by the insensitivity of men who take both her love and her hard work for granted. But of course the crisis is glossed over; not only does Alice go back to Ray (the real Alice recently got a divorce), she goes back because he needs her to cook Thanksgiving dinner for all their friends!

* * *

Another subject barely touched on in *Easy Rider* that *Alice's Restaurant* explores at length is the meaning of family and home and the possibilities of redefining them. Again the tone is basically negative. Although older people are not lumped together as the enemy—Arlo's deep love for Woody and compassion for his mother are apparent and touching—home is a place to get away from. Arlo is comfortable only on the road or alone in his apartment in New York. And though he loves Alice and Ray, too, he feels no more at ease in the church they have set up as headquarters for the communal family they desperately want to establish. He is forever commuting back and forth from the city. When he's gone, he misses the church, but when he's there, he feels suffocated and restless. Alice nags him to stay, luring him with chicken soup, and he makes excuses and leaves.

Ray Brock is the pivotal character and the most interesting. Halfway between Arlo's generation and Woody's, he craves tradition, stability, and community and can't find or create them, except for the moment in a huge Thanksgiving dinner or the mock church wedding with which he and Alice celebrate their reunion. In the last scene he is caught up in the back-to-the-land dream. He talks enthusiastically of selling the church and buying enough acreage so that people can be together without being on each other's necks. "I bet they wouldn't all drift off if we had land," he muses. But he has lost his audience. Arlo is bored and a little sad, getting ready to drive away. Yeah, Ray, see you later. Meanwhile, back on the road, see what happens. And maybe if he's lucky, he won't get his father's fatal hereditary disease after all . . .

The church family's most spectacular failure is its inability to prevent a speed freak named Shelly from cracking up and finally killing himself with an overdose. Ray beats him up, Alice falls in love with him, and the kids try to make him feel at home. They are about as effective as a middle-class family from Scarsdale, and he flees. But mostly the mistakes are less dramatic, just a matter of the beautiful people being very much like ordinary people. In a moment of anger Ray, who has an autocratic streak, tries to silence disagreement by invoking private property: this is *my* church you're in.

Neither *Easy Rider* nor *Alice's Restaurant* ever considers a political solution to the social chaos. The most Guthrie can conceive of is individual resistance; he wonders at one point whether he would have the courage to refuse induction. Fonda and Hopper never think politically at all. The temptation is to credit the media with a sinister plot to give the impression that there is no alternative to individualism, but that is a convenient cop-out. In private life Guthrie, Fonda, and Hopper are all more or less apolitical and the movies reflect their personalities. Furthermore, I'm not at all sure that their attitude is not shared by the majority of adherents to the hip life style. It may be that those of us who still have some faith in collective action are simply indulging an insane optimism. Nevertheless, it is clear to me that if we want to survive the seventies, we should learn to draw strength from something more solid than a culture that in a few years may be just a memory: "Remember hair down to your shoulders? Remember Janis Joplin? Remember *grass*, man? Wow, those years were really, uh, *far out!*"

December 1969

Janis Joplin

The hippie rock stars of the late sixties merged two versions of that hardy American myth, the free individual. They were stars, which meant achieving liberation by becoming rich and famous on their own terms; and they were, or purported to be, apostles of cultural revolution, a considerably more ambitious and romantic vision of freedom that nevertheless had a similar economic foundation. Young Americans were in a sense the stars of the world, drawing on an overblown prosperity that could afford to indulge all manner of rebellious and experimental behavior. The combination was inherently unstable—Whitman's open road is not, finally, the Hollywood Freeway, and in any case neither stardom nor prosperity could deliver what it seemed to promise. For a fragile historical moment rock transcended those contradictions; in its aftermath, our pop heroes found themselves grappling, like the rest of us, with what are probably enduring changes in the white American consciousness—changes that have to do with something very like an awareness of tragedy. It is in this context that Janis Joplin developed as an artist, a celebrity, a rebel, a woman, and it is in this context that she died.

Joplin belonged to that select group of pop figures who mattered as much for themselves as for their music; among American rock performers she was second only to Bob Dylan in importance as a creator-recorder-embodiment of her generation's history and mythology. She was also the only woman to achieve that kind of stature in what was basically a male club, the only sixties culture hero to make visible and public women's experience of the quest for individual liberation, which was very different from men's. If Janis's favorite metaphors—singing as fucking (a first principle of rock-and-roll) and fucking as liberation (a first principle of the cultural revolution)—were equally approved by her male peers, the congruence was only on the surface. Underneath—just barely —lurked a feminist (or prefeminist) paradox.

The male-dominated counterculture defined freedom for women almost exclusively in sexual terms. As a result, women endowed the idea of sexual liberation with immense symbolic importance; it became charged with all the secret energy of an as yet suppressed larger rebellion. Yet to express one's rebellion in that limited way was a painfully literal form of submission. Whether or not Janis understood that, her dual persona—lusty hedonist and suffering victim—suggested that she felt it. Dope, another term in her metaphorical equation (getting high as singing as fucking as liberation) was, in its more sinister aspect, a pain killer and finally a killer. Which is not to say that the good times weren't real, as far as they went. Whatever the limitations of hippie rock star life, it was better than being a provincial matron—or a lonely weirdo.

For Janis, as for others of us who suffered the worst fate that can befall an adolescent girl in America—unpopularity—a crucial aspect of the cultural revolution was its assault on the rigid sexual styles of the fifties. Joplin's metamorphosis from the ugly duckling of Port Arthur to the peacock of Haight-Ashbury meant, among other things, that a woman who was not conventionally pretty, who had acne and an intermittent weight problem and hair that stuck out, could not only invent her own beauty (just as she invented her wonderful sleazofreak costumes) out of sheer energy, soul, sweetness, arrogance, and a sense of humor, but have that beauty appreciated. Not that Janis merely took advantage of changes in our notions of attractiveness; she herself changed them. It was seeing Janis Joplin that made me resolve, once and for all, not to get my hair straightened. And there was a direct line from that sort of response to those apocryphal burned bras and all that followed.

Direct, but not simple. Janis once crowed, "They're paying me $50,000 a year to be like me." But the truth was that they were paying her to be a personality, and the relation of public personality to private self—something every popular artist has to work out—is especially problematic for a woman. Men are used to playing roles and projecting images in order to compete and succeed. Male celebrities tend to identify with their maskmaking, to see it as creative and—more or less—to control it. In contrast, women need images simply to survive. A woman is usually aware, on some level, that men do not allow her to be her "real self," and worse, that the acceptable masks represent men's fantasies, not her own. She can choose the most interesting image available, present it dramatically, individualize it with small elaborations, undercut it with irony. But ultimately she must serve some male fantasy to be loved—and then it will be only the fantasy that is loved anyway. The female celebrity is confronted with this dilemma in its starkest form. Joplin's revolt against conventional femininity was brave and imaginative, but it also dovetailed with a stereotype—the ballsy, one-of-the-guys chick who is a needy, vulnerable cream puff underneath—cherished by her legions of hip male fans. It may be that she could have pushed beyond it and taken the audience with her; that was one of the possibilities that made her death an artistic as well as human disaster. There is, for instance, the question of her bisexuality. People who knew Janis differ on whether sexual relationships with women were an important part of her life, and I don't know the facts. In any case, a public acknowledgment of bisexual proclivities would not necessarily have contradicted her image; it could easily have been passed off as more pull-out-the-stops hedonism or another manifestation of her all-encompassing need for love. On the other hand, she could have used it to say something new about women and liberation. What makes me wonder is something I always noticed and liked about Janis: unlike many other female performers whose acts are intensely erotic, she never made me feel as if I were crashing an orgy that consisted of her and the men in the audience. When she got it on at a concert, she got it on with everybody.

Still, the songs she sang assumed heterosexual romance; it was men who made her hurt, who took another little piece of her heart. Watching men groove on Janis, I began to appreciate the resentment many black people feel toward whites who are blues freaks. Janis sang out of her pain as a woman, and men dug it. Yet it was men who caused the pain, and if they stopped causing it, they would not have her to dig. In a way their adulation was the cruelest insult of all. And Janis's response—to sing harder, get higher, be worshiped more—was rebellious, acquiescent, bewildered all at once. When she said, "Onstage I make love to 25,000 people, then I go home alone," she was not merely repeating the cliché of the sad clown or the poor little rich girl. She was noting that the more she gave, the less she got, and that honey, it ain't fair.

Like most women singers, Joplin did not write many songs; she mostly interpreted other people's. But she made them her own in a way few singers dare to do. She did not sing them so much as struggle with them, assault them. Some critics complained, not always unfairly, that she strangled them to death, but at her best she whipped them to new life. She had an analogous adversary relationship with the musical form that dominated her imagination —the blues. Blues represented another external structure, one with its own contradictory tradition of sexual affirmation and sexist conservatism. But Janis used blues conventions to reject blues sensibility. To sing the blues is a way of transcending pain by confronting it with dignity, but Janis wanted nothing less than to scream it out of existence. Big Mama Thornton's classic rendition

64

of "Ball and Chain" carefully balances defiance and resignation, toughness and vulnerability. She almost pities her oppressor: "I know you're gonna miss me, baby. . . . You'll find that your whole life will be like mine, all wrapped up in a ball and chain." Her singing conveys, above all, her determination to survive abuse. Janis makes the song into one long frenzied, despairing protest. Why, why, *why*, she asks over and over, like a child unable to comprehend injustice. "It ain't fair . . . this can't be. . . . I just wanted to hold you. . . . All I ever wanted to do was to love you." The pain is overwhelming her, "draggin' me down . . . maybe, maybe you can help me—c'mon *help me*." There are similar differences between her recording of "Piece of My Heart" and Erma Franklin's. When Franklin sings it, it is a challenge: no matter what you do to me, I will not let you destroy my ability to be human, to love. Joplin seems rather to be saying, surely if I keep taking this, if I keep setting an example of love and forgiveness, surely he has to understand, change, give me back what I have given.

Her pursuit of pleasure had the same driven quality; what it amounted to was refusal to admit of any limits that would not finally yield to the virtue of persistence—*try just a little bit harder* —and the magic of extremes. This war against limits was largely responsible for the electrifying power of Joplin's early performances; it was what made *Cheap Thrills* a classic, in spite of its unevenness and the impossibility of duplicating on a record the excitement of her concerts. After the split with Big Brother, Janis retrenched considerably, perhaps because she simply couldn't maintain that level of intensity, perhaps for other reasons that would have become clear if she had lived. My uncertainty on this point makes me hesitate to be too dogmatic about my conviction that her leaving Big Brother was a mistake.

I was a Big Brother fan. I thought they were better musicians than their detractors claimed, but more to the point, technical accomplishment, in itself, was not something I cared about. I thought it was an ominous sign that so many people did care—

including Janis. It was, in fact, a sign that the tenuous alliance between mass culture and bohemianism—or, in my original formulation, the fantasy of stardom and the fantasy of cultural revolution—was breaking down. But the breakdown was not as neat as it might appear. For the elitist concept of "good musicianship" was as alien to the holistic, egalitarian spirit of rock-and-roll as the act of leaving one's group the better to pursue one's individual ambition was alien to the holistic, egalitarian pretensions of the cultural revolutionaries. If Joplin's decision to go it alone was influenced by all the obvious professional/commercial pressures, it also reflected a conflict of values within the counterculture itself—a conflict that foreshadowed its imminent disintegration. And again, Janis's femaleness complicated the issues, raised the stakes. She had less room to maneuver than a man in her position, fewer alternatives to fall back on if she blew it. If she had to choose between fantasies, it made sense for her to go with stardom as far as it would take her.

But I wonder if she really had to choose, if her choice was not in some sense a failure of nerve and therefore of greatness. Janis was afraid Big Brother would hold her back, but if she had thought it was important enough, she might have been able to carry them along, make them transcend their limitations. There is more than a semantic difference between a group and a back-up band. Janis had to relate to the members of Big Brother as spiritual (not to mention financial) equals even though she had more talent than they, and I can't help suspecting that that was good for her not only emotionally and socially but aesthetically. Committed to the hippie ethic of music-for-the-hell-of-it—if only because there was no possibility of their becoming stars on their own—Big Brother helped Janis sustain the amateur quality that was an integral part of her effect. Their zaniness was a salutary reminder that good times meant silly fun—remember "Caterpillar"?—as well as Dionysiac abandon; it was a relief from Janis's extremism and at the same

66

time a foil for it. At their best moments Big Brother made me think of the Beatles, who weren't (at least in the beginning) such terrific musicians, either. Though I'm not quite softheaded enough to imagine that by keeping her group intact Janis Joplin could somehow have prevented or delayed the end of an era, or even saved her own life, it would have been an impressive act of faith. And acts of faith by public figures always have reverberations, one way or another.

Such speculation is of course complicated by the fact that Janis died before she really had a chance to define her post–San Francisco, post–Big Brother self. Her last two albums, like her performances with the ill-fated Kozmic Blues Band, had a tentative, transitional feel. She was obviously going through important changes; the best evidence of that was "Me and Bobby McGee," which could be considered her "Dear Landlord." Both formally— as a low-keyed, soft, folkie tune—and substantively—as a lyric that spoke of choices made, regretted and survived, with the distinct implication that compromise could be a positive act—what it expressed would have been heresy to the Janis Joplin of *Cheap Thrills*. "Freedom's just another word for nothing left to lose" is as good an epitaph for the counterculture as any; we'll never know how—or if—Janis meant to go on from there.

Janis Joplin's death, like that of a fighter in the ring, was not exactly an accident. Yet it's too easy to label it either suicide or murder, though it involved elements of both. Call it rather an inherent risk of the game she was playing, a game whose often frivolous rules both hid and revealed a deadly serious struggle. The form that struggle took was incomplete, shortsighted, egotistical, self-destructive. But survivors who give in to the temptation to feel superior to all that are in the end no better than those who romanticize it. Janis was not so much a victim as a casualty. The difference matters.

1976

67

Hard to Swallow:

Deep Throat

It gets harder and harder to find someone who will say a good word for pornography. Angry feminists, chagrined liberals, Henry Miller and Pauline Réage fans, all agree that this is not what we meant, not what we meant at all, while the legions who never wanted to let the genie out of the bottle in the first place feel both outraged and vindicated. Die-hard (so to speak) porn liberationists like Al Goldstein of *Screw* are embarrassments to what is left of the hip subculture that spawned them—as out-of-date as skirts up to the thighs or inspirational speeches hailing groupies as the vanguard of the cultural revolution. Yet in spite of this ecumenical disapproval, pornography may well be the characteristic mass art form of this decade. What could be a better icon of the Nixon years than a fiftyish, balding businessman in suit and tie, briefcase on lap, hands chastely folded over briefcase (I checked), watching with solemn absorption a pair of larger-than-life genitals copulating in close-up to the strains of—was it really "Stars and Stripes Forever," or am I making that up?

The ironies may be painful, but they are hardly surprising. The revolt against Victorian morality has always had its left and right wings. On the one hand, it has been part of a continuing historical process, the economic and social emancipation of women; more narrowly, it has both reflected and facilitated the shift from a production-centered (hence austere) to a consumption-centered (and hedonistic) capitalism. At this point the feminist version of the sexual revolution has been incorporated into the broader program of the women's movement, while the consumerist version has ended up on Forty-second Street, which is as American as cherry pie—and as masculine as chewing tobacco.

For men the most obvious drawback of traditional morality was the sexual scarcity—actual and psychic—created by the enforced abstinence of women and the taboo on public acknowledgment of sexuality. Sex was an illicit commodity, and whether or not a sexual transaction involved money, its price almost always included hypocrisy; the "respectable" man who consorted with prostitutes and collected pornography, the adolescent boy who seduced "nice girls" with phony declarations of love (or tried desperately to seduce them), the husband who secretly wished his wife would act like his fantasies of a whore, all paid in the same coin. Men have typically defined sexual liberation as freedom from these black-market conditions: the liberated woman is free to be available; the liberated man is free to reject false gentility and euphemistic romanticism and express his erotic fantasies frankly and openly; by extension, the liberated entrepreneur is free to cater to those fantasies on a mass scale.

Understandably, women are not thrilled with this conception of sexual freedom. In a misogynist culture where male sexuality tends to be confused with dominance and corrupted by overt or covert sadism—read any one of the endless spew of male confessional novels that have come out of the closet (or the bathroom) since Portnoy's notorious liver-fuck—its potential is frightening. Nor have men allowed themselves or each other to push their "liberation" to its logical extreme (that is, fascism). The sexual revolution has simply institutionalized a more advanced form of hypocrisy: instead of saying one thing and doing another, the game is to say and do the same thing but feel another, or not feel at all. Of course this is no news in 1973. Everybody knows it—"everybody" being middle-class intellectuals, bohemians, and feminists. Which is exactly what's so embarrassing about pornography. As an ideology the fuck-it-and-suck-it phase of the sexual revolution may be passé; as a mentality it is nonetheless big business.

Like all popular culture, pornography is shaped by its social setting, and the relaxation of the obscenity laws has not only brought it out in the open but inspired new genres, chief of which is the X-rated movie. Partly because of the logistics of moviegoing, which is a communal rather than a private experience, and partly because the movie industry has only recently thrown off censorship of the crudest and most anachronistic sort, porn movies have retained an air of semirespectability, fuzzing the line between liberated art and out-and-out smut. They turn up at art houses, where they are known as "erotic films"; they occasionally get reviewed; in time of need a stray professor or two can be induced to testify to their redeeming social value. If there is such a thing as establishment porn, these movies are it. They apotheosize the middle-American swinger's ethic: sex is impersonal recreation, neither sacred nor dangerous; above all, it has no necessary connection to any human emotion, even the most elemental lust, frustration, or fulfillment.

While pornography has never been known for its emotional subtlety, this ultradeadpan style is distinctively contemporary; watching a "documentary" history of stag films that came out some time ago, I was struck by the difference between the earliest clips, which were amusingly, whimsically naughty, and later sequences, which contained progressively less warmth and humor and more mechanical sex. Traditional pornographers reveled in the breaking of taboos, the liberation of perverse and antisocial impulses. Today's porn is based on the conceit that taboos are out-dated, that the sexual revolution has made us free and innocent—a fiction that can be maintained, even for the time span of a movie, only at the cost of an aggressive assault on all feeling.

Since the image on the screen is so inescapably *there*, imposing strict limits on the spectator's imagination, film is an ideal medium for this assault. Not only do most porn movies fail to build tension or portray people and situations in a way that might involve the viewer; they use a variety of techniques to actively discourage involvement. Clinical close-ups of sexual acts and organs, reminiscent of the Brobdingnagians, are one such ploy; a Brechtian disjunction between visual image and soundtrack is another. The first commercial porn movies often presented themselves as documentaries about sex education, the history of sexual mores, pornographic film making, and so on—a device that had an important formal function as well as the obvious legal one. Narrators' pedantic voices would superimpose themselves on orgy scenes, calling our attention to the grainy texture of the film; blank-faced young girls would explain in a bored monotone why they acted in porn movies—"It's the bread, really. . . . I guess I dig it sometimes. . . . It's hard work, actually"—while in the background, but still on camera, another actress fellated a colleague with the businesslike competence of a plaster-caster.

These days, the narrators' voices have mostly given way to music, which generally sounds as if it were composed by a Chamber of Commerce committee just returned from a performance of *Hair*. Sexual partners in porn movies rarely make noise, and I've never heard one talk sex talk; most often they perform silently, like fish in an aquarium. When there is dialogue, its purpose is generally to break the mood rather than heighten it. In the opening scene of *Deep Throat*, for instance, the heroine enters her apartment and is cheerfully greeted by her roommate, who just happens to have a man's head buried in her crotch. He looks up to see what's happening, but roomie firmly guides his head back down to business. Then she lights a cigarette and says, "Mind if I smoke while you're eating?"—a line that just might be the definitive statement of the porn aesthetic.

Throat is the first porn movie to become a cultural event. Besides being a huge money-maker, it has been widely acclaimed as an artistic triumph. Allegedly, *Throat* is "different," the porn movie everybody has been waiting for—the one that has a plot and characters and humor and taste and really gets it on. It has been playing at "legitimate" movie theaters around the country, and in New York, where its run at the New Mature World has lasted seven months so far, the *Post* reported that lots of women were going to see it, with other women, yet—an unprecedented phenomenon. When the managers of the World were charged with obscenity, Arthur Knight, film critic for *Saturday Review* and professor at the University of Southern California, testified for the defense, praising the movie for its concern with female sexual gratification and its socially valuable message that "the so-called missionary position is not the only way to have sex." He also liked the photography.

There is something decidedly creepy about all this fanfare, which—Professor Knight's remark about the missionary position excepted—has no discernible relation to what's actually on the screen. I suspect a lot of ambivalent libertarians of hedging by badmouthing porn in general while rallying around an "exception," but that they should pick *Throat* for the honor suggests that they have been missing the point all along.

True, *Throat* has certain peculiarities that distinguish it from the average porn flick. It may not have a plot, but it should get some sort of award for the most grotesque premise: the heroine's clitoris is in her throat. It's not hard to figure out how *that* fantasy got started; needless to say, I couldn't identify with it, though I did feel like gagging during a couple of scenes. Or am I being too literal? Is *Throat* really a comment of the psychology of oral fixation? (It does have one of those socially redeeming blurbs at the beginning, about Freud's stages of psychosexual development and the use of suggestion in curing sexual hang-ups.) Is that what the bit with the doctor blowing bubbles is all about? And near the end, when Linda Lovelace shaves her pubic hair to the accompaniment of science fiction music and the Old Spice theme, does that represent a ceremonial transition to the genital stage?

Linda is fresh-and-freckle-faced, comes on like a cut-rate Viva, sighs, "There must be more to life than screwing around," gets genuinely upset about her predicament, and hangs around for the entire movie, all of which I guess makes her a character, at least by porno standards. *Throat* also boasts lots of moronic jokes. (Linda to doctor, who is making light of her problem: "Suppose your balls were in your ear!" Doctor: "Then I could hear myself coming.") What all this means is that in ten years I may appreciate *Throat* as an artifact, but for now I find it witless, exploitative, and about as erotic as a tonsillectomy.

The last point is really the crucial one: movies like *Throat* don't turn me on, which is, after all, what they are supposed to do. On the contrary, I find them a sexual depressant, partly because they are so unimaginative, partly because they objectify women's bodies and pay little attention to men's—American men are *so* touchy about you-know-what—but mostly because they deliberately and perversely destroy any semblance of an atmosphere in which my sexual fantasies could flourish. Furthermore, I truly can't comprehend why they excite other people—a failure of empathy that leads straight into the thickets of sexual polarization. I know there are men who don't respond to these movies, and I'm sure it's possible to find a woman here or there who does. Still, the fact remains that their audience is overwhelmingly male—the *Post* notwithstanding, I counted exactly three other women in the *Throat* audience, all of them with men—and that most men seem to be susceptible even when, like the letter writer who complained to the *Times* that *Teenage Fantasies* was erotically arousing but spiritually degrading, they hate themselves afterward.

My attempts to interrogate male friends on the subject have

73

never elicited very satisfying answers ("I don't know . . . it's sexy, that's all. . . . I like cunts"). I suppose I shouldn't be so mystified; "everybody" knows that men divorce sex from emotion because they can't afford to face their real emotions about women. Nevertheless, it baffles and angers me that men can get off on all those bodies methodically humping away, their faces sweatless and passionless, their consummation so automatic they never get a chance to experience desire.

I've often had fantasies about making my own porn epic for a female audience, a movie that would go beyond gymnastics to explore the psychological and sensual nuances of sex—the power of sexual tension and suspense; the conflict of need and guilt, attraction and fear; the texture of skin; the minutiae of gesture and touch and facial expression that can create an intense erotic ambience with a minimum of action. Not incidentally, the few porn movies I've seen that deal with these aspects of the erotic were made by gay men. A classic underground example is Jean Genet's *Un Chant d'Amour*, an unbearably romantic and arty movie that nevertheless had a strong effect on me when I saw it in 1964. Aside from a few masturbation scenes the sex is almost entirely in the minds of the characters (prison inmates and a guard); the overriding mood is frustration. Yet it is exactly this thwarted energy that makes *Chant* exciting. It works on two levels: it is serious anguish, and it is also a tease. Either way, Genet makes the point that sex is a head trip as much as it is anything else. Similarly, in Wakefield Poole's currently popular *Bijou*, the coming-out process is presented—again too romantically for my taste—as a kind of psychedelic theater in which the hero discovers his various sexual personalities and accepts the male body in all its aspects.

Women have no pornographic tradition, and at the moment it doesn't look as if anybody's about to start one. The New York Erotic Film Festival recently scheduled an evening of movies by women, but they turned out to be more about self than about sex, which pretty much sums up a lot of women's priorities right now. I enjoyed them; in the middle of the whole dying culture of swingerism they radiated life. Still, I was disappointed that no one had made my movie. Maybe next year.

1973

It's Later Than You Think

Don't look back (Idi Amin may be gaining on you), but the seventies are behind us. Sometime during 1976 they just faded out. Historians will recall the seventies as nasty and brutish, but mercifully short. The eighties, contrary to a lot of people's gloomy expectations, are going to be different. Not fun and games, by any means, but an active, energetic decade that we can really live in, not just live through.

How do I know? Well, to explain I have to try to convey what life has been like these many months in occupied New York. The city, as you probably know—some of you may even care—is broke. We are being governed by a junta of bankers who do not look kindly on such decadent luxuries as police and fire protection, public education, and a functioning transit system. Without massive federal aid, which does not appear to be forthcoming, our economic future looks pretty grim. Furthermore, the sludge that hit Long Island's beaches last summer is undoubtedly lurking out there ready to strike again. And the weather has been terrible. In short, New Yorkers have every reason to be totally demoralized.

Yet mysteriously, the spirit in this city is better, the energy level higher, than it's been in years.

I first realized this around the time of the Bicentennial. I had fully expected the Bicentennial to be a depressing experience. The official booster bullshit was embarrassing; so was the unimaginative whining of the People's Bicentennial Commission, the left's only countereffort. Where were the Yippies, now that we needed them to organize a Festival of Life in San Clemente, or something? But by the weekend of the Fourth I discovered that I was not depressed at all. Along with most of my cynical radical friends, I was turned on by the Tall Ships, but even more by a new electricity in the air. It seemed as if every unemployed folk singer, magician, and chamber-music ensemble in the city was performing on the street, attracting lively crowds. People radiated a secret solidarity, a communal grin that translated, "Don't let the bastards get you down!"

After that I began to notice how many people were saying things like "A year ago I was bored, nothing was happening, now I'm involved in this project and that relationship, my life is coming together again—don't get me wrong, I know we're in the middle of a depression. . . ." I also noticed that at a time when I would have expected the more footloose members of my generation to start deserting New York like rats leaving the *Titanic*, people who had left were coming back! "I don't know," they would say when I asked. "I was getting tired of San Francisco/Washington/Boston. New York seemed like the right place to be." I agreed, but I wasn't sure why until I caught on about the eighties.

New Yorkers are justly reputed to be tough-minded survivors. But when they are true to their best selves, they refuse to settle for mere survival—they believe in survival with élan. In the seventies what we refugees from the sixties euphemistically called survival was really more like shell shock. Here we were, bravely marching into the New Age when all of a sudden we found ourselves on our asses, wondering what hit us. Under those circumstances anyone who didn't commit suicide or move to Florida and become an orange was counted a survivor.* In the eighties that title will be reserved for those of us who can recover our wind, our fight, and our sense of humor. And I'm convinced that New York, which has a long tradition in such matters, has already begun leading the recovery. I even have a nomination for the first eighties culture hero: the unknown guerrilla who recently stalked the sidewalks of Greenwich Village planting tiny red flags in the piles of dogshit.

Note that the eighties are as different from the sixties as from the seventies. The eighties are a decade of maturity rather than youth, of experience rather than innocence. You have to have been through the sixties to truly appreciate the eighties. Kids who have grown up in a depressed economy and an atmosphere of political-cultural reaction and quietism are likely to accept dogshit as the central fact of life; their attention must be directed to the red flags. (They won't listen, of course. Never trust anybody under thirty.)

My script for politics (you remember politics) in the eighties includes a revived radical movement, seasoned by adversity, chastened by its mistakes, prepared to learn from and build on the sixties revolt while eschewing dope-crazed visions of instant revolution. (Dope-crazed visions of eventual revolution are acceptable.) Admittedly, this phase of the new decade has been slow to arrive, even in New York. Most of us are still reacting to each new round of layoffs and budget cuts with groans instead of demonstrations. Establishment politics have been equally sluggish. Bella Abzug, New York's most promising eighties politician, is out of a

---

* Sensitized by Greil Marcus's lonely but fanatical campaign against this self-inflating use of the word—whereby the deaths, breakdowns, and burnouts that attended the struggles of the sixties are converted into moral credit for the rest of us—I am embarrassed at having contributed, even backhandedly, to one of the past decade's more inane clichés. The concept of emotional or spiritual survival has an honorable history, but it does invite self-indulgence. In my own case, the worst I survived was severe personal and political confusion, the temptation to various sorts of craziness, and a couple of bad acid trips. It felt pretty horrendous at the time, and some of it was even dangerous, but Auschwitz it wasn't.

job. Ford's defeat (spearheaded by live New York City voters) was clearly a repudiation of the seventies, but unfortunately, Carter doesn't seem to have noticed; Griffin Bell is a seventies appointment if there ever was one. Still, I'm not too discouraged. It takes a little time to turn a decade around.

I know what you're thinking: what about 1984? My theory is that 1984 has already happened. Orwell originally wanted to call the book *1974*, but his editor made him change it on the naive assumption that 1974 wasn't far enough in the future.

Happy New Year!

January 1977

Tom Wolfe's Failed Optimism

My deepest impulses are optimistic, an attitude that seems to me as spiritually necessary and proper as it is intellectually suspect. In college and for some time afterward, my education was dominated by modernist thinkers and artists who taught me that the supreme imperative was courage to face the awful truth, to scorn the soft-minded optimism of religious and secular romantics as well as the corrupt optimism of governments, advertisers, and mechanistic or manipulative revolutionaries. I learned that lesson well (though it came too late to wholly supplant certain critical opposing influences, like comic books and rock-and-roll). Yet the modernists' once-subversive refusal to be gulled or lulled has long since degenerated into a ritual despair at least as corrupt, soft-minded, and cowardly—not to say smug—as the false cheer it replaced. The terms of the dialectic have reversed: now the subversive task is to affirm an authentic postmodernist optimism that gives full weight to existent horror and possible (or probable) apocalyptic disaster, yet insists—credibly—that we can, well, overcome. The catch is that you have to be an optimist (an American?) in the first place not to dismiss such a project as insane.

Tom Wolfe's Failed Optimism

A subtheme of sixties utopianism was the attempt—often muddled, at times self-negating—to arrive at some sort of honest optimism. This concern was also implicit in the antiutopian sensibility first self-consciously articulated by the pop artists. Pop sensibility—loosely defined as the selective appreciation of whatever is vital and expressive in mass culture—did more than simply suggest that life in a rich, capitalist, consumption-obsessed society had its pleasures; the crucial claim was that those pleasures had some connection with genuine human feelings, needs, and values and were not—as both conservative and radical modernists assumed—mere alienated distraction. Pessimists like Herbert Marcuse argued that advanced capitalism destroyed the autonomous self and with it the possibility of authentic pleasure, let alone happiness; pop implied a more sanguine view of the self as guerrilla, forever infiltrating territory officially controlled by the enemy, continually finding new ways to evade and even exploit the material and psychic obstacles that the social system continually erected. I shared this view; I doubted that either Marx or Freud would quarrel with the proposition that a human being who had the urge to build a castle, and found that the only material available was shit, would soon learn how to build shit castles—and how to use the unique properties of shit to advantage. Pop was about the ways in which the spirit of the people invaded the man's technology: restrict us to three chords, a back beat, and two minutes of air time, and we'll give you—rock-and-roll.

The pop stance was honest up to a point. But its commitment to making the most of the existing reality excluded painful or dangerous questions about systemic change. Not that pop optimism was devoid of political content: it was by definition populist (while modernist pessimism was, at least in part, an aristocratic vote of no-confidence in the lower orders), and it gleefully offended upper bourgeois pieties about art, taste, and the evils of consumerism. Nor did the pop sensibility deny or defend the various forms of oppression that at once hedged our pleasures and made them possible; its very celebration of human resilience implied an awareness of such barriers to fulfillment. But it took that tension for granted. The price of pop optimism was a deeper fatalism; in a way Andy Warhol's silk-screened electric chair was more chilling than anything in *One Dimensional Man*. Those of us who were unwilling to pay that price looked for ways to integrate the pop impulse with political and cultural radicalism and with the parallel experience of the immanence of the spirit—best described as religious—that had become a mass phenomenon because of a technological achievement called LSD. Yet pop remained central, if only because mass culture was the bloodstream in which other influences had to circulate if they were to have much effect.

I had no more than an inkling of the importance of all this when, in the fermenting mid-sixties, I first came across *The Kandy-Kolored Tangerine-Flake Streamline Baby*. The book—particularly the title piece and the one on Las Vegas, neither of which I'd read in their original *Esquire* incarnations—made a strong impression on me. Tom Wolfe had pulled off the remarkable feat of not only describing but embodying pop consciousness—an essentially aliterate phenomenon—in print. The baroque extravagance of his prose mirrored the cultural styles he was writing about; his narrative voice captured the single-minded vision, the manic enthusiasm, the confident, idiosyncratic genius of their inventors. He even played around with his own mass art, journalism, borrowing not only from fiction but from advertising and pulp jargon. His introduction laid out assumptions that had already begun to affect my view of the world: "Here was this incredible combination of form plus money in a place nobody ever thought about finding it. . . . Suddenly classes of people whose styles of life had been practically invisible had the money to build monuments to their own styles. . . . Stock car racing, custom cars—and, for that matter, the jerk, the monkey, rock music—still seem beneath serious consideration, still the preserve of ratty people with ratty hair and dermatitis. . . . Yet all these rancid people are creating new styles all the time and changing the life of the whole country in ways that nobody even bothers to record, much less analyze. . . . The new sensibility—*Baby baby baby where did our love go?*—the new world, submerged so long, invisible and now arising, slippy, shiny, electric—Super Scuba-man!—out of the vinyl deeps."

In comparison, Wolfe's second collection, *The Pump House Gang*, fell curiously flat. It was full of repetitious variations on the proliferation-of-styles theme, which in 1968 was no longer either new or neglected, and Wolfe's enthusiasm seemed forced, his rhetorical devices mechanical, as if he himself were bored with it all. Most of the pieces had been written two or three years earlier, and the gap showed. A lot had happened to overshadow, or at least complicate, all that churning of the vinyl deeps—the Vietnam escalation, black power, the burgeoning of radical and bohemian dissidence. Wolfe was not unaware of those events; on the contrary, he devoted a page of introduction to defensive ridicule of intellectuals' avidity for disaster: "War! Poverty! Insurrection! Alienation! O Four Horsemen, you have not deserted us entirely. The game can go on." He recalled that during a symposium on the sixties, a few years ago, the other panelists had been so obsessed with gloomy maunderings that he had been moved to protest. " 'What are you talking about?' I said. 'We're in the middle of a . . . Happiness Explosion!' " Elsewhere in the introduction Wolfe announced the imminent spontaneous demise of the class structure, already accomplished in New York.

Though I did not expect incisive radical analysis from Tom Wolfe, any more than I expected it from Mick Jagger, I did think a touch of the Stones'—or even the Beatles'—irony was in order. By indulging in mindless yea-saying, Wolfe betrayed the tension at the core of pop, converting it to a more sophisticated version of the traditional American booster mentality, whose purpose was, as it had always been, cosmetic. It was this betrayal, I suspected, that made *The Pump House Gang* so lifeless. There was some truth in Wolfe's complaint; intellectuals did have an emotional investment in apocalypse, for reasons that rightly offended his populism. But it was hard to take seriously a populism that willfully ignored certain discomfiting facts. Such as that the ratty-haired, dermatitic kids whose creativity Wolfe so admired, and who populated the lower ranks of the class structure he so jauntily pronounced dead, were providing most of the bodies for the war.

Still, the book contained one piece that confounded all these judgments—"The Pump House Gang," Wolfe's account of the La Jolla surfers who hung out and hung loose on the beach, creating a hedonistic subculture based on physical perfection, daring, contempt for the straight life, mystical rapport with the ocean, above all youth and a horror of age. The story paid Wolfe's usual loving attention to surface minutiae, but it also had an underside. There was the *mysterioso* Pacific, which had somehow drowned this fantastic surfer, who should have been . . . *immune*; there was the ineluctable aging process, which would sooner or later consign the Pump House Gang to the cruel obsolescence they themselves had decreed. The piece made me shiver; it hovered on the edge of a metaphorical wave that suggested both the danger and the lure of the American ride. It also suggested that Wolfe was basically too talented and too honest to practice the complacency he preached.

That suggestion was justified, and then some, by *The Electric Kool-Aid Acid Test*. I think *Acid Test* is a great book, certainly the best to come out of the sixties. Again Wolfe uses his reportorial gifts to get down a sensibility based largely on a revolt against the supremacy of words. But there is something more: *Acid Test* is about the whole sticky problem of optimism, of how to pursue the elusive synthesis. What makes the book so powerful —and so brave—is the way Wolfe allowed the Pranksters' vision to challenge and stretch his own. Ken Kesey and his friends created a wondrous new style, rooted in American history, myth, technology, and popular culture, but their aim was not only aesthetic—it was messianic. If Wolfe's pop sympathies were engaged by the style, his antiutopianism must have been equally offended by the aim. Yet the two could not be separated, for they were complementary aspects of a central unifying impulse—to live out and spread the psychedelic experience. If Wolfe was really to do his job—report accurately on what the Pranksters' trip was about—he could not take them seriously on one level, dismiss them as silly hippies on another. Like everyone else he had in some sense to choose: was he on the bus or off?

For Wolfe, getting on did not mean taking acid—apparently he did not—or abdicating his particular role in the Pranksters' movie, which was to be a reporter. *Acid Test* always keeps the proper critical distance; it carefully documents the Pranksters' confusions, fuck-ups, and ultimate failure. But Wolfe does not hold himself aloof from the pain of that failure. From his first meeting with Kesey at the beginning of the book to the "WE BLEW IT!" litany at the end, he never shirks the recognition that there was a real chance to blow.

Wolfe has never risked or achieved so much since; in the seventies his writing has increasingly reflected and served the decade's characteristic failures of imagination and will. On its own terms, Wolfe's first seventies book, *Radical Chic and Mau-Mauing the Flak-Catchers*, is successful, even brilliant; his demolition of rich liberals and of the charades that so often pass for left-wing politics in this country is maliciously accurate and irresistibly funny. Yet the terms themselves represent a retreat from the complex blend of identification and objectivity that informs the best of his earlier work to a more conventional stance as critic of manners and mores. And the pieces are a moral retreat as well. Like the *Pump House Gang* introduction, they offer specific truths in the service of a larger lie. Their underlying assumption is that political action is inherently ridiculous and irrelevant, nothing more than a ritual designed—like, say, a demolition derby—to meet the psychological needs of its participants. But while Wolfe has always regarded demolition derbies and most other American rituals with tolerance if not positive fondness, the very idea of social conscience pisses him off, and he takes a mean-spirited pleasure in discrediting it.

In his most recent work Wolfe's wit has declined as his crankiness has increased. *The Painted Word* parlays a slight and dubious thesis into a long and boring polemic. And *Mauve Gloves & Madmen, Clutter & Vine*, Wolfe's latest and weakest anthology, hits a note of asperity that suggests nothing so much as the curmudgeonly irritation of an old Tory. The title piece is a heavy-handed, son-of-radical-chic exposé of that ungrateful wretch, the rich West Side writer who finances his rich West Side existence with jeremiads about repression and recession. "The Intelligent Co-Ed's Guide to America," a frankly conservative attack on radical intellectuals cum defense of American democracy, could have been lifted, minus a few exclamation points, from the pages of *Commentary*.

Then there is "The Me Decade and the Third Great Awakening," in which Wolfe attempts to graft his standard happiness-is-postwar-prosperity number to a report on the popularity of various therapeutic/sexual/religious invitations to self-fulfillment. The result has an oddly schizophrenic quality. On the one hand, the current preoccupation with "me" is a product of leisure and money, hence to be applauded as further evidence against the disaster mongers. On the other hand, it is not lower-class kids who show up at Esalen and EST but West Side writers who are bored with Martha's Vineyard, and anyway, all that silly self-absorption —all that psychic muckraking—what is it, really, but a form of internal disaster mongering? Wolfe does not try to reconcile these opposing trains of thought; he just scatters cheap shots in all directions and ends up saying less about middle-class narcissism than any random Feiffer cartoon.

The one memorable piece in *Mauve Gloves* is "The Truest Sport: Jousting with Sam and Charlie," a day-in-the-life account of Navy bomber pilots flying missions over North Vietnam. Wolfe's greatest strength is his ability to write from inside his subjects, even when they are inarticulate, and since that skill requires empathy rather than spleen, he has always written best about people he admires. He admires the bomber pilots. They are prototypical American heroes—not eccentric offshoots of the genre, like Kesey, but the real thing: men who do much and say little, who master rather than submit to machines, who test their skills to the limit, keep their cool in the face of death, and enjoy a mystical confrontation with the universe denied ordinary mortals.

A few years ago, Wolfe wrote about the same brand of heroism in his *Rolling Stone* series on the Apollo 17 astronauts. But astronauts are one thing, bomber pilots quite another. The real suspense of "The Truest Sport" is not whether Dowd and Flint will make it back from their deadly trip over Haiphong harbor, but whether Wolfe can compel his readers—most of whom, he knows, are inclined to regard Vietnam bomber pilots as war criminals—to see these men as complex human beings who are in certain ways admirable, more admirable perhaps than you or I. Improbably, he succeeds, at least with me. "The Truest Sport" is an impressive tour de force. It has, however, one rather disturbing flaw: the Vietnamese are as invisible to Wolfe as they were to the pilots.

What bothers me is not that Wolfe didn't write an antiwar tract but that the issue of whether the war was right or wrong, the bombings necessary or criminal, is not even an implicit issue in the piece. What matters to Wolfe is that he prefers the pilots' stoic style to that of whiny, bad-sport peaceniks who never put their lives on the line but whose influence on the conduct of the war— particularly the restrictions placed on bombing raids—made the pilots' task more difficult and dangerous. I wish I could believe that Wolfe's use of the sporting metaphor (it is one of the pilots who compares the bombing missions to jousting) is at least a bit ironic. But I'm afraid the truth is that Wolfe simply refuses to entertain the possibility that there are times when style is beside the point.

The continuing inability of someone as intelligent and perceptive as Tom Wolfe to confront unpleasant political realities in any serious way—even to admit that, like it or not, they exist—strikes me as not just obtuse but neurotic. It comes, I think, from Wolfe's failure to resolve the contradiction between his populist faith in human possibility and his essentially conservative political instincts. The cultural excitement of the sixties allowed Wolfe to avoid facing that conflict; it was possible then to nourish the illusion that politics didn't matter, that the real action was elsewhere. For all the prominence of political movements, it was the idea of cultural revolution—whether in its right-wing (pop) or left-wing (psychedelic) versions—that dominated the sixties imagination; Kesey was antipolitical, in his way a classic American individualist, and Wolfe loved the way the Pranksters' anarchism befuddled the straight left. But the times changed, abruptly and rudely exposing the fragility of that idea—and of the prosperity on which it had depended. Cultural revolution had been a side effect of expanding American empire; thanks to the Vietnamese, the expansive days were over. The vaunted postscarcity economy, which would make all that nasty conflict between classes academic, had failed to arrive; if you believed the projections of ecologists, it never would. And in the absence of a political spark the happiness explosion was fizzling out.

Deprived of cultural fireworks to celebrate, Wolfe diverted his energy to attacking the left—to, as it were, killing the bearer of bad news. But the repressed always returns. At this point Wolfe's optimism, such as it is, denies rather than affirms. The voice he raises against his archenemies, the disaster mongers, is the strident, defensive, I'm-all-right-Jack voice of official rationalization, a negative voice worthy of the archenemies themselves. It is, one might say, the sound of the . . . old sensibility . . . once again having the last whine. For the time being.

*1*977

Beginning to See the Light

O n November 7, I admitted I was turned on by the Sex Pistols. That morning I had gone from my shrink to my office and found that a friend who takes an interest in my musical welfare had sent me a package of British punk singles and albums. He had been urging me to listen to the stuff, and I had been resisting; I was skeptical about punk, in both its British and American versions. The revolt against musical and social pretension, the attempts to pare rock to its essentials, the New York bands' Velvetesque ironic distance had a certain *déjà vu* quality: Wasn't all that happening five years ago? When I had first heard "God Save the Queen" on the radio, my main reaction had been, "They sound like Mott the Hoople—what's the big deal?" And the Ramones bored me; I felt they were not only distanced but distant, apologists for coldness as a world view. I had dutifully gone to see them at CBGB's and bought their first album, hoping to be interested in what they were trying to do, but duty goes only so far. I was also put off by the heavy overlay of misogyny in the punk stance.

In October I had gone to an art show opening in Queens and

had run into another punk evangelist, Bob Christgau. He argued that people who put down the punk bands as "fascist" were really objecting to their lack of gentility. The English bands, he said, were overtly antifascist, and after all it was in England that fascism was a serious threat, not here. I wasn't so sure, I said, either that fascism wasn't a threat here or that the punk rockers were incapable of flirting with it.

I wasn't referring to the swastikas or sadomasochistic regalia that some punk bands affected to prove they were shocking, though I felt that to use Nazi symbolism for any purpose was both stupid and vicious. I meant that sexism combined with anger was always potentially fascistic, for when you stripped the gentility from the relations between the sexes, what too often remained was male power in its most brutal form. And given the present political atmosphere, that potential was worrisome. The American right was on the move; the backlash against feminism was particularly ominous. Jimmy Carter, with his opposition to abortion, his fundamentalist religion, and his glorification of the traditional (i.e., male-dominated) family, was encouraging cultural reaction in a way that was all the more difficult to combat because he was a Democrat and supposedly a populist. Closer to home, I found it deeply disturbing that so many liberal and leftist men I knew considered Mario Cuomo* some sort of working-class hero—that they were at best willing to ignore, at worst secretly attracted to, Cuomo's antifeminist attitudes. The punk rockers were scarcely defenders of the family, or of tradition, but like pseudopopulist politicians they tended to equate championing the common man with promoting the oppression of women. That the equation was as inherently contradictory as "national socialist" was unlikely to deter men from embracing it.

The following week I went hiking in the Blue Ridge Mountains. At the inn where I was staying I took a lot of more or less friendly kidding about being from New York, to which I responded with more or less friendly defensiveness: no, there had been no looting

* A candidate for mayor of New York in 1977.

in my neighborhood during the blackout, and yes, I walked around at night by myself. Back in the city, in the early morning, my clock-radio clicked on to wake me up. I lay in bed drifting. The dee jay delivered a commercial about a *Voice* article on punk rock: "A cult explodes and a movement is born!" Then came the news: The West German commandos had made their triumphant raid on the terrorists at Mogadishu. I lay in bed confused. Were the punk rockers the terrorists or the raiders?

Some friends of mine were giving a Halloween costume party. I decided to go as a punk. I wore a black T-shirt that read in yellow letters "Anarchy in Queens" (I would love to be able to say I found it somewhere, but in fact I had it made up), a huge safety-pin earring, pasty white makeup, green food coloring on my teeth, and fake vomit that I had bought in a magicians' supply store.

Around the same time I was beginning to emerge from a confusing and depressing period in my life. I had a problem I needed to face, a painful and scary choice to make, and I had been refusing to think about it. In such circumstances, music was my enemy. It had a way of foiling my attempts at evasion; when I was least prepared, some line or riff or vocal nuance would invariably confront me with whatever I was struggling to repress. And so I had simply stopped listening. I told myself that the trouble was I was tired of old music, and there was no new music that excited me. I wondered if I were coming to the end of an era—was rock-and-roll no longer going to be important in my life?

Then I gave up trying to censor my thoughts. Immediately there were plenty of records I needed to hear: *Blood on the Tracks; Loaded; Heat Treatment* and *Howlin Wind; Astral Weeks; Exile on Main St.; The Bessie Smith Story, Volume 4,* which includes "Send Me to the 'Lectric Chair" and "Empty Bed Blues." I realized with a shock that although I'd listened to "Send Me to the 'Lectric Chair" hundreds of times over the years, I had never really heard it before. It was a fierce, frightening song: a woman described how she had killed her lover, reeling off the brutally graphic details with almost casual defiance, saying in effect "I lost my temper and I blew it and I'm sorry now but it's too late so fuck it." Bessie had concentrated more intensity in that one song than Janis Joplin had achieved in her whole career. I played it over and over.

And now I had all these punk-rock records, by the Sex Pistols, the Clash, Slaughter and the Dogs, the Unwanted, Wire, the Adverts, Johnny Moped, Eater, X-Ray Spex, the Buzzcocks, Chelsea, the Rezillos. I liked them; they made most of what passed for rock these days sound not only genteel but out of focus. And I was knocked out by the Sex Pistols. How could I have denied that they had a distinctive sound? I knew I might react differently if I saw them live, or if I could hear more than about 1 percent of their lyrics, but for the moment—as had so often happened in the past— my conceptual reservations were overwhelmed by the immediate, angry force of the music. WE DON'T CARE!—but they cared about not caring.

Later I listened to my Ramones album and found that it moved me more than it had before. It seemed that the British had done it again—beamed my culture back at me in a way that gave it new resonances. The last time (when "swinging London" was prosperous and euphoric) they had done this by achieving an aesthetic distance—based on their detachment from America's racial history —that was also a kind of innocence. This time (when England was in deep economic and political trouble) they were doing it by ignoring—or more precisely smashing—the distance the American punk bands had taken uninnocent pains to achieve. It was not that groups like the Sex Pistols and the Clash had no irony of their own, that their punk persona was not a calculated creation. But the passion with which they acted out that persona reflected England's unambiguously awful situation; the Ramones were stuck with the American dilemma, which is that the system is bad enough to piss us off, and not bad enough so that we can make up our minds what to do about it.

Months before my capitulation to the Sex Pistols I was talking to an editor and we got on the subject of pop music. I said that I still felt involved with the increasingly distinct subgenre of contemporary rock-and-roll, but there wasn't that much of it around, and what there was was often disappointing. The editor asked what sort of music I was talking about. "Well, the bands that play CBGB's . . . Graham Parker . . . Springsteen . . ." "Patti Smith?" "Yes." The editor shook her head. "All these people," she said, "are still caught up in the past, in the myth of the sixties." "I disagree," I said, feeling a bit prickly because I'd had this argument before. "It's just that they *acknowledge* the sixties, instead of trying to pretend all that stuff never happened."

The argument bothered me. Talk about irony: the worst insult you could throw at those of us who had been formed by the sixties was to imply that we were living in the past; not to be totally wired into the immediate moment meant getting old, which we hoped we would die before. The thing was, I really felt not guilty. In the last couple of years, especially, the sixties had seemed very distant to me. When I thought of the person I had been in 1967, or even 1970, she was almost as much of a stranger as my college-student self. I rarely played music that had been popular in the sixties; most of it lacked a certain dour edge that felt necessary in this crabbed decade. It was nevertheless true that many of my favorite records had been made by veterans of the sixties, just as it was true that I was still interested in my past, felt a continuing need to understand and absorb it. Was this need regressive?

I had once raised the question in a letter to Greil Marcus, and he had replied: "Well, we're caught in our own trap. We promoted and got across a myth of the '60s and now we're paying for it—having it thrown back on us as some sort of strange aberration that we all caught a disease from—i.e. it wasn't a real era, wherein real things happened, it was some giant anomaly. Well, it can seem like that, because so much of such intensity happened so fast. . . . more happened in rock and roll in six months of '65 than in all of the '70s. . . . More happened politically in 1968–in terms of stuff we will live with and think about all our lives with great emotion and puzzlement—than since. Etc."

That was part of the problem—too much had happened to assimilate all at once. Culturally and politically, the seventies had been at best dull, at worst grim, yet for me the retreat into work and introspection had its positive side; it was a chance to consolidate what I'd learned, live down some of the egregious silliness I'd been party to. How else was I to figure out where I was heading? Feminism, drugs, Vietnam, the flowering of pop culture had changed me. They were no longer "the sixties"; they were part of my baggage.

Yet what was finally most insidious about the whole "You're caught in the myth of the sixties" business was not its denial that the sixties were real—and therefore consequential—as well as mythical, but its use of "the sixties" as a dismissive label with which to quarantine certain ideas and attitudes. What, for instance, did it really mean to relegate Patti Smith or the Ramones to the sixties? True, seventies rock and roll had roots in the sixties, but then so did disco, which editors and other cultural arbiters agreed was quintessential seventies music: the original disco audience—middle-class blacks who retained a black cultural identity rather than imitating whites—had been created by the civil rights movement and black nationalism. The difference was that rock-and-roll, as a musical language, was always on some level about rebellion, freedom, and the expression of emotion, while disco was about cooling out as you move up, about stylizing and containing emotion.* I knew I was supposed to consider the first set of concerns as outdated as the miniskirt. Yet owing to the parlous state of New

---

* While this is all true as far as it goes, it is a bit beside the point. Despite its base in minority subcultures (black and gay), disco is a mass cultural phenomenon and so inevitably embodies the spirit of the times in a more immediate and central way than rock-and-roll, which has become a somewhat abstracted comment on itself and (like jazz in the fifties) an essentially bohemian taste. In any case, seventies rock-and-roll is obsessed with its formal tradition, a concern that links it to the past in a special way. Finally, there are distinctions to be made: Bruce Springsteen is far more tied into the sixties than the punk and new wave bands. (For elucidation of these last two points, see my essay on the Velvet Underground.)

York's economy, I was, for the first time ever, somewhat downwardly mobile; I aspired to have less control over my feelings, not more; liberation was still a potent idea for me, not because I was clinging to the utopian sixties but because I was still oppressed as a woman—and still angry about it—in the conservative seventies. In short, though I had nothing against disco, rock-and-roll had a lot more to do with my life. And I couldn't help suspecting that "You're still living in the sixties" was often nothing more than code for "You refuse to admit that what really matters to you is to stake out a comfortable position in the upper middle class." Well, not only did I refuse to admit that: I didn't even think it was true.

I was grappling with my uncensored thoughts, finding them no less scary and painful, the night I went to see Ms. Clawdy at the Women's Coffee House. Ms. Clawdy is a singer-songwriter from Oakland. In the early seventies she managed and wrote songs for an all-female rock-and-roll band called Eyes; later she sang with another women's band, Rosie and the Riveters; now she performs alone, accompanying herself on the piano. She has a local following, particularly though not exclusively in the San Francisco Bay Area's lesbian/feminist/alternative-women's-culture community, but she is unknown outside California. I've rooted for Ms. Clawdy for years, not only because she is good but because of what she is good at. Her music successfully combines two of my main passions: feminism and rock-and-roll. The Women's Coffee House gig was her first performance in New York, and to see it I had passed up Graham Parker at the Palladium.

For those of us who crave music by women who will break out of traditional molds, write and sing honestly about their (and our) experience, and create art so powerful that men and the society in general will have to come to terms with it whether they want to or not, the seventies have offered scant comfort. Though many women performers give me pleasure, few have touched those specifically feminist yearnings. There is the Joy of Cooking, whose music endures but whose lyrics seem dated and sentimental now; Joni Mitchell's "Blue," ditto; some of Yoko Ono's stuff; great songs here and there like Helen Reddy's "Summer of '71," Carly Simon's "You're So Vain," Patti Smith's "Redondo Beach" . . . give me an hour and I'll think of a dozen more examples, but that only proves my point.

As a woman who has made a significant contribution to what I've called contemporary rock-and-roll, Patti Smith stands alone. Her best songs are as good as any in rock-and-roll, and she is capable of an electrifying live performance. But she is erratic; in concerts she has a habit of generating enormous energy, then diffusing it with rambling, pointless raps. I've always wondered if she were afraid of her considerable power. I'm also uncomfortable with her androgynous, one-of-the-guys image; its rebelliousness is seductive, but it plays into a kind of misogyny—endemic to bohemian circles and, no doubt, to the punk-rock scene—that consents to distinguish a woman who acts like one of the guys (and is also sexy and conspicuously "liberated") from the general run of stupid girls.

So Patti Smith may be a rock-and-roll hero, but she is not quite a feminist heroine. Ms. Clawdy, on the other hand . . . I watched her with an avidity that came from discovering someone who was distinctively herself, yet fit my generic fantasy. Her style was at once functional and matter-of-factly sensual; her plump, womanly body was encased in red mechanic's overalls. She was funny, ironic, passionate, self-deprecating without being masochistic, vulnerable without being pathetic, and political in the best sense—that is, willing to tell the truth about the conditions of her life. I enjoyed her funny songs—especially a discourse on compulsive eating called "Ice Cream Cone"—but I liked her best at her most serious. Of her newest songs the one that most compelled me was "The Dark Side," which she introduced by noting that Chairman Mao had urged revolutionary artists to emphasize the bright side of life and that she hadn't followed his advice. But my favorite was still her signature song, "Night Blindness." Whenever she sang it I heard something new. This time, the lines that got to me were "We all need love, it's worth any price you pay/ That's what my mother said, and she lives alone today."

I had gone to the show with a woman friend, and afterward we were so high that we ran down the street, shouted, and hugged. Some weeks later, I had dinner with Ms. Clawdy, a.k.a. Ella Hirst, and we talked about the possibilities for an alternative women's culture. I had once been attracted to the idea but had long since become convinced that it was unworkable and even reactionary. It was, I believed, inseparable both in theory and in practice from political ideas I had rejected: that sexual and cultural separatism were a solution to the oppression of women or an effective strategy for ending that oppression. For me feminism meant confronting men and male power and demanding that women be free to be themselves everywhere, not just in a voluntary ghetto. Separatists argued that a consistent feminist had to break all sexual and emotional ties with men, yet it seemed to me that not to need men for sex or love could as easily blunt one's rage and pain and therefore one's militance; I also had the feeling that there was a lot of denial floating around the separatist community—denial that breaking with men did not solve everything, that even between women love had its inescapable problems. I suspected that a culture based on separatist assumptions was unlikely to be angry enough, or truthful enough, to be revolutionary.

I had arrived at these conclusions not by thinking about the issue abstractly, but by trying to answer a specific question: why did I like so little of the women's-culture music I had heard? The feminist music scene had two main tendencies. One was a women's version of political folk music, which replicated all the virtues (simplicity, intimacy, community) and all the faults (sentimentality, insularity, heavy rhetoric) of the genre. Some of it was fun to listen to, but the idiom was too well worn to promise anything exciting or original. The other tendency actively turned me off: it was a slick, technically accomplished, rock-influenced but basically conventional pop. I believed that this music could be a commercial success; supposedly the product of a dissident culture, it struck me as altogether compatible with the MOR blandness of most white pop music.

What disturbed me most about both brands of women's-culture music was that so much of it was so conventionally feminine. Years ago Ella Hirst had told me that she thought most female performers did not have a direct line to their emotions, the way men did—they were too busy trying to please. It seemed to me that too many of the women's-culture people had merely switched from trying to please men to trying to please other women.

A couple of years ago I had gone to see the feminist folk-rock group, the Deadly Nightshade, at a lesbian bar in Boston. They sang "Honky Tonk Women" with rewritten, nonsexist lyrics. Someone in the audience sent them an outraged note, attacking them for singing an antiwoman song. The lead singer read the note aloud and nervously and defensively complained that the writer hadn't been listening. The incident had helped me understand why I wasn't enthusiastic about the group. They did not have the confidence, or the arrogance, to say or feel "If you don't like it, tough shit." It was not that I thought performers should be indifferent to the response of their audience. I just thought that the question they ought to ask was not "How can I make them like me?" but "How can I make them hear me?"

Ella protested that I was harder on these women, who were at least trying to create an alternative system of values, than on traditional female performers. She had a point. Why did the Deadly Nightshade's wimpiness bother me more than Linda Ronstadt's sex-kitten routine? For the same reason, probably, that the radical left's offenses against women always incensed me more than everyone else's.

But rock-and-roll, as always, posed a more troublesome paradox. Listening to the Sex Pistols, trying to figure out if "Bodies" was really an antiabortion song, I discovered that it was something even worse. It was an outburst of loathing for human physicality, a loathing projected onto women because they have babies and abortions and are "a fucking bloody mess," but finally recoiling against the singer himself: "I'm not an animal!" he bellowed in useless protest, his own animal sounds giving him the lie. It was an outrageous song, yet I could not simply dismiss it with outrage. The extremity of its disgust forced me to admit that I was no stranger to such feelings—though unlike Johnny Rotten I recognized that the disgust, not the body, was the enemy. And there lay the paradox: music that boldly and aggressively laid out what the singer wanted, loved, hated—as good rock-and-roll did—challenged me to do the same, and so, even when the content was antiwoman, antisexual, in a sense antihuman, the form encouraged my struggle for liberation. Similarly, timid music made me feel timid, whatever its ostensible politics. What I loved most about Ms. Clawdy was that I could have liberating form and content both; I could respond as a whole person. Listening to most rock-and-roll was like walking down the street at night, automatically checking out the men in my vicinity: this one's okay; that one could be trouble, watch out. Listening to most feminist music was like taking a warm bath. Ms. Clawdy did not make me wary—but that didn't mean she let me relax.

The other day, I was sitting on a bench in front of the laundromat on my corner. While I waited for my wash, I thought about the choice I still had to make. For some reason I happened to glance upward, and my eyes hit a stop sign. I laughed; if my life had to be a series of metaphors, I ought to pick some better ones. Like, say, the last verse of "Night Blindness": "I never thought that anyone would know me like you do./ If I let you make me happy you could make me unhappy too./ I told my friend, she said she knows just how I feel/ But I have to take a chance and find out if it's real."

November 1977

How's the Family?

hristmas week: if Phyllis Schlafly and her cohorts could observe my friends right now, they might conclude that the plot against the American family is a paper tiger. As a group, the people I know are surely in the vanguard of the plot if it exists at all; they travel light, have sharp elbows, and are deeply ambivalent about marital and parental bliss. But come December and they all seem as obsessed with family as if they had never read Marcuse: they worry about aging parents and confused siblings, haggle with ex-spouses over who gets the kids for which holidays, have second thoughts about arriving in their mid-thirties unencumbered—and unconnected. They are sensitive to the need for friends to be family to each other; careful to make sure no one is unwillingly alone on Christmas or New Year's. They joke seriously about getting together when they're seventy-five and starting a commune.

As usual, I'm feeling somewhat insulated from the seasonal angst; since my family, being Jewish, has never made a big deal of Christmas, it doesn't have a lot of heavy associations for me. Rather, I think of the holidays as a period when the pace of the city slows down, the phone rings less, people I have to talk to aren't in their offices, and I have more time than usual to read, go to the movies, wander around, shop. On Christmas Eve, with a modicum of conscious perversity, I go alone to see *Looking for Mr. Goodbar.* Everyone has been warning me against it; the consensus is that it's bad in an uninteresting way. I'm stubborn—the movie has Diane Keaton, it's a cultural event, and it's playing three blocks from my house. But the consensus is right: *Mr. Goodbar* is a study in incoherence untrammeled by notions of motivation, though I'm willing to believe that the strain of being a saintly guru to cherubic deaf children is enough to drive anyone to singles bars. I leave the theater feeling irritated, wishing I had stayed home with the Margaret Drabble novel I just bought. But reading *The Realms of Gold,* I get irritated all over again. The book has a marvelous, dense texture; its world is real, its characters alive; yet its craft cannot hide a certain, well, banality. What do I (or the characters) learn from the anthropologist heroine's relationship with a married man? That love is mysterious, that lovers accept each other's imperfect humanity? No shit. Drabble avoids moral complexity by making the wife a dedicated pain in the ass. I cheat and turn to the end: the wife conveniently becomes a lesbian. I get it—it's the plot against the family (British, in this case) with no plotters and no victims.

Christmas day: a man I used to live with has invited me to dinner. He has roasted a turkey. I have never roasted a turkey because I can't seem to shake the idea that turkey roasting is an infinitely complicated process that only my mother can handle.

Later in the week I try another movie—*Close Encounters of the Third Kind.* It's a matinee; the audience is full of obstreperous kids. I love the movie. It's not just that I'm a sucker for science-fiction movies, though I am. What moves me is that, for all his sentimentality, Spielberg has managed—with certain shots of Richard Dreyfuss's face and François Truffaut's smile; with Dreyfuss's dirt-and-shrub replica of the mountain; with the interplanetary duet; even with a sensual, charismatic version of that stock character, the practical wife who stands in the hero's way—to convey the frustration of struggling to follow a vision others don't share and the triumph of vindication. The movie's view of the family has a nice (if sexist) balance. Dreyfuss leaves his wife and children to pursue the vision. But Melinda Dillon pursues it by pursuing her child, who is, of course, visionary by definition.

New Year's Eve: having considered and rejected the idea of organizing an expedition to see Patti Smith and Richard Hell and the Voidoids, I have a choice of three parties—two large ones and a small one. I go to the small one, where the order of the night is shameless indulgence in champagne and old rock-and-roll. Sometime after midnight with Guy Lombardo's brother, the Stones are crooning "She comes in colors." "I wonder how you do that?" I muse. A silly question—obviously you have to take some evil drug.

The last time I took an evil drug on New Year's Eve I was living with three other people in a small town in the Catskills. Before we dropped our little pink tabs we had a conference about our cat, Molly (short for Molotov Cocktail). She was in heat, and we had been keeping her in the house. It occurred to us that once we were high, we might feel sorry for her and decide that it was absurd to be so uptight about letting nature take its course. We solemnly agreed that no matter how expansive we felt, we would be responsible and not let Molly out. But in the morning we realized that at some point in our revels we had simply forgotten about the whole thing and left the door open. Molly was gone; she didn't come back for two days. She had two kittens. One of them died last fall, of a liver ailment, but Molly is still around. The man I used to live with has custody; I didn't want the bother of keeping a cat in the city. But I still think of her as partly mine.

February 1978

Jackie, We Hardly Knew You

They say that Jackie's father, "Black Jack" Bouvier, was flamboyant, sexy, and irresponsible, while her stepfather, Hugh Auchincloss, was kind, solid, and dull. Kitty Kelley's *Jackie Oh!* is the sort of book Black Jack might have grinned at; Hugh would no doubt have preferred *Jacqueline Bouvier Kennedy Onassis*, by Stephen Birmingham, author of *The Right People*. All the trappings of the Kelley book—the title, the garish cover, the Lyle Stuart imprint, photographs by the intrepid Ron Galella—shout juicy trash; Birmingham's book exudes a claustrophobic aura of good taste. The content of both books corresponds to their packaging. The result is that while *J.B.K.O.* may be more faithful to the provable facts, *Jackie Oh!* makes a more convincing stab at the unprovable truth.

As a participant in public life—in history—Jackie is insignificant. No one has ever claimed that she has had the slightest influence on public affairs, and although her style contributed to the glamor of the Kennedy era, it has had no enduring impact on the way Americans behave or think. Jackie was an icon to admire, not a model to emulate. As first lady she charmed Charles de Gaulle, redecorated the White House, played the role of heroic national widow, and that was about it. The source of the public's (particularly the female public's) continuing obsession with Jackie is her private life as the wife of spectacularly rich and powerful men. Which means that the prurient details *J.B.K.O.* discreetly plays down are of the essence. Birmingham is obtuse about this. He can go on for pages about Jackie's busy-work in the White House while expending all of a paragraph on the observation that "the marriage had become, by now, little more than a matter of mutual convenience." "Some of the rumors were no doubt true" is his word on JFK's womanizing. But what anyone who would bother to pick up the book wants to know is: Was the marriage ever more than convenient? Did she marry power, he an ornament, or was it more complicated? Was she jealous of his affairs? And so on.

Birmingham's attitude toward Jackie is embarrassingly respectful, as is his attitude toward the upper classes generally. He seems most in his element when he is chronicling (at excessive length) the history of the Bouviers and the Auchinclosses, and he has a fondness for remarks like "[Jackie] bore the genes of designers and decorators." His take on the Jackie myth is an updated version of the familiar idea that she fulfilled America's craving for an aristocracy; he implies that her celebrity survived her inelegant second marriage and its aftermath because she was too classy to be dragged down.

Kitty Kelley is not respectful. If her book leaves one overriding impression, it is that morality is indeed a middle-class concern, alien to the rich. Jackie, the Kennedy family, and especially John F. himself are portrayed—not with disapproval but with wicked relish—as strong-willed, self-centered, greedy, hedonistic, and totally untrammeled by anything we might recognize as a system of values or a notion of other people's rights. Proprieties and rules of behavior are for public relations; power is the only law that counts.

Jackie Oh! is as vivid and as broadly drawn as a popular novel.

Jackie, We Hardly Knew You

Even its minor characters are full of obsessive passions: Jackie's mother hates her ex-husband and allegedly sees to it that Black Jack is too drunk to make it to his daughter's wedding; the indignant landlady of one of JFK's girlfriends embarks on a one-woman crusade to discredit him. But Kelley's best creations are the fascinating and appalling Kennedys. They appear in the first chapter, forcing an ostentatious Catholic politician's wedding on the impeccably genteel WASP Auchinclosses, and they dominate most of the book. JFK emerges as a larger-than-life egomaniac whose compulsive Don Juanism—according to Kelley, he was a lousy lover, interested only in conquest—serves as a metaphor for his pursuit of power. Jackie's character develops through coping with him, getting around him, making her position work for her. If their marriage is one of convenience for him, it is, as Kelley sees it, less cynical and more bitter for her. Still, she learns to apply a Kennedyesque stubbornness to her hatred of politics, her contempt for the official duties of a first lady, her love of luxury, her outrageously expensive restoration project, her war with the hapless Bill Manchester.

Kelley gives little space to Jackie's years with Onassis. Too bad, because those years provide the necessary climax to the Jackie myth: the shy, insecure debutante who was intimidated by the overbearing Kennedys has become a determined woman whose "classiness" does not inhibit her from fighting hard for what she wants—a sizable chunk of the Onassis estate. Jackie is the mirror image of her closest rival for preeminent female celebrity, Elizabeth Taylor. While Liz broke all the rules, had her own work, flaunted her sexuality, and engaged in open, equal combat with her men, Jackie played the game, took traditional femininity as far as it could go, and managed to end up on her own with 20 million bucks. In a way, she beat the system. Which could be why Kelley —like most women I know—regards her with a kind of covert glee.

December 1978

Classical and Baroque Sex

in Everyday Life

There are two kinds of sex, classical and baroque. Classical sex is romantic, profound, serious, emotional, moral, mysterious, spontaneous, abandoned, focused on a particular person, and stereotypically feminine. Baroque sex is pop, playful, funny, experimental, conscious, deliberate, amoral, anonymous, focused on sensation for sensation's sake, and stereotypically masculine. The classical mentality taken to an extreme is sentimental and finally puritanical; the baroque mentality taken to an extreme is pornographic and finally obscene. Ideally, a sexual relationship ought to create a satisfying tension between the two modes (a baroque idea, particularly if the tension is ironic) or else blend them so well that the distinction disappears (a classical aspiration). Lovemaking cannot be totally classical unless it is also totally baroque, since you can't abandon all restraints without being willing to try anything. Similarly, it is impossible to be truly baroque without allowing oneself to abandon all restraints and so attain a classical intensity. In practice, however, most people are more inclined to one mode than to the other. A very classical person will be incompatible with a very baroque person unless each can bring out the other's latent opposite side. Two people who are very one-sided in the same direction can be extremely compatible but risk missing a whole dimension of experience unless they get so deeply into one mode that it becomes the other.

Freud, the father of the sexual revolution, was a committed classicist who regarded most baroque impulses as infantile and perverse. Nevertheless, the sexual revolution, as it is usually defined, has been almost exclusively concerned with liberating those impulses from the confines of an exaggeratedly classical puritanism. The result, to my mind, has been an equally distorting cultural obsession with the baroque. Consider, for example, that quintessential expression of baroque angst (a contradiction in terms, the product of Jewish guilt; Christian guilt is classical all the way), Lenny Bruce's notorious monologue about fucking a chicken. Or, come to think of it (puns are baroque), Portnoy's adventures with liver. I mean seriously (classically, that is), is fucking chickens and livers what sex is all about?

Curiously, contemporary sexual "experts" never mention this crucial polarity. This is because they have a vested interest in what might be called establishment or middlebrow baroque—really an attempt to compromise with proclassical traditionalists who insist that sex should be somehow worthwhile, not just fun. Thus the basic axiom of establishment baroque is that consensual sex in any form is wholesome and good for you; a subsidiary premise is that good sex depends on technical skill and is therefore an achievement. Kinsey, with his matter-of-fact statistical approach to his subject, was a pioneer of establishment baroque. Masters and Johnson belong in this category, as do all behavior therapists. The apotheosis of multiple orgasm is an establishment baroque substitute for the old-fashioned classical ideal of coming together. Real baroque sex has no ideals. Much as I hate to admit it, what I have in mind here is a sort of middlebrow baroque project—to report on the two kinds of sex in everyday life.

Time: Night is classical; so are sunrise and sunset. High noon and half an hour before dinner (or during dinner) are baroque.

Location: Outdoors is classical, except for crowded nude beaches. The back seat of a car is classical if you're a teen-ager, baroque otherwise. The shower is classical; the bathtub is baroque.

Number: Two is classical. One or three or more is baroque.

Lighting: Total darkness is ultraclassical except when it's a baroque variation. Dim lights and candlelight are classical. Floodlights and fluorescent lights are definitely baroque.

Clothing: The only truly classical outfit is nothing. Clothing evokes fantasy and fantasies are baroque. Black lace underwear is of course the classic baroque outfit. Red is baroque, as is anything see-through. Frilly white nightgowns are a baroque impulse with classical content.

Food: Eating in bed is baroque, although artichoke hearts and sour cream are more classical than potato chips and pizza. Tongues, tastes, and flavors are inherently baroque. Comparing sex with food is usually middlebrow baroque, except when a classicist, quarreling with the baroque idea that getting off is getting off no matter how you do it, points out that "Steak and hamburger may both be protein but they still taste different." Putting food anywhere but in your mouth is superbaroque.

Drugs: Wine and marijuana are classical. Cocaine and quaaludes are baroque.

Music: Comparisons between sex and music are classical even if the music itself is baroque. Rock-and-roll is a good mixture of both sensibilities. My favorite classical sex song is Rod Stewart's "Tonight's the Night"; my favorite baroque sex song is "Starfucker." Rock-and-roll is usually more classical than disco.

Pornography: Porn is basically a baroque phenomenon. Much of it (*Hustler*, most X-rated movies) is belligerently anticlassical and therefore a form of inverted puritanism. Some of it (*Playboy*) is pure middlebrow baroque. Many porn classics (like *Fanny Hill*) have a fairly large classical element. The larger the classical element, the likelier that a piece of pornography will be judged to have redeeming social value. If it is classical enough, it stops being porn altogether and becomes art, but this is a very subjective and relative matter. *Lady Chatterley's Lover* was once considered pornographic because it used certain baroque words, but by contemporary standards it is cornball classical. (Actually, Lawrence seems to have intended a classical celebration of the joy of the baroque, and he might have pulled it off if it weren't for all that solemn phallic worship and particularly those ridiculous flowers. One thing he did accomplish, though: he made "fuck" into a classical word without sacrificing its baroque connotations.) Pornography also becomes art when it is so baroque it is classical, like *The Story of O.*

Sex manuals: *Love Without Fear* is echt-classical. The *Kama Sutra* is baroque with classical trappings (all that religious overlay). *The Joy of Sex*, with its sections headed "Starters," "Main Courses," and "Sauces and Pickles," is middlebrow baroque except for its rather classical illustrations.

Devices: All technology is baroque, including contraceptives, vibrators, and air conditioning.

Sexism: Classical sexism is the mystique of yin and yang, masculine strength and feminine surrender, noble savage and earth mother, D. H. Lawrence, Norman Mailer. Baroque sexism is the objectification of women, black garter belts and six-inch heels, Larry Flynt, Helmut Newton.

Feminism: Classical feminism is a vision of total equality, the transcendence of artificial social roles, love and respect for one's partner as an individual. Baroque feminism asserts women's right to be baroque, traditionally a male prerogative; rejects preconceptions about what is natural and moral; insists that anything goes for either sex so long as it feels good.

National characters: The Italians are classical. So are the French, though they pretend otherwise. The Communist countries and Sweden are middlebrow baroque. As a rule, wildly baroque countries exist only in their conquerors' imagination. Americans have classical leanings, but the world headquarters of baroque is New York City. In Manhattan you can eat a chicken and the waiter won't even notice.

May 1979

Velvet Underground

This essay originally appeared in *Stranded*, an anthology of critics' responses to the question "What rock and roll album would you take to a desert island?"

I'LL LET YOU BE IN MY DREAM

A change of fantasy: I have just won the first annual Keith Moon Memorial Essay Contest. (This year's subject was "Is Ecstasy Dead?") The prize is a fallout shelter in the bowels of Manhattan, reachable only through a secret entrance in CBGB's basement. It is fully stocked: on entering the contest I was asked to specify my choice of drugs (LSD), junk food (Milky Way), T-shirt ("Eat the Rich"), book (*Parade's End*), movie (*The Wizard of Oz*),* rock-and-roll single ("Anarchy in the U.K."), and rock-and-roll album. The album is *Velvet Underground*, an anthology culled from the Velvets' first three L.P.s. (My specially ordered version of this collection is slightly different from the original; for "Afterhours," a song I've never liked much, it substitutes "Pale Blue Eyes," one of my favorites.) The songs on *Velvet Underground* are all about sin and salvation. As luck would have it,

---

* On second thought, I'd rather have *Gone With the Wind*, or maybe *The Harder They Come*.

I am inspecting my winnings at the very moment that a massive earthquake destroys a secret biological warfare laboratory inside the Indian Point nuclear power plant, contaminating New York City with a virulent, radioactive form of legionnaire's disease. It seems that I will be contemplating sin and salvation for a long time to come.

I LOVE THE SOUND OF BREAKING GLASS

In New York City in the middle sixties the Velvet Underground's lead singer, guitarist, and *auteur*, Lou Reed, made a fateful connection between two seemingly disparate ideas—the rock-and-roller as self-conscious aesthete and the rock-and-roller as self-conscious punk. (Though the word "punk" was not used generically until the early seventies, when critics began applying it to unregenerate rock-and-rollers with an aggressively lower-class style, the concept goes all the way back to Elvis.) The Velvets broke up in 1970, but the aesthete-punk connection was carried on, mainly in New York and England, by Velvets-influenced performers like Mott the Hoople, David Bowie (in his All the Young Dudes rather than his Ziggy Stardust mode), Roxy Music and its offshoots, the New York Dolls and the lesser protopunk bands that played Manhattan's Mercer Arts Center before it (literally) collapsed, the antipunk Modern Lovers, the archpunk Iggy Stooge/Pop. By 1977 the same duality had surfaced in new ways, with new force, under new conditions, to become the basis of rock-and-roll's new wave.

There are important differences, both temperamental and musical, that divide today's punks and punkoids from the Velvets and other precursors and from each other; American punk (still centered in New York) and its British counterpart are not only different but in a sense opposed. Yet all this music belongs to a coherent genre, implicitly defined by the tension between the term "punk" and the more inclusive "new wave," with its arty connotations. If the Velvets invented this genre, it was clearly anticipated by the

Who: Pete Townshend, after all, is something of an aesthete, and Roger Daltrey something of a punk. It was not surprising that the impulse to make music that united formal elegance and defiant crudity should arise among working-class Englishmen and take shape among New York bohemians; each environment was, in its own way, highly structured and ridden with conflict. And as a vehicle for that impulse, rock-and-roll had unique advantages: it was defiantly crude, yet for those who were tuned in to it it was also a musical, verbal, and emotional language rich in formal possibilities.

The Who, the Velvets, and the new wave bands have all shared this conception of rock-and-roll; their basic aesthetic assumptions have little to do with what is popularly known as "art rock." The notion of rock-as-art inspired by Dylan's conversion to the electric guitar—the idea of making rock-and-roll more musically and lyrically complex, of combining elements of jazz, folk, classical, and avant-garde music with a rock beat, of creating "rock opera" and "rock poetry"—was from the rock-and-roll fan's perspective a dubious one. At best it stimulated a vital and imaginative eclecticism that spread the values of rock-and-roll even as it diffused and diluted them. At worst it rationalized a form of cultural upward mobility, concerned with achieving the appearance and pretensions of art rather than the reality—the point being to "improve" rock-and-roll by making it palatable to the upper middle class. Either way, it submerged rock-and-roll in something more amorphous and high-toned called rock. But from the early sixties (Phil Spector was the first major example) there was a countertradition in rock-and-roll that had much more in common with "high" art—in particular avant-garde art—than the ballyhooed art-rock syntheses: it involved more or less consciously using the basic formal canons of rock-and-roll as material (much as the pop artists used mass art in general) and refining, elaborating, playing off that material to produce what might be called rock-and-roll art. While art rock was implicitly based on the claim that rock-and-roll was or could be as worthy as more established art forms, rock-and-roll art came out of an obsessive commitment to the language of rock-and-roll and an equally obsessive disdain for those who rejected that language or wanted it watered down, made easier. In the sixties the best rock often worked both ways: the special virtue of sixties culture was its capacity for blurring boundaries, transcending contradictions, pulling off everything at once. But in the seventies the two tendencies have increasingly polarized: while art rock has fulfilled its most philistine possibilities in kitsch like Yes (or, for that matter, Meat Loaf), the new wave has inherited the countertradition, which is both less popular and more conscious of itself *as* a tradition than it was a decade ago.

The Velvets straddled the categories. They were nothing if not eclectic: their music and sensibility suggested influences as diverse as Bob Dylan and Andy Warhol, Peter Townshend and John Cage; they experimented with demented feedback and isolated, pure notes and noise for noise's sake; they were partial to sweet, almost folk-like melodies; they played the electric viola on Desolation Row. But they were basically rock-and-roll artists, building their songs on a beat that was sometimes implied rather than heard, on simple, tough, pithy lyrics about their hard-edged urban demimonde, on rock-and-roll's oldest metaphor for modern city life—anarchic energy contained by a tight, repetitive structure. Some of the Velvets' best songs—"Heroin," especially—redefined how rock-and-roll was supposed to sound. Others—"I'm Waiting for the Man," "White Light/White Heat," "Beginning to See the Light," "Rock & Roll"—used basic rock-and-roll patterns to redefine how the music was supposed to feel.

The Velvets were the first important rock-and-roll artists who had no real chance of attracting a mass audience. This was paradoxical. Rock-and-roll was a mass art, whose direct, immediate appeal to basic emotions subverted class and educational distinctions and whose formal canons all embodied the perception that mass art was not only possible but satisfying in new and liberating ways. Insofar as it incorporates the elite, formalist values of the avant-garde, the very idea of rock-and-roll art rests on a contradiction. Its greatest exponents—the Beatles, the Stones, and (especially) the Who—undercut the contradiction by making the surface of their music deceptively casual, then demolished it by reaching millions of kids. But the Velvets' music was too overtly intellectual, stylized, and distanced to be commercial. Like pop art, which was very much a part of the Velvets' world, it was antiart art made by antielite elitists. Lou Reed's aesthete-punk persona, which had its obvious precedent in the avant-garde tradition of artist-as-criminal-as-outlaw, was also paradoxical in the context of rock-and-roll. The prototypical rock-and-roll punk was the (usually white) working-class kid hanging out on the corner with his (it was usually his) pals; by middle-class and/or adult standards he might be a fuck-off, a hell-raiser, even a delinquent, but he was not really sinister or criminal. Reed's punk was closer to that bohemian (and usually black) hero, the hipster: he wore shades, took hard drugs, engaged in various forms of polymorphous perversity; he didn't just hang out on the corner, he lived out on the street, and he was a loner.

As white exploitation of black music, rock-and-roll has always had its built-in ironies, and as the music went further from its origins, the ironies got more acute. Where, say, Mick Jagger's irony was about a white middle-class English bohemian's (and later a rich rock star's) identification with and distance from his music's black American roots, his working-class image, and his teen-age audience, Lou Reed's irony made a further leap. It was not only about a white middle-class Jewish bohemian's identification with and distance from black hipsters (an ambiguity neatly defined when Reed-as-junkie, waiting for his man on a Harlem street corner, is challenged, "Hey white boy! Whatchou doin' uptown?") but about his use of a mass art form to express his aesthetic and social alienation from just about everyone. And one of the forms that alienation took pointed to yet another irony. While the original, primal impulse of rock-and-roll was to celebrate the body, which meant affirming sexual and material pleasure, Reed's temperament was not only cerebral but ascetic. There was nothing resembling lustiness in the Velvets' music, let alone any hippie notions about the joys of sexual liberation. Reed did not celebrate the sadomasochism of "Venus in Furs" any more than he celebrated heroin; he only acknowledged the attraction of what he saw as flowers of evil. Nor did he share his generation's enthusiasm for hedonistic consumption—to Reed the flash of the affluent sixties was fool's gold. Like Andy Warhol and the other pop artists he responded to the aesthetic potency of mass cultural styles; like Warhol he was fascinated by decadence—that is, style without meaning or moral content; but he was unmoved by that aspect of the pop mentality, and of rock-and-roll, that got off on the American dream. In a sense, the self-conscious formalism of his music—the quality that made the Velvets uncommercial—was an attempt to purify rock-and-roll, to purge it of all those associations with material goodies and erotic good times.

Though it's probable that only the anything-goes atmosphere of the sixties could have inspired a group like the Velvets, their music was prophetic of a leaner, meaner time. They were from—and of—hard-headed, suspicious New York, not utopian, good-vibes California. For all Lou Reed's admiration of Bob Dylan, he had none of Dylan's faith in the liberating possibilities of the edge—what he had taken from *Highway 61 Revisited* and *Blonde on Blonde* was the sound of the edge fraying. Like his punk inheritors, he saw the world as a hostile place and did not expect it to change. In rejecting the optimistic consensus of the sixties, he prefigured the punks' attack on the smug consensus of the seventies; his thoroughgoing iconoclasm anticipated the punks' contempt for all authority—including the aesthetic and moral authority of rock-and-roll itself.

Throughout this decade rock-and-roll has been struggling to reclaim its identity as a music of cultural opposition, not only distinct from but antagonistic to its own cultural conglomerate, rock. The chief accomplishment of the punks has been to make that antagonism explicit and public in a way that is clearly contemporary—that is, has nothing to do with "reviving" anything except the spirit of opposition itself. What is new in rock-and-roll—what is uncomfortable and abrasive and demanding—is the extent to which it insists on a defensive stance; the authentic late seventies note is nothing so much as cranky. Though the British punk movement was in some respects a classic revolt of youth—a class-conscious revolt, at that—its self-mocking nihilism is a classic crank attitude, while the American new wave makes up in alienated smart-assism for what it lacks in shit-smearing belligerence. The power and vitality of the crank posture are attested to by the way it makes less discordant sensibilities sound corny, even to those of us who might prefer to feel otherwise. Bruce Springsteen may still pull off a credible mélange of fifties teen-age-street-kid insurgency, sixties apocalyptic romance, and early/mid-seventies angst, but he is an anomaly; so is Graham Parker, whose stubborn and convincing faith in traditional rock-and-roll values recalls John Fogerty's. Patti Smith, on the other hand, is a transitional figure, half cranky messiah, half messianic crank. The rock-and-rollers who exemplify the current aesthetic do so with wide variations in intensity, from Johnny Rotten (maniacal crank) to Elvis Costello (passionate crank) to Nick Lowe or Talking Heads (cerebral cranks) to the Ramones (cranks of convenience). (The Clash, one convolution ahead, is boldly anti- or post-crank—the first eighties band?) The obvious core of their crankiness is their consciousness of themselves as a dissident minority, but it's more complicated than that. Real, undiluted rock-and-roll is almost by definition the province of a dissident minority (larger at some times than at others); it achieved its cultural hegemony in the sixties only by becoming rock—by absorbing competing cultural values and in turn being absorbed, making a new rebellion necessary. What is different now is that for the first time in the music's twenty-five-year history, rock-and-rollers seem to accept their minority status as given and even to revel in it. Which poses an enormous contradiction, for real rock-and-roll almost by definition aspires to convert the world.

In some ways the crankiness of current rock-and-rollers resembles the disaffection of an earlier era of bohemians and avant-gardists convinced they had a vision the public was too intractably stupid and complacent to comprehend. But because the vision of rock-and-roll is inherently populist, the punks can't take themselves seriously as alienated artists; their crankiness is leavened with irony. At the same time, having given up on the world, they can't really take themselves seriously as rock-and-rollers, either. They are not only antiart artists but antipeople populists—the English punks, especially, seem to abhor not only the queen, America, rich rock stars, and the uncomprehending public but humanity itself. The punks' working-class-cum-lumpen style is implicitly political; it suggests collective opposition and therefore communal affirmation. But it is affirmation of a peculiarly limited and joyless sort. For the new wave's minimalist conception of rock-and-roll tends to exclude not only sensual pleasure but the entire range of positive human emotions, leaving only what is hard and violent, or hard and distanced, or both: if the punks make sex an obscenity, they make love an embarrassment.

In reducing rock-and-roll to its harshest essentials, the new wave took Lou Reed's aesthete-punk conceit to a place he never intended. For the Velvets the aesthete-punk stance was a way of surviving in a world that was out to kill you; the point was not to glorify the punk, or even to say fuck you to the world, but to be honest about the strategies people adopt in a desperate situation. The Velvets were not nihilists but moralists. In their universe nihilism regularly appears as a vivid but unholy temptation, love and its attendant vulnerability as scary and poignant imperatives. Though Lou Reed rejected optimism, he was enough of his time to crave transcendence. And finally—as "Rock & Roll" makes explicit —the Velvets' use of a mass art form was a metaphor for transcendence, for connection, for resistance to solipsism and despair. Which is also what it is for the punks; whether they admit it or not, that is what *their* irony is about. It may be sheer coincidence, but it was in the wake of the new wave that Reed recorded "Street Hassle," a three-part, eleven-minute antinihilist anthem that is by far the most compelling piece of work he has done in his post-Velvets solo career. In it he represents nihilism as double damnation: loss of faith that love is possible, compounded by denial that it matters. "That's just a lie," he mutters at the beginning of part three. "That's why she tells her friends. 'Cause the real song—the real song she won't even admit to herself."

THE REAL SONG, OR I'LL BE YOUR MIRROR

If the Velvets suggested continuity between art and violence, order and chaos, they posed a radical split between body and spirit. In this way too they were closer to the Who than to any other contemporaries. Like the Velvets the Who were fundamentally ascetic; they too saw the world as hostile—particularly the world as organized by the British class system. Their defiance was cruder than the Velvets', their early music as hard and violent as any to come out of the new wave. But they were not cranks; they were determined to convert the world, and Townshend's guitar-smashing expressed his need to break through to his audience as well as his contempt for authority, including the authority of rock-and-roll itself. That need to connect also took another form: even before Townshend discovered Meher Baba, the Who's music had a side that could only be called religious. If it seemed, at first, surprising that the same band could produce music as uncompromising in its bitterness as "Substitute" and as miraculously transcendent as the "You are forgiven!" chorus of "A Quick One," it was no contradiction; on the contrary, it was precisely Townshend's sense of the harshness of life, the implacability of the world, that generated his spiritual hunger.

The same can be said of Lou Reed, except that "spiritual hunger" seems too self-important a phrase to apply to him; the Velvets' brand of spirituality has little in common with the Who's grand bursts of mystical ecstasy or Townshend's self-conscious preoccupation with the quest for enlightenment. It's impossible to imagine Lou Reed taking up with a guru, though he might well write a savagely funny (and maybe chillingly serious) song about one. The aesthete-punk and his fellow demimondaines are not seeking enlightenment, though they stumble on it from time to time; like most of us they are pilgrims in spite of themselves. For Townshend moral sensitivity is a path to spiritual awareness; for Reed awareness and the lack—or refusal—of it have an intrinsically moral dimension. While he is not averse to using the metaphors of illusion and enlightenment—sometimes to brilliant effect, as in "Beginning to See the Light" and "I'll Be Your Mirror"—they are less central to his theology than the concepts of sin and grace, damnation and salvation. Some of his songs ("Heroin," "Jesus," "Pale Blue Eyes") explicitly invoke that Judeo-Christian language; many more imply it.

But "theology" too is an unfairly pretentious word. The Velvets do not deal in abstractions but in states of mind. Their songs are about the feelings the vocabulary of religion was invented to describe—profound and unspeakable feelings of despair, disgust, isolation, confusion, guilt, longing, relief, peace, clarity, freedom, love—and about the ways we (and they) habitually bury those feelings, deny them, sentimentalize them, mock them, inspect them from a safe, sophisticated distance in order to get along in the hostile, corrupt world. For the Velvets the roots of sin are in this ingrained resistance to facing our deepest, most painful, and most sacred emotions; the essence of grace is the comprehension that our sophistication is a sham, that our deepest, most painful, most sacred desire is to recover a childlike innocence we have never, in our heart of hearts, really lost. And the essence of love is sharing that redemptive truth: on the Velvets' first album, which is dominated by images of decadence and death, suddenly, out of nowhere, comes Nico's artless voice singing, "I'll be your mirror/ . . . The light on your door to show that you're home./ When you think the night has seen your mind/ That inside you're twisted and unkind/ . . . Please put down your hands, cause I see you."

For a sophisticated rock-and-roll band with a sophisticated audience this vision is, to say the least, risky. The idea of childlike innocence is such an invitation to bathos that making it credible seems scarcely less difficult than getting the camel of the gospels through the needle's eye. And the Velvets' alienation is also problematic: it's one thing for working-class English kids to decide life is shit, but how bad can things be for Lou Reed? Yet the Velvets bring it off—make us believe/admit that the psychic wounds we inflict on each other are real and terrible, that to scoff at innocence is to indulge in a desperate lie—because they never succumb to self-pity. Life may be a brutal struggle, sin inevitable, innocence elusive and transient, grace a gift, not a reward ("Some people work very hard/ But still they never get it right," Lou Reed observes in "Beginning to See the Light"); nevertheless we are responsible for who and what we become. Reed does not attempt to resolve this familiar spiritual paradox, nor does he regard it as unfair. His basic religious assumption (like Baudelaire's) is that like it or not we inhabit a moral universe, that we have free will, that we must choose between good and evil, and that our choices matter absolutely. If we are rarely strong enough to make the right choices, if we can never count on the moments of illumination that make them possible, still it is spiritual death to give up the effort.

That the Velvets are hardly innocents, that they maintain their aesthetic and emotional distance even when describing—and evoking—utter spiritual nakedness, does not undercut what they are saying; if anything, it does the opposite. The Velvets compel belief in part because, given its context, what they are saying is so bold: not only do they implicitly criticize their own aesthetic stance—they risk undermining it altogether, ending up with sincere but embarrassingly banal home truths. The risk is real because the Velvets do not use irony as a net, a way of evading responsibility by keeping everyone guessing about what they really mean. On the contrary, their irony functions as a metaphor for the spiritual paradox, affirming that the need to face one's nakedness and the impulse to cover it up are equally real, equally human. If the Velvets' distancing is self-protective (hence in their terms damning), it is also revelatory (hence redeeming); it makes clear that the feelings being protected are so unbearably intense that if not controlled and contained they would overwhelm both the Velvets and their audience. The Velvets' real song is how hard it is to admit, even to themselves.

That song in its many variations is the substance of *Velvet Underground*. This album can be conceived of—nonlinearly; the cuts are not at all in the right order—as the aesthete-punk's *Pilgrim's Progress*, in four movements. ("Sha la la, man, whyn't you just slip away?" I can hear Lou Reed say to that.)

One: Worldly Seduction and Betrayal. "Sunday Morning," a song about vague and ominous anxiety, sums up the emotional tone of this movement: "Watch out, the world's behind you." "Here She Comes Now" and "Femme Fatale," two songs about beautiful but unfeeling women (in the unlovable tradition of pop—not to mention religious—misogyny, Lou Reed's women are usually demonic or angelic icons, not people), sum up its philosophy: "Aah, it looks so good/ Aah, but she's made out of wood." These songs underscore the point by juxtaposing simple, sweet, catchy melodies with bitter lyrics sung in flat, almost affectless voices (in "Sunday Morning," Reed's voice takes on a breathiness that suggests suppressed panic). "White Light/ White Heat," a song about shooting speed, starts out by coming as close as any Velvets song does to expressing the euphoria of sheer physical energy; by the end of the trip the music has turned into bludgeoning, deadening noise, the words into a semiarticulate mumble.

Two: The Sin of Despair. "Heroin" is the Velvets' masterpiece —seven minutes of excruciating spiritual extremity. No other work of art I know about has made the junkie's experience so powerful, so horrible, so appealing; listening to "Heroin" I feel simultaneously impelled to somehow save this man and to reach for the needle. The song is built around the tension between the rush and the nod—expressed musically by an accelerating beat giving way to slow, solemn chords that sound like a bell tolling; metaphorically by the addict's vision of smack as a path to transcendence and freedom, alternating with his stark recognition that what it really offers is the numbness of death, that his embrace of the drug ("It's my wife and it's my life") is a total, willful rejection of the corrupt world, other people, feeling. In the beginning he likens shooting up to a spiritual journey: he's gonna try for the Kingdom; when he's rushing on his run he feels like Jesus' son. At the end, with a blasphemous defiance that belies his words, he avows, "Thank your God that I'm not aware/ And thank God that I just don't care!" The whole song seems to rush outward and then close in on itself, on the moment of truth when the junkie knowingly and deliberately chooses death over life—chooses damnation. It is the clarity of his consciousness that gives the sin its enormity. Yet the clarity also offers a glimmer of redemption. In the very act of choosing numbness the singer admits the depths of his pain and bitterness, his longing for something better; he is aware of every nuance of his rejection of awareness; he sings a magnificently heartfelt song about how he doesn't care. (A decade later, Johnny Rotten will do the same thing in an entirely different way.) A clear, sustained note runs through the song like a bright thread; it fades out or is drowned out by chaotic, painful distortion and feedback, then comes through again, like the still small voice of the soul. Reed ends each verse with the refrain, "And I guess that I just don't know." His fate is not settled yet.

Three: Paradise Sought, Glimpsed, Recollected. This movement consists of four songs about world-weary sophistication and the yearning for innocence. "Candy Says" defines the problem: "I've come to hate my body and all that it requires in this world/ . . . I'd like to know completely what others so discreetly talk about." "Jesus" is a prayer: "Help me in my weakness, for I've fallen out of grace." In "I'm Set Free" the singer has his illumination, but even as he tries to tell about it, to pin it down, it slips away: "I saw my head laughing, rolling on the ground/ And now I'm set free to find a new illusion." In "Pale Blue Eyes" the world has gotten in the way of the singer's transcendent love: "If I could make the world as pure and strange as what I see/ I'd put you in the mirror I put in front of me."

Musically these songs are of a piece. They are all gentle, reflective. They all make use of the tension between flat, detached voices and sweet melodies. They all have limpid guitar lines that carry the basic emotion, which is bittersweet: it is consoling to know that innocence is possible, inexpressibly painful that it always seems just out of reach. In "Pale Blue Eyes" a tambourine keeps the beat, or rather is slightly off where the beat ought to be, while a spectacular guitar takes over completely, rolling in on wave after wave of pure feeling.

Four: Salvation and Its Pitfalls. "Beginning to See the Light" is the mirror held up to "Heroin." I've always been convinced that it's about an acid trip, perhaps because I first really heard it during one and found it utterly appropriate. Perhaps also because both the song and the acid made me think of a description of a peyote high by a beat writer named Jack Green: "a group of us, on peyote, had little to share with a group on marijuana the marijuana smokers were discussing questions of the utmost profundity and we were sticking our fingers in our navels & giggling." In "Beginning to See the Light" enlightenment (or salvation) is getting out from under the burden of self-seriousness, of egotism, of imagining that one's sufferings fill the universe; childlike innocence means being able to play. There is no lovelier moment in rock-and-roll than when Lou Reed laughs and sings, with amazement, joy, gratitude, "I just wanta tell you, *everything* is all right!"

But "Beginning to See the Light" is also wickedly ironic. Toward the end, carried away by euphoria, Reed cries, "There are problems in these times/ But ooh, none of them are mine!" Suddenly we are through the mirror, back to the manifesto of "Heroin": "I just don't care!" Enlightenment has begotten spiritual pride, a sin that like its inverted form, nihilism, cuts the sinner off from the rest of the human race. Especially from those people who, you know, work very hard but never get it right. Finally we are left with yet another version of the spiritual paradox: to experience grace is to be conscious of it; to be conscious of it is to lose it.

CODA: I'D LOVE TO TURN YOU ON

Like all geniuses, Lou Reed is unpredictable. In "Street Hassle" he does as good a job as anyone of showing what was always missing in his and the Velvets' vision. As the song begins, a woman (or transvestite?) in a bar is buying a night with a sexy young boy. This sort of encounter is supposed to be squalid; it turns out to be transcendent. Reed's account of the odd couple's lovemaking is as tender as it is erotic: "And then sha la la la la he entered her slowly and showed her where he was coming from/ And then sha la la la la he made love to her gently, it was like she'd never ever come." Of course, in part two he almost takes it all back by linking sex with death. Still.

What it comes down to for me—as a Velvets fan, a lover of rock-and-roll, a New Yorker, an aesthete, a punk, a sinner, a some-time seeker of enlightenment (and love) (and sex)—is this: I believe that we are all, openly or secretly, struggling against one or another kind of nihilism. I believe that body and spirit are not really separate, though it often seems that way. I believe that redemption is never impossible and always equivocal. But I guess that I just don't know.

1978

Part Two

American Girls Want Everything

Learning from Chicago

The Chicago protest was one of those rare political events that is not merely attended, but lived. What was most remarkable about it was how much living was concentrated in such a short time; the week of the Democratic Convention summed up a period of movement history as no other action has done since the historic Mississippi Summer Project. Chicago was an emotional marathon; between bouts of rage and fear, exhaustion and boredom, pessimism and euphoria, we slept little and badly. It was an experience from which, as I write this, I am still learning.

It started out badly. The Mobilization had never recovered from the confusion following President Johnson's withdrawal (was the war over? was Robert Kennedy going to lead us into the light?), while Mayor Daley's scare campaign was a triumph of reverse public relations. McCarthy and Lowenstein urged their supporters to stay home; SDS was noncommittal; hippies accused the Yippies of luring kids to a bloodbath instead of a "Festival of Life"; local radical organizers worried about repression that would make it more difficult for them to operate within their communities. Only a tiny fraction of the expected 200,000 people showed up, and some of the local organizers even left town to make sure the police couldn't blame them for anything. Poor organization resulted in potentially disastrous gaffes: centering the protest in isolated Lincoln Park rather than a downtown site; staging an illegal march in the middle of a park, with the only escape routes a few easily blocked bridges.

Yet sometimes a political demonstration (like a play, or a love affair) just miraculously jells. Chicago jelled. All our mistakes somehow turned into assets; all Daley's mistakes got him deeper in trouble. We succeeded in disrupting the convention—spiritually at least—and demoralizing the Democratic Party. But this was secondary; like typical Americans, we got our biggest kicks from contemplating our image in the media. The publicity was graphic and slanted in our favor, and we obtained it at notably little cost: no one died demonstrating, and most injuries were painful rather than disabling. Instead of the bitterness, political infighting, and accusations of contrived martyrdom that would have followed killings, there was a feeling of community that almost transcended ideological differences; added to the comradeship that came from spending so much time on the streets of a strange city was the solidarity forced on us by the authorities, who treated us all—hardcore street-fighters, McCarthy liberals, and those somewhere between (me)—with equal animus.

After Black Wednesday we walked the streets grinning, greeting strangers "Peace, brother," and meaning it, flashing the V sign at every opportunity. Our expansiveness was accentuated by the unexpected friendliness of local people. Blacks radiated especially welcome sympathy. I had not experienced such genuine interracial good will in years; genuine, I say, because looking suspiciously for sarcasm and secret glee at white injuries, I found only respect for kids willing to put their bodies on the line. But white workers (not necessarily under thirty) also gave us the V; even a young cop, directing traffic on Michigan Avenue, spread two fingers and winked and smiled. Then there were the Chicago kids. All week they had been coming up to Lincoln Park to play dialogue with the weirdos—tensely polite high school footballers arguing solemnly with revolutionaries, teenies asking half-seriously how to go about breaking away from their parents. There wasn't much overt hostility from the public. I heard that a few demonstrators got beaten up in the white working-class neighborhood near the International Amphitheater. Thursday night some white vocational students lay in wait for Dick Gregory's march up Michigan and chanted, without much enthusiasm, "Hippies go home." But that was about it.

I went to Chicago mainly for negative reasons. I thought that the movement could not, without looking foolish, allow the Democrats to play their game in a complacent, business-as-usual atmosphere; further, to have panicked in the face of Daley's threats would have been to display weakness and invite a general crackdown on dissent. I left knowing that something very positive had happened to me. Specifically: never had I been so conscious that what I was involved in was a rebel *community*, whose emotions and sensations had a collective life of their own; although I didn't always agree with what was happening, I was always part of it. At the same time I became more acutely sensitive than ever before to our problematic relations with the larger community. In its name we had been clubbed and gassed, yet in some ways it had been far more hospitable to us than we deserved. For we were and still are too much disposed to see ourselves as the beautiful green planet around which the vast body of the American people sluggishly revolves. What we need, if we are to understand and change this society, is a Copernican theory of politics.

II

The Yippies saw the Chicago action as theater, and they were right. The clashes between demonstrators and police—four major "confrontations," from the first skirmish in Lincoln Park on convention eve to the Wednesday night extravaganza, and dozens of minor conflicts—were theater that bordered on religious ritual. This is not to imply that the emotions and the injuries were in any sense unreal; on the contrary, they were superreal—not only personal and concrete but collective and symbolic. On the streets and in the parks of Chicago the movement lived two of its most potent myths: the myth of insurrection (let's stop talking about it and *do* it) and the myth of revelation (this time we're going to make everyone *see* the whole motherfucking mess once and for all).

The insurrectionary myth could be seen at its purest in Lincoln Park. Since the atmosphere of the city, as well as direct restrictions, had squelched the Yippies' counterconvention festival before it began, and since the Mobilization had planned no activities early in the week, the focus of the protest had shifted completely away from the convention and Vietnam to a battle over turf. What made the battle mythic was that so many of the participants believed—or at least convinced themselves they believed—that its outcome was in doubt. In fact, the main argument among the militants in the crowd was whether the three thousand of us should concentrate on liberating the park or taking over the city. Would-be organizers who tried to give advice on how to get out of the park in a hurry, or information on free housing, were received with almost universal hostility. It was as if stagehands were to interrupt a play to tell the actors where the emergency exit was or to set up props for the next scene.

During the tense precurfew hours, against a background of garbage fires and African drumming, the militants' exhortations and responses functioned as an improvised Greek chorus:

"If one of us dies, how many pigs will die?"

"Ten!"

"Twenty!"

"They got the guns, but we got the numbers."

"We gonna stay in the park. We all gonna stay together, right?"

"Yes! Yes!"

"Let's get out on the streets. Fuck over the city. Do them in."

"The park is ours!"

"The streets are ours!"

The images on everyone's mind were Paris and Columbia; the presiding spirit was Ché's. But no one seemed to realize that Paris was a defeat, leaving de Gaulle stronger than before; that Columbia was still a slumlord and still part of the war machine; that Ché had died without creating a single Vietnam. Nor in all the self-congratulatory talk about the courage of "the people"—meaning us, not the 70 percent of Chicagoans who had given Mayor Daley his last election victory—was there any recognition that revolution is a matter of life and death, not split scalps and dented police cars. The mythic impulse disdained such practical details.

The drama of insurrection developed more or less spontaneously as a reflex response to Mayor Daley's ban on camping in the park. The drama of revelation, on the other hand, was carefully planned —produced and directed by the movement's most inventive image maker, Jerry Rubin. Not only were the Festival of Life and Pig-for-President ploys more effective than any of Mobe's efforts in getting people to come to Chicago, but Rubin's nominal organization of perhaps a dozen activists impressed the media so much that "Yippie" became virtually a generic term for demonstrator. (In the aftermath of the protests, police claimed that TV officials had told Rubin where cameras would be located so that he could plan accordingly—a not implausible charge.) The Yippie conception of the demonstrations as radical theater for a mass audience was a more sophisticated, imaginative extension of the line espoused by straight radicals like Tom Hayden and Rennie Davis—that the purpose of confrontation was to prove to millions that our putative democracy is governed not by consent but by force.

This rationale has always made me uncomfortable, because I don't believe that confrontations, in themselves, prove anything of the sort. The government has never pretended not to back its laws with force; what radicals must demonstrate is that the laws do not represent the majority will or—what is even more complicated— that the majority will is consistently manipulated to oppose its own interests. The Chicago confrontations showed only that Daley's actions were possibly unconstitutional and certainly vindictive and that the police were unnecessarily violent. Liberals might easily argue that it was not the inherent repressiveness of the system that had been exposed, but the stubbornness of a particularly dictatorial, xenophobic politician and the general benightedness of policemen; the remedy, then, was not revolution but reform of the Democratic Party and a college education for cops. As for the mass of Americans, they could be expected to conclude that the troublemaking freaks—and after all, none of us denied that we came to make trouble, to disrupt a national convention, no less—simply got what they asked for.

Nevertheless, the theory of revelation-through-confrontation was tenaciously defended. When it was suggested to Tom Hayden that Mayor Lindsay would have given the demonstrators Central Park, let them march wherever they wanted, and ordered the police to keep hands off, Hayden replied that since Lindsay would not have scared away potential demonstrators, a New York action would have drawn 750,000 people, too many to be peacefully contained. Besides, he said, the prevalent belief that the war was going to end because corporate liberals had decided it was a mistake was all wrong; on the contrary, the war was going to be pressed, and the reaction of the Chicago police showed that the power structure had decided to crush dissent. I thought Hayden's statistic was fanciful—after all, the highest total estimate of demonstrators in Chicago had been 15,000 ("And that," remarked one disappointed radical, "is if you count everybody twice"). His analysis of the political situation struck me as equally facile. The outcome of the war was still in doubt, but the extent and respectability of the opposition, which had split the nation's ruling party, could not help but reflect bitter conflicts of interest among the powerful—conflicts that were reflected not only in differing policies but in differing styles. Hayden underestimated the ability of the Lindsay-style politician to neutralize dissent by avoiding conspicuous abrasion. After Martin Luther King's death the New York police had stood by while arsonists gutted several blocks of Lenox Avenue stores. Many peculiar things were possible in this peculiar moment of history.

Of course, I am oversimplifying. For one thing, most big-city mayors are more like Daley than Lindsay. For another, the security measures at the convention and Daley's prohibition of the march on the amphitheater were not simply whim, but were rooted in the social crisis: the danger of assassinations was real, and so was the possibility of a violent clash between demonstrators and angry residents of the stockyards neighborhood. And in calling on the National Guard and federal troops, Daley was merely behaving like a conscientious liberal—the Kerner Report had recommended the use of large numbers of police to intimidate rioters without bloodshed. If the Chicago convulsion was no metaphysical necessity, neither was it just a fluke. In a sense it did reveal the system— though only at its crudest, at its most rigid, inflammatory, and provincial. Radicals who took that part for the whole were making an understandable inductive leap to a not improbable future. The problem was, it was not ourselves we had to convince—it was those people Out There.

It soon became clear that favorable publicity could not be equated with favorable public opinion; poll after poll showed that a large majority supported the police action. Publicity had been sympathetic because Daley had tried to restrict television coverage, because newsmen had been manhandled by police and security guards, and most of all because the average reporter is a good liberal, with the proper aristocratic prejudices against cops and machine politicians. But people who are not good liberals—that is, most people—do not necessarily take their cues from the media any more than radicals do. More likely, they lump reporters with those pseudointellectuals George Wallace reviled. Anyway, the honeymoon between the media and the demonstrators ended almost simultaneously with the convention. Under pressure from indignant citizens as well as Mayor Daley, his police chief, the

Democratic Party, and the United States government (ominously, the FCC announced it would investigate charges of bias in television coverage of the demonstrations), the newspapers and TV stations went into paroxysms of self-doubt: Did we get too involved instead of maintaining our objectivity? Were we unfair to the police? If "the other side of the story" had indeed been stinted, it soon came into its own; September was the month of the On-the-Other-Hand press. Besides atoning for real or imagined misfeasances, the media had the burden of reporting all the evidence various police and government sources were accumulating to show that the disturbances had been engineered by "a handful of dedicated revolutionaries": an undercover cop accused Jerry Rubin of plotting to kill a policeman; a cache of vituric acid (the active ingredient in stink bombs) was discovered in a bus-station locker; and so forth and so on.

Yet the reaction that many dreaded has so far turned out to be rather mild, its tone more propolice than antidemonstrator. The HUAC hearings were a joke, and the President's Commission on Violence even labeled the events in Chicago a "police riot." It may be that neither the radical left nor the right benefited as much from Chicago as the Democratic doves. The one thing the demonstrations certainly accomplished was to strengthen the anti-Humphrey forces in the party and galvanize local reformers. And since the movement to the right is more one of desperation than of positive enthusiasm—in the preelection polls a significant percentage of Wallace voters revealed that their second choice had been Robert Kennedy or even Gene McCarthy—the antiwar liberals could mop up in 1972.* The way the week ended—with dissenting liberal delegates sitting in the dirt, singing "We Shall Overcome," getting arrested, and otherwise adopting the style of

* Though I had enough sense to hedge, this piece of wishful thinking stands as the worst prediction I ever made, except perhaps for a rock review in which I suggested that David Bowie did not have much of a future in America.

protest politics circa 1963 (liberals have their myths, too)—seems
a portent. Radicals have been accused of duping hordes of innocent McCarthy kids into risking life and limb. But suppose it's just
the opposite—suppose the street-fighters were really only shock
troops for the reform Democrats, stalking-horses for Teddy Kennedy? Suppose the power structure isn't preparing to crush us,
only to absorb us, as usual? America—and we ought to know
this by now—is not a gun but a gigantic vacuum cleaner.

No matter. We forced a national political conclave under the
gun. Every such activity saps the efficiency of government, divert-
ing energy, money, manpower. More, it forces the authorities to
keep taking us into account. If they know that whenever they do
A we will do B, they have to stop each time and calculate: is it
worth the trouble? And whether or not the publicity created any
new radicals, if it just showed some kid in Des Moines that we
exist, it served its purpose. Visibility is the difference between a
movement and ten thousand people in search of one.

III

The Chicago project cannot be judged simply by its concrete
political results. In the long run, its influence on the attitudes of
the participants may be more important. For all of us it was,
among other things, a week-long exercise in political education, in
which tactical experiments succeeded or failed, in which prejudice
—and myth-making—came up against experience. The street
community provided a continuing forum for gut-level debate
about what had been and what should be done. Spokesmen for a
variety of issues—Huey Newton, the Chicago transit strike, the
California grape boycott, chemical and biological warfare—came
to state their cases and mobilize subsidiary demonstrations. The
constant argument and exchange of information, which meshed
with the action in a way that should have delighted progressive
educators as well as revolutionaries, was extended and amplified by

the street media: the *Ramparts*-sponsored *Wallposter*, the best source of street news and analysis;* SDS's polemical broadside, *Handwriting on the Wall*, which was tacked to trees in the park; the usual underground and radical press; and leaflets on every conceivable subject.

For obvious reasons, our most impassioned discussion concerned the police. Before I go on, I should say that I am a policeman's daughter. My father is atypical (Jewish, liberal, educated) and anyway, since cops distrust all civilians, my entrée to the police subculture is limited. But from years of parental inside-dopesterism and personal contact with policemen I have learned many things. One of the simplest is that cops are not by definition vicious subhumans. This is not a truth generally accepted among political activists. In Chicago the street fighters saw the demonstrations almost exclusively in terms of "the people" versus the cops, who were, depending on one's favorite metaphor, either animals or machines. For most of the week this attitude dominated, at least on a rhetorical level. Shouted in anger, "pig" was a relatively mild epithet; used as a routine synonym in the Black Panther mode ("And then three pigs got out of their car . . ."), it became monstrous. I thought it was self-deceptive—another pretense that white bohemians and radicals are as oppressed as ghetto blacks; and arrogant—a special case of that fierce bohemian contempt for all those slobs who haven't seen the light. Many cops thought it was funny; they made jokes about "bringing home the bacon" and "Lincoln Pork."

First to question the cop-hating orgy were the McCarthy kids and the few genuine hippies. With no revolutionary machismo to protect, they could afford to observe that most of the cops were doing their job with no special zeal, that some of them were even friendly ("We're all different—you're a nonconformist, and I'm a conformist"), and that in any case, the practice of reading whole groups of people out of the human race has a bad history. For

* For the first few days; later, *Ramparts* editor Warren Hinckle insisted on playing up convention gossip and the Chicago staff quit in protest.

many radicals, second thoughts began when the National Guard arrived. An important recent development on the left has been the discovery that servicemen are people—that a soldier is not necessarily a fascist because he would rather serve than go to jail, or because he thought he would get good training in the army, or because he believed what the government said about our mission in Vietnam. And though there were shouts of "Sieg Heil!" at the troops in Chicago, the consensus was that these boys were not our enemies; they were only being used. Although there are obvious differences between soldiers and cops—a policeman's job is permanent and always voluntary—there are also obvious analogies. The police-baiting began to cool, and the crowd to hear don't-blame-the-cops-but-the-system speeches with increasing frequency. At the Mobilization rally on Wednesday afternoon a line of cops rushed into the bewildered crowd, sending at least two people to the hospital; the cause of the disturbance, it turned out, was an attempt—which most of the demonstrators had not even seen—to lower an American flag and run up a red flag in its place. Shortly after this incident, Dick Gregory spoke: "At least after World War II, people blamed Hitler first and the troops second. The police are worse off than you—at least you can demonstrate. The police are the new niggers. They can whup your heads, but it won't get them a raise—they gotta go downtown and ask." Though antipolice feeling had been aggravated by the gratuitous violence, Gregory got an enthusiastic ovation and inspired cries of "More pay for cops!" and "Join us!"

The reaction was a good sign. The police issue is really part of the much larger problem of anti-working-class prejudice. The authoritarian character, far from being a special affliction of the policeman, is endemic to the lower socioeconomic brackets.* (If

* Though the idea of this piece was to defend American workers against the condescending bigotry of middle-class radicals, my own middle-class bias permeates it. The "authoritarian character" comes in more than one guise, and sixties leftists were hardly free of authoritarian tendencies; the left's arrogance toward the working class was, among other things, symptomatic of its implicit faith in its own superior enlightenment. There is, for example,

anything, cops are *more* tolerant of deviant behavior than the average workingman—they see so much of it they get calloused.) The policeman happens to be doing the dirty work; the others just wish they could. Liberals and radicals dislike cops not only because they have the guns and the clubs, but because they are under-educated proles who like television and think Negroes are lazy. And almost invariably, virulent cop-haters have little use for ordinary people. The guerrilla mentality that came to full flower in Chicago denies the first principle of guerrilla warfare—that the population must be sympathetic or at least not actively hostile. The street-fighters think they can and should do it all by themselves; Mark Rudd has put down organizing as a cowardly alternative to rebellion.

Before the Wallace campaign, most radicals assumed that white workers were too well integrated into the system to be an important force for change. Those leftists who did insist on the importance of working-class organizing tended to explain away workers' conservative, racist attitudes as a superficial aberration, the result of ruling-class divide-and-conquer tactics. The flaw in this analysis was its failure to observe that divide-and-conquer tactics work both ways: radicals also lashed out at the white working class because their real enemies were beyond reach. White workers, economically and psychologically ill equipped to cope with change, were the group most affected by domestic social upheaval. They suffered most from increasing crime, paid most—percent-agewise—for welfare and poverty programs, depended most on the disintegrating public school.* But the left, preoccupied with its

---

the underlying assumption of this article that radical organizing is basically a public relations problem. Nowhere do I suggest that workers' resistance to the left might have anything to do with justified skepticism about some of our ideas.

* Actually, poor black people are the most frequent victims of crime. And for blacks the public schools were a disaster long before 1968.

own oppression, could not see them as human beings with real grievances. Liberal politicians (with the concurrence of radicals) dismissed the workingman's fear of crime as racist paranoia and his resentment at having to support people who did not work as social backwardness. Liberal experts (with the silent complicity of radicals) proclaimed that poor blacks and students must be consulted on policies that affected them, but treated white workers like inert material to be socially engineered at will.

It took George Wallace to make radicals understand that white workers were in fact a vast disaffected constituency that had been fairly begging for someone to care about its problems. Then, just as this new consciousness began to make a substantial impact on the left, Chicago happened. For anyone who wanted to look at it that way, Chicago was a case study in the indifference-cum-contempt that radicals, especially posthippies, reserved for ordinary Americans. Many of us felt the contradiction very deeply.

Talking to local activists, I began to realize that the problem of elitism was at least partly a function of geography. Most radicals came from New York or San Francisco, where dissidents were numerous enough to develop subcultures and where even larger numbers of liberal sympathizers stood ready to support mass demonstrations. In such an environment an emphasis on cultural radicalism and confrontation politics came naturally. But outside the coastal enclaves and their microcosms, the university campuses, radicals found themselves isolated. If they wanted to have any effect at all, they had to go to the people. In Chicago itself there were several fairly sophisticated projects aimed at improving relations between radicals and white workers. Organizers lived in working-class city and suburban neighborhoods, worked with the people on consumer problems, taught in local schools. Cities like Cleveland had similar programs. But for the cosmopolite left this was unexplored territory; it was hard even to imagine a typical New York radical cutting off his hair and moving to Queens. Given these social facts, it meant something that the demonstrations took place in Chicago, without a Lindsay or 900,000 liberals to act as a buffer between us and the people—as represented by Daley's cops but also, let us not forget, by the construction workers who gave us the V sign and the high school kids who asked us why we liked the, uh, Viet Cong. We could not have learned nearly so much from a New York protest.

In recent months radicals have been increasingly critical of confrontation politics—not as one sometimes-useful tactic among others, but as an all-purpose religious rite. Discussion about working whites has become at once more sympathetic and more realistic. The next step is for radicals in significant numbers to break out of their ghettos and go live in America. It's too late to do anything about the cops—most of them, anyway. But we need their children.

1968

Herbert Marcuse,

1898–1979

When I heard that Herbert Marcuse had died, I immediately thought, "The same year as John Wayne." For people like me Marcuse was something of a star, a presence, a symbol of certain values. I felt connected to him, though not in any simple way. I discovered his books at a time when I was groping toward a radicalism that would make sense of my experience as a middle-class American. *Eros and Civilization* and *One Dimensional Man* excited me because they were about problems I was struggling with—the relation of psychology to politics, the idea of a cultural revolution, the prospects for radical change in a society where most people had enough to eat. Still, my copies of the books are filled with comments like "European elitism" and "glib" and "what bullshit!" As my politics matured, I found that I disagreed with most of what Marcuse said and hated what the new left made of his ideas. In some ways I defined my political outlook in reaction to Marcuse's, an acknowledgment that he'd made certain territory his own.

In his monolithically bleak view of advanced capitalism and his contempt for American workers' enjoyment of their material gains, Marcuse was hardly distinguishable from conservative critics of mass culture. His version of that perennial aristocratic nightmare, "mass man," was the passive, manipulated consumer who had no autonomous desires, only socially imposed "false needs" for the system's products and spectacles. He could see no value in the formal political liberties that might seem to give American rebels room to maneuver, or in the prosperity that encouraged cultural experiment as well as consumption; he argued that, on the contrary, this society's superficial tolerance only reinforced ruling-class power, maintaining an illusion of freedom and harmlessly absorbing dissent. From Marcuse's standpoint the only revolutionary act was to stand outside the system and say no; to try to make positive changes was to be taken over and used. The line between his sort of apocalyptic utopianism and nihilistic pessimism is not easy to draw. Though Marcuse refrained from pursuing the rougher edges of his vision, many who shared his assumptions were less cautious. According to his obituary in the *Times*, Marcuse "despised" being called "father of the new left." I doubt that, say, the Weather Underground would particularly appreciate being called "children of Marcuse." But I don't think it's unfair to make the connection.

What Marcuse had most obviously in common with many of his new left children, or cousins, was the alienated snobbery of the middle-class intellectual. Classes that take money for granted are always horrified at the naive delight of the "vulgar" nouveau riche in getting and spending. But a deeper, more complicated kind of class bias defined the relationship between the new left and the rest of America. Marcuse and like-minded radicals simply assumed that their perception of social reality was more accurate than that of the average nonrevolutionary worker. It did not occur to them that in some ways the opposite might be true. Yet I think their one-dimensional view of American life, their obsession with consumer goods as the root of all evil, and their conviction that most people were satisfied robots had less to do with the objective workings of the system than with the way many middle-class intellectuals experienced themselves. Trapped in abstractions, cut off from a sense of their own autonomous desires, they projected their self-estrangement onto others. Their hatred of things—which was mixed with a fascination that bordered on prurience—was a form of identification; while they felt impotent, objectified, they endowed objects with seductive power. I say "they," but I don't want to claim too much distance. I can remember, some fifteen years ago, having a screaming fight with my then-husband because he wanted to buy a TV set to watch the news and I didn't want to have one in the house. Secretly I felt a bit foolish. A TV set was just a TV set— what was I so afraid of? The answer was simple: I knew that the morning after the set arrived I would wake up and find myself transformed into a suburban housewife. This fantasy of demonic possession by *things*, of paralyzed inability to resist (except by saying no! television get thee hence!) what an all-powerful system chose to make of me, did not really jibe with my life, in which I acted, complained, fought, directly or deviously tried to get what I wanted, sometimes even succeeded. In the same way the left distorted reality by denying that people were agents.

Not that I didn't learn a good deal from Marcuse; his analysis had its core of truth. (So, for that matter, did my fantasy.) He was right in his contention that the modern capitalist state has immense resources for social control, that it operates as much by manipulation as by direct coercion. He was right, certainly, in thinking that the American ruling class uses liberalism as one of its many weapons, trying whenever it can to pass off the appearance of freedom as the reality. But for a Marxist he was a curiously undialectical thinker, despite his fondness for oxymorons like "repressive tolerance." Liberalism, after all, is a strategy forced on the state by people's pressure for greater freedom and a higher standard of living; rulers do their best to take back liberal concessions whenever they have the opportunity—as the last few years surely prove. If American workers have not hated their lives enough to make a revolution, it is in part because liberalism meets some genuine human needs. But it is also because however pissed off they may be (and Americans usually are), most people, understandably, don't want to risk what they have unless they see a practical alternative and feel they have a real chance at it. In the meantime, there is struggle in small, daily ways and the opportunity to sneak out to a movie now and then.

The *Times* quotes Marcuse wistfully referring to the "heroic period" of "the hippies and yippies." I wonder if he understood how thoroughly his heroes' values were rooted in mass culture. What did he think it meant when the Yippies got the Chicago police and the news media to cooperate in bringing revolutionary theater to millions? But then, he may have been more appreciative of such ironies than I tend to assume. I met Marcuse once; a friend and I were in La Jolla, so we went to see the great man. I liked him. The main thing I remember is that at one point he demanded, "Tell me—is there a way to define the difference between art and nonart?" I felt like a student being tested; anyway, I suspected him of thinking rock-and-roll was trash. With trepidation, I said "No." He nodded and looked pleased. "I agree with you!"

August 1979

Glossary for the Eighties

As the seventies draw to a close, it is painfully obvious that militant critics of our society have fallen on hard times. Young, eager, and sexy only a decade ago, they have aged badly. By now the least perceptive of them have realized that radical is no longer chic; where once crowds of people hung on their every word, now the same words are almost certain to elicit an uncomfortable silence, a tactful change of subject, or an outright sneer. But most radicals have not yet caught on that "the same words" are actually at the root of their problem. In keeping with a general tendency to cling to the manners and mores of their beloved sixties (radicals are a conservative lot), they have failed to master the subtleties of contemporary discourse. It's impossible for people to communicate if they don't speak the same language. And so, for those who would rather not spend the eighties standing alone in a corner muttering "The country is swinging to the right!" I've compiled a basic vocabulary.

DOGMA: a political belief one is unreasonably committed to, such as the notion that freedom is good and slavery is bad.

BIAS: predilection for a particular dogma. For example, the feminist bias is that women are equal to men and the male chauvinist bias is that women are inferior. The unbiased view is that the truth lies somewhere in between.

IDEOLOGY: a body of dogma, usually based on the stubborn belief that some social injustice exists and ought to be corrected. Not to be confused with "ideas," which are common-sense propositions like "The truth lies somewhere in between" and "Life is unfair."

IDEOLOGICAL FANATIC: a compulsive purveyor of ideology. In particular, one who can't resist bringing up pet dogmas at awkward or inappropriate moments, such as during a sensible discussion of more important issues or at a social gathering where someone has unwittingly offended the fanatic's beliefs (see SUPERSENSITIVE, below). The term is often applied to women who drag feminism into everything, as when they make a fuss because some terrific populist politician thinks abortion is murder. Also used of people who make themselves into terrible bores by repeatedly criticizing the same social evil, simply because nothing has been done about it.

PARTY LINE: an opinion shared by three or more ideological fanatics.

INDEPENDENT THINKERS: people who refuse to do the easy thing, the popular thing, who boldly repudiate party lines. For example, women who declare that it's okay to be a sex object again; straight liberals who confess that the scene on Christopher Street makes them sick.

STALINIST: a particularly abrasive ideological fanatic. One who hews to the party line and accuses independent thinkers of telling the people in power what they want to hear. Stalinists can never get it through their heads that a person can be sympathetic to their cause without being an ideological fanatic; a typical Stalinist trick is to insinuate that such people are not as sympathetic as they

146

pretend. For instance, Stalinists invariably get their backs up when male friends of the women's movement refer to Bella Abzug as "that loudmouthed bitch." (cf. popular sixties epithet, "fascist")

HUMORLESS: what you are if you do not find the following subjects funny: rape, big breasts, sex with little girls. It carries no imputation of humorlessness if you do not find the following subjects funny: impotence, castration, vaginas with teeth.

SUPERSENSITIVE: in the habit of hearing insult and bigotry where none is intended. Jews are traditionally the worst offenders, being inclined to take constructive criticism like "Pale-faced Jew-boy, I wish you were dead" as evidence of anti-Semitism. The especially supersensitive may even react angrily to compliments, such as "I prefer liberated women, they're better fucks."

SHRILL: female.

PARANOID: Jewish.

ZIONIST: paranoid.

CRANK: see IDEOLOGICAL FANATIC. Also SUPERSENSITIVE.

OPPRESSION: the endless abuses committed by ideological fanatics—especially pushy blacks, women, Jews, and homosexuals—against long-suffering regular people. Oppressors have often been known to corner their victims at dinner parties and subject them to Stalinist harangues. Another common form of oppression consists of asking the victim tactless personal questions, such as "Do you share child care with your wife?"

SURVIVOR: a white middle-class person who manages to function despite recurrent nightmares about being chased by giant black lesbians with pitchforks.

147

DECADENT: preoccupied with insignificant matters of Life Style, such as one's need for a satisfying sexual relationship; frivolous. (It carries no imputation of decadence if you are frivolous about rape, big breasts, or sex with little girls.)

NARCISSIST: (thanks to Tom Wolfe, this clinical term is beginning to be supplanted by the more colorful "child of the me decade"): one who selfishly pursues personal freedom and pleasure instead of buckling down to the grim but necessary duties of a mature adult. Specifically, anyone who gets a divorce, has an abortion, sleeps with someone of the same sex, lives alone, lives with a lover with no intention of getting married, leaves a moribund relationship for a vital one, or is reluctant to have children (unless there is a good reason for the reluctance, such as having had a hysterectomy). Also, a woman who thinks it's important that she have orgasms, complains about being cooped up at home with her kids, insists that even middle-class women have problems, or believes that freeing women is more important than strengthening the family. Contradictory as it may seem, many narcissists are also ideological fanatics.

January 1979

The Family:

Love It or Leave It

When I talk about my family, I mean the one I grew up in. I have been married, lived with men, and participated in various communal and semicommunal arrangements, but for most of the past six years—nearly all of my thirties—I have lived alone. This is neither an accident nor a deliberate choice, but the result of an accretion of large and small choices, many of which I had no idea I was making at the time. Conscious or not, these choices have been profoundly influenced by the cultural and political radicalism of the sixties, especially radical feminism. The sense of possibility, of hope for great changes that pervaded those years affected all my aspirations; compromises that might once have seemed reasonable, or simply to be expected, felt stifling. A rebellious community of peers supported me in wanting something other than conventional family life; feminist consciousness clarified and deepened my ambivalence toward men, my skepticism about marriage. Single women were still marginal, but their position was dignified in a way it had never been before: it was possible to conceive of being alone as a choice rather than a failure.

For me the issue was less the right to be alone, in itself, than the right to take as much time and room as I needed to decide what kind of life I wanted, what I could hold out for. Intimate connections are important to me. I want a mate, or so I believe, and possibly a child. Before the counterculture existed I was attracted to the idea of communal living and I still am. Yet obviously other priorities have intervened: I haven't found what I supposedly want on terms I can accept. The psychologist in me suggests that I don't want it as wholeheartedly as I think, the feminist retorts that it's not my fault if a sexist society keeps offering me a choice between unequal relationships and none, and I'm sure they're both right. Anyway, I wouldn't take back the choices I've made. I would not wish to be a different person, or to have been shaped by a different time.

Still, I can't help being uneasy about the gap between the lessons I learned during that time and the rules of the game in this one. As the conservative backlash gains momentum, I feel a bit like an explorer camped on a peninsula, who looks back to discover that the rising tide has made it into an island and that it threatens to become a mere sandbar, or perhaps disappear altogether. If there is one cultural trend that has defined the seventies, it is the aggressive resurgence of family chauvinism, flanked by its close relatives, antifeminism and homophobia. The right's impassioned defense of traditional family values—the common theme of its attacks on the Equal Rights Amendment, legal abortion, gay rights, sexual permissiveness, child care for working mothers, and "immoral" (read unattached female) welfare recipients—has affected the social atmosphere even in the liberal, educated middle class that produced the cultural radicals. The new consensus is that the family is our last refuge, our only defense against universal predatory selfishness, loneliness, and rootlessness; the idea that there could be desirable alternatives to the family is no longer taken seriously. I've also noticed a rise in the level of tension between married and single people. Over the years family boosters have subjected me to my share of hints that I'm pathetic, missing out on real life, or that the way I live is selfish and shallow, or both; I've indulged an unworthy tendency to respond in kind, flaunting my independence and my freedom from the burdens of parenthood while implying that I see through their facade of happiness to the quiet desperation beneath. Lately these exchanges have become edgier; sometimes they explode into fights. As I said, I'm uneasy.

Of course, "family" is one of those concepts that invite stretching. One might reasonably define a family as any group of people who live under the same roof, function as an economic unit, and have a serious commitment to each other—a definition that could include communes and unmarried couples of whatever sexual preference. But the family as it exists for most people in the real world—in a social and historical context—is nothing so amorphous or pluralistic. It is an institution, a set of laws, customs, and beliefs that define what a family is or ought to be, the rights and duties of its members, and its relation to society. This institution embraces only households of people related by birth or marriage. It is rooted in the assumption of male authority over dependent women and children, the sexual double standard, and the traditional exchange of the husband's financial support for the wife's domestic and sexual services. It defines the pursuit of individual freedom as selfish and irresponsible ("narcissistic" in current jargon), the subordination of personal happiness to domestic obligations as the hallmark of adulthood and the basis of morals. Above all, the family is supposed to control sex and legitimize it through procreation; family morality regards sensual pleasure for its own sake as frivolous, sexual passion as dangerous and fundamentally antisocial. In a family-centered society prevailing attitudes toward people who live differently range from pity to indifference to hostile envy to condemnation. Women who step outside the home into the world become fair game for economic and sexual exploitation; children who have no parents, or whose parents cannot or will not give them adequate care, get minimal attention from a community that regards them as aliens in a land where only citizens have rights.

On the left, family chauvinism often takes the form of nostalgic declarations that the family, with its admitted faults, has been vitiated by modern capitalism, which is much worse (at least the family is based on personal relations rather than soulless cash, etc., etc.). Christopher Lasch's *The Culture of Narcissism* is the latest polemic to suggest that radicals who criticize the family are beating a dead (and presumably mourned) horse. True, capitalism has eroded patriarchal authority; the family has been drastically altered by modern developments from industrialism to women's participation in the labor force to the hedonism implicit in mass culture. (Personally, I prefer the present system, with its admitted faults, to one that allowed women no rights at all.) But it is perverse to deny that the family and its ideology continue to shape our lives. Most of us have been brought up by parents or other relatives. It is in the family that children discover their sexuality and learn how women and men are supposed to behave, toward the world and each other. The family is still the main source of women's oppression and the main focus of feminist politics, which is probably why male leftists are so inclined to premature announcements of its demise.

Whether or not they work outside the home, most women base their lives on marriage and motherhood; since job discrimination ensures that women earn roughly half as much as men and lack of public child-care facilities is a further deterrent to single motherhood, women's employment has not ended their dependence on marriage, nor has it relieved them of the chief responsibility for housework and child rearing. Though families who conform to the classic patriarchal pattern are now in the minority, most domestic-relations laws define the obligations of husband and wife in terms of their traditional roles. So does the government. Nixon vetoed federally funded child care on the grounds that the state should not usurp the prerogative of the family, code for "Mothers should stay home where they belong and if they don't, it's their children's tough luck." The Carter administration's response to the poverty of families dependent on a female breadwinner was to suggest that federal job programs employ *men*, the assumption being that women should be married to men who can support them. Despite all the activism of the past ten years, our society still regards wife beating as a private domestic matter, condones rape within marriage, hesitates to condemn men for raping independent or sexually active women, restricts women's access to contraception and abortion, discriminates against homosexuals and even throws them in jail. In most states it is still legal to punish a spouse by using evidence of sexual "immorality" as a weapon in contested divorces and child-custody disputes. Social prejudice against single people remains pervasive: we are immature, unreliable, and incapable of deep attachments, we don't own property, we like loud music, our sexual activities are offensive, and if too many of us are allowed in we'll ruin the neighborhood. (The stereotype goes double for homosexuals.) Unmarried couples and groups also encounter various forms of discrimination, from difficulty in renting apartments, obtaining mortgages, and buying insurance to ordinances that limit or ban communal housing to tax laws that allow only the legally married to file joint returns. Nor do "illegitimate" children have equal legal rights.

The relation of capitalism to the family is in fact far more dialectical than analyses like Lasch's suggest. When families were economically self-sufficient, they provided jobs for those who could work and took care of those who could not. In an industrial economy, where workers must find buyers for their labor, anyone who cannot command a living wage faces a grim existence; even the white middle-class man at the height of his earning power may find that a technological advance, an economic downturn, or an illness has made him unemployable. While government services like unemployment insurance and social security purport to fill the gaps, in practice they offer a bare minimum of protection against disaster and do nothing to alleviate the day-to-day anxiety of coping with a hostile system. For most people the only alternative to facing that anxiety alone is to be part of a family. At least in theory, family members are committed to each other's survival; small, unstable, and vulnerable as the contemporary nuclear family may be, it is better than nothing.

Capitalists have an obvious stake in encouraging dependence on the family and upholding its mythology. If people stopped looking to the family for security, they might start looking to full employment and expanded public services. If enough parents or communal households were determined to share child rearing, they might insist that working hours and conditions be adapted to their domestic needs. If enough women refused to work for no pay in the home and demanded genuine parity on the job, our economy would be in deep trouble. There is a direct link between the conservative trend of American capitalism and the backlash on so-called cultural issues. During the past decade, the loss of the Vietnam War, the general decline in American influence, and the growing power of the oil industry have led to an intensive corporate drive to increase profits by reducing social services, raising prices faster than wages and convincing the public to have "lower expectations"; in the same period blatant family chauvinism has become official government policy. Under the circumstances it is not surprising that most people are less inclined to demand change —with all the risk and uncertainty such demands entail—than to cling to what they have and defend it against attack. These days "my family first" is only a slightly less insular version of the "me first" psychology the insecurity of capitalism provokes. Both are based on the dismaying knowledge that if you and your family are not first, they are all too likely to be last. People who are clinging are never eager to share their branch, nor do they look kindly on anyone who insists it's rotten wood.

Like most educated white middle-class women of my generation, I did not grow up worrying about economic survival. My central problems had to do with the conflict between a conservative upbringing and the "sexual revolution," between traditional definitions of femininity and a strong desire for worldly achievement and independence. For me the cultural revolt began in the late fifties with the libertarian campaign against obscenity laws and conventional sexual morality. I was for it, but I was also suspicious, and no wonder: quite aside from my own internal conflicts, the sexual freedom movement was full of contradictions. The libertarians did not concern themselves with the quality of sexual relationships or the larger social and emotional causes of sexual frustration. They were less influenced by feminism than their counterparts in the twenties; in theory they advocated the sexual liberation of women, but in practice their outlook was male-centered and often downright misogynist. They took for granted that prostitution and pornography were liberating. They carried on about the hypocrisy of the sexual game—by which they meant men's impatience with having to court women and pay lip service to their demands for love, respect, and commitment. No one suggested that men's isolation of sex from feeling might actually be part of the problem, rather than the solution.

Around the same time, more radical ideas were beginning to surface. While I was in high school, I was fascinated by the beats and their rejection of the "square" institution of marriage. Later I began to read and learn from radical Freudians like Paul Goodman, Norman Mailer, Herbert Marcuse, and—especially—the original radical Freudian, Wilhelm Reich. Where Freud contended that civilization required instinctual repression, Reich argued that what Freud took to be civilization, in some absolute sense, was a specific, changeable social structure—authoritarian, patriarchal, class-bound. In Reich's view the incestuous fantasies, perverse impulses, and sadistic aggression that dominated the Freudian unconscious were themselves the product of repression—the child's response to the frustration of its natural sexual needs. He claimed that when his patients managed to overcome their neurotic sexual inhibitions they became spontaneously decent, rational, and cooperative; the problem, from the conservative moralist's standpoint, was that they also developed a sense of independence and self-respect that made them question arbitrary authority, compulsive work, passionless marriage, and conventional moral and religious ideas. The function of sexual repression, Reich concluded, was to instill in children the submissive attitudes demanded by patriarchal "civilization." Thus a truly revolutionary program could not be limited to economic issues, but must include demands for sexual liberation, the emancipation of women, and the transformation of the family. (Unsurprisingly, Goodman, Mailer, and other cultural radicals heavily influenced by Reich's work did not pick up on his feminism.)

To my mind, Reich's most revolutionary assertion was also his simplest (some would say most simpleminded): that natural sexuality is the physical manifestation of love. He insisted that the perception of tenderness and sensuality as separate, even antagonistic phenomena was the collective neurosis of an antisexual culture, that pornography, prostitution, rape, and other forms of alienated sex were the by-products of ascetic moralism, the underside of patriarchy, the social equivalent of the Freudian unconscious. These ideas have encountered near-universal resistance; the belief in an intrinsic split between lust and love is one of our most deeply ingrained and cherished prejudices. Most people agree that untrammeled pursuit of sexual pleasure is one thing, socially responsible relationships quite another; debate is usually over the proper ratio of license to repression. Though all democratic thought is based on the premise that freedom is compatible with civilization, that under the right conditions people are capable of self-regulation, even dedicated democrats hesitate to apply this premise to sex and family life. Radicals criticize the conservative assumption that people are innately acquisitive, violent, and power-hungry; yet most swallow the parallel idea that the sexual drive is innately solipsistic. Sex, they assume, is different. Why? It just is. Everybody knows *that*.

What everybody knows is not necessarily wrong. But it seems clear to me that if there were no inherent opposition between freedom and responsibility, pleasure and duty, "mere" sex and serious love, the patriarchal family would create it. I believe that sexual love in its most passionate sense is as basic to happiness as food is to life and that living and sleeping with a mate one does not love in this sense violates fundamental human impulses. Which is to say that since passion is by definition spontaneous—we can behave in ways that inhibit or nurture it, but finally we feel it or we don't—a marital arrangement based on legal, economic, or moral coercion is oppressive. But the whole point of marriage is to be a binding social alliance, and it cannot fulfill that function unless mates are forced or intimidated into staying together. Traditional patriarchal societies dealt with this contradiction by refusing to recognize passionate love as a legitimate need. For men it was seen as an illicit disruptive force that had nothing to do with the serious business of family; for women it was usually proscribed altogether. The modern celebration of romantic love muddled the issue: now we want marriage to serve two basically incompatible purposes, to be at once a love relationship and a contract. We exalt love as the highest motive for marriage, but tell couples that of course passion fades into "mature" conjugal affection. We want our mates to be faithful out of love, yet define monogamy as an obligation whose breach justifies moral outrage and legal revenge. We agree that spouses who don't love each other should not have to stay together, even for the sake of the children; yet we uphold a system that makes women economic prisoners and condone restrictive adversary divorce laws. We argue that without the legal and moral pressure of marriage lovers won't make the effort required to live intimately with someone else; but by equating emotional commitment with the will to live up to a contract, we implicitly define passion as unserious, peripheral to real life.

Another equally insoluble conflict is built into the nuclear family. Children are a twenty-four-hour-a-day responsibility, yet parents have legitimate needs for personal freedom, privacy, and spontaneity in their lives. The brunt of this conflict falls on mothers, but even if fathers shared child care equally, the basic problem would remain. Child rearing is too big a job for one or even two people to handle without an unnatural degree of self-sacrifice, destructive for both generations.

A different kind of family structure could solve or ease these problems. In matrilineal societies mothers, children, and their blood relatives were the ongoing social unit; the permanence of sexual relationships apparently became an issue with the rise of patriarchy. In traditional patriarchies the extended family at least gave parents some relief from responsibility for their offspring. The logical postpatriarchal unit is some version of the commune. Groups of people who agreed to take responsibility for each other, pool their economic resources, and share housework and child care would have a basis for stability independent of any one couple's sexual bond; children would have the added security of close ties to adults other than their biological parents (and if the commune were large and flexible enough, parents who had stopped being lovers might choose to remain in it); communal child rearing, shared by both sexes, would remove the element of martyrdom from parenthood.

I realize that the kind of change I'm talking about amounts to a social and psychic revolution of almost inconceivable magnitude. Yet to refuse to fight for love that is both free and responsible is in a sense to reject the possibility of love itself. I suspect that in a truly free society sexual love would be at once more satisfying and less terrifying, that lovers would be more spontaneously monogamous but less jealous, more willing to commit themselves deeply yet less devastated if a relationship had to end. Still, there is an inherent, irreducible risk in loving: it means surrendering detachment and control, giving our lovers the power to hurt us by withdrawing their love, leaving, or wanting someone else. The marriage contract appeals to our self-contradictory desire to negate that risk, nullify that power. I don't mean to suggest that people who reject marriage are less afflicted with this desire than anyone else; remaining single can be an excellent way of distancing oneself from love, or avoiding it altogether. But I am convinced that contrary to its myth, the institution supports our fear of love rather than our yearning for it. We can embrace marriage, hoping to transcend its contradictions, or reject it, hoping to find something better; either way we are likely to be disappointed.

The Family: Love It or Leave It

Until recently I had no doubt which route I preferred. I had married at twenty, left three years later, and though I did not rule out marrying again if I had some specific practical reason, the idea bothered me the way the thought of signing a loyalty oath always had. It was not the public, ceremonial aspect of marriage I objected to—I thought the decision to share one's life with a lover was worth celebrating—but the essence of marriage, the contract. Whatever two people's private view of their relationship, however they might adapt the ceremony, in getting legally married they officially agreed to be bound by the rules of a patriarchal institution—one of which was that the state defined the circumstances in which they could be unbound. Besides, most people made endless assumptions about married couples and treated them accordingly; it wasn't so easy to get married and pretend you weren't.

I was also put off by the marriages I observed; domestic life as most of my peers lived it made me feel claustrophobic. What disturbed me was the degree of emotional repression most "successful" (that is, stable and reasonably contented) marriages seemed to involve. Given the basic contradictions of the family, it inevitably provoked conflicts that had to be submerged. But the conditions of contemporary middle-class marriage—the prevalence of divorce and infidelity, the emergence of feminism, the nagging ambivalence about whether we were supposed to enjoy life or be Adults—tended to bring those conflicts into the open, requiring a whole extra layer of evasions to keep them at bay. While some couples had managed to fight out the battle of the sexes to a real understanding instead of a divorce, most successful marriages I knew of were based on a sexist détente: the husband had made it clear that he would not give up certain prerogatives and the wife pretended not to hate him for it. Add a bit of sexual and emotional boredom in an era when not to be madly in love with your spouse was a social embarrassment, and it was not surprising that so many "happy" couples radiated stifling dependence or low-level static. No, I would think, with a fair amount of smugness, better alone than trapped.

But the year I turned thirty-five, an odd thing happened: I had a persistent fantasy about getting married. It was—on the surface at least—a fantasy of triumph. At the time of my actual marriage, I had felt that my life was totally out of control. I was a scared kid making a promise I suspected I wouldn't keep, at a conventional wedding I didn't want, in a dress I'd been talked into getting. A rabbi I hardly knew presided over the traditional Jewish ritual, in which the bride gets to say precisely nothing. Since then I had, as they say, come a long way, but it had been a rocky trip. While I had rebelled against the idea that a woman needs a man to run her life, I had struggled with an undertow of conviction that such rebellion was disastrous hubris. On the level of social reality this made perfect sense; if feminism had taught me anything, it was that the liberated woman was a myth, that women who deviated from prescribed feminine behavior always paid a price. But the connection between the personal and the political is usually more convoluted than it seems. In fact, my conflict had less to do with the real social consequences of nonconformity than with an un-conscious fear that I could not, after all, be female and yet compe-tent to make my way through the world. In my relationships I had found it hard to draw the essential line between the power men have over women and the power all lovers have over each other—but I had begun to understand that what I was really fighting, more often than not, was the power of my own worst impulses to give in, give up, and be dependent.

That year, I felt the struggle was paying off. Some balance had shifted; emotionally I was on my own in a way I had not been before. And so my marriage fantasy was a kind of exorcism. Now that I was strong enough to love a man and preserve my identity, confident enough to make a choice that wouldn't be easy to get out of, I would do it over again and do it right—I would get to talk, play rock-and-roll, wear what I pleased. By marrying I would beat the system, give the lie to all the old farts who insisted that women could not have autonomy and love too. As the noted femi-nist Mick Jagger was to put it a couple of years later, American girls want everything—and I was no exception.

The Family: Love It or Leave It

Though I sensed an underside to all this, I was too proud of my psychic victory to realize I was doing yet another version of the liberated woman tap dance, one that contained its own negation. These days the formula is familiar: women, we are told (often by women themselves) are now free enough so that they can choose to be sex objects/wear six-inch heels/do the housework without feeling oppressed. The unspoken question, of course, is whether women can refuse to be sex objects/wear six-inch heels/do the housework without getting zapped. When women start answering, in effect "We've made our point—let's not push our luck," it is a sure sign of backlash. And in retrospect it seems clear that my sudden interest in marriage (it's just a silly fantasy, I kept telling myself) was an early sign that the backlash was getting to me. As it intensified, I found myself, in moments of rank self-pity, thinking about marriage in a very different spirit. Okay (I would address the world), I've fought, I've paid my dues. I'm tired of being a crank, of being marginal. I want in!

As a single woman, and a writer who will probably never make much money, I feel more vulnerable now than I ever have before. My income has not kept up with inflation. I am approaching the biological deadline for maternity, confronting the possibility that the folklore of my adolescence—if a woman doesn't settle down with a man before she's thirty, forget it—may turn out to apply to me after all. I am very conscious of the sustenance I have always gotten (and mostly taken for granted) from the family I grew up in: the intense bonds of affection and loyalty; the acceptance born of long intimacy; the power of "we," of a shared slant on the world, a collective history and mythology, a language of familiar jokes and gestures. In some ways I have recreated these bonds with my closest friends, but it is not quite the same. The difference has to do with home being the place where when you have to go there they have to take you in—and also being (as the less-quoted next line of the poem has it) something you haven't to deserve. I have friends who would take me in, but on some level I think I have to deserve them.

Around the time I began having these feelings, but before I

had quite faced them, I broke a long-standing taboo and had a love affair with a married man. At night I would sit in my kitchen arguing with myself, debates that usually began with the reflection that what I was doing was selfish, irresponsible, and an egregious breach of female solidarity. But goddammit, I would protest, I refuse to define it that way! I really believe there's such a thing as a basic human right to love whom you love and act on it.

But if you're hurting another woman? Making her unequal struggle with this whole fucked-up system more difficult?

Well, the fact is, it hurts if your mate wants someone else! That's an inescapable part of life—no matter what the almighty contract says!

Oh, yeah, right—life is unfair. And the children?

Silence, more coffee.

I never did resolve that argument; it just settled undigested in my stomach. Afterward, I had to admit I could not come up with a handy moral, except perhaps that there is no such thing as a free lunch. Morals aside, there was the matter of all those unacknowledged illusions about what I could get away with—humiliating perhaps, humbling certainly. At odd moments an old image would float into my mind. Once, as a bus I was riding in pulled out of a station, a silly-looking dog danced alongside, coming dangerously close to the wheels and yapping its lungs out. The bus rolled on.

Recently a friend reminded me that in the early, heady days of feminist activism I had said to her, "We're not going to see the results of this revolution in our lifetime; we're making it for the women who come after us." A judicious and sensible comment, but I'm not sure I ever really meant it. The reason feminism touched me so deeply was that I wanted the revolution for myself; I can't help being disappointed and angry that it is turning out to be every bit as difficult as I claimed to believe. Reaction is always temporary, I know that—what I'm afraid of is that it won't end in time to do me any good. But I also realize that kind of pessimism feeds the reaction and is in fact part of it. For all the external pressures that have contributed to the retrenchment of the erstwhile dissident community, in a sense reaction was built into its passionate optimism. The mentality that currently inspires sixties veterans to say things like "We didn't succeed in abolishing the family. This proves we were wrong—the family is necessary" is of a piece with the counterculture's notorious impatience. Our ambitions outstripped both the immediate practical possibilities and our own limitations. People turned themselves and each other inside out; terrible bitterness between women and men came to the surface; everything seemed to be coming apart, with no imminent prospect of our finding a better way to put it back together. A lot of people were relieved when the conservative mood of the seventies gave them an excuse to stop struggling and stretching themselves to uncertain purpose; a lot of men were particularly relieved when the backlash gave them support for digging in their heels against feminism. Some former rebels have turned against their past altogether, dismissing their vision as adolescent extravagance, reducing a decade of history to the part of it that was—inevitably —foolish and excessive. Many more have responded to the reaction with confusion and malaise. If women must reconcile their raised consciousness with the limits of a conservative time, men are torn between their more regressive impulses and their desire to be (or be thought) good guys. Increasingly, both sexes tend to define feminism and related cultural questions not as public issues calling for political action but as a matter of private "life styles" and "options." This sort of individualism is not only a retreat from sixties radicalism but in very real ways an extension of it—a more modest liberal version of the counterculture's faith that simply by dropping out of the system we could have the world and have it now.

That we did not manage in a few years to revolutionize an institution that has lasted for thousands, serving indispensable functions as well as oppressive ones, is hardly something to be surprised at or ashamed of. Rather, what needs to be repudiated is the naive arrogance implicit in slogans like "abolish the family" and "smash monogamy," in the illusion of so many counterculturists that revolution meant moving in with a bunch of people and calling it a commune. Far from being revolutionary, the cultural left was basically apolitical. That so much of its opposition was expressed in terms of contempt for capitalism and consumerism only confirms how little most sixties radicals understood the American social system or their own place in it. There is a neat irony in the fact that leftists are now romanticizing the family and blaming capitalism for its collapse, while ten years ago they were trashing the family and blaming capitalism for its persistence. Ah, dialectics: if an increasingly conservative capitalism has propelled the seventies backlash, it was a dynamic liberal capitalism that fostered the sixties revolt. The expansion of the American economy after World War II produced two decades of unprecedented prosperity, which allowed masses of people unprecedented latitude in making choices about how to live. Just as more and more people could afford to buy houses, cars, and appliances, they could choose to work less—or at less lucrative occupations—and still earn enough to survive without undue hardship, especially if they didn't have kids to support. As a result a growing minority—particularly among the children of the upper middle class—felt free to question the dominant social arrangements, to experiment and take risks, to extend student life with its essentially bohemian values into adulthood rather than graduate to professional jobs, nuclear families, and the suburbs.

What most counterculture opposition to capitalism amounted to was this minority's anger at the majority for refusing to make the same choice. Even the organized left, which should have known better, acted as if the way to change American society was for each person individually to renounce the family, material comfort, and social respectability. That most people were doing no such thing was glibly attributed to sexual repression, greed, and/or "brainwashing" by the mass media—the implication being that radicals and bohemians were sexier, smarter, less corrupt, and generally more terrific than everyone else. Actually, what they mostly were was younger and more privileged: it was easy to be a self-righteous antimaterialist if you had never known anxiety about money; easy to sneer at the security of marriage if you had solicitous middle-class parents; easy, if you were twenty years old and childless, to blame those parents for the ills of the world. Not that radicals were wrong in believing that a sexually free, communal society was incompatible with capitalism, or in perceiving connections between sexual repression, obsessive concern with material goods, and social conformity. But they did not understand that, psychology aside, most people submit to the power of institutions because they suffer unpleasant consequences if they don't. It made no sense to talk of abolishing the family without considering the genuine needs it served and organizing against the social pressures that inhibited us from satisfying those needs in other ways. In the seventies the left itself would provide the best illustration of that truth: it was when economic conditions worsened, around the time most sixties rebels were reaching an age where anxieties about the future were not so easy to dismiss, that radicals began to change their line on the family.

But if the political myopia of the counterculture was partly a matter of class and age, it was even more a matter of sex. Like every other segment of society, the counterculture was dominated by men, who benefited from the male privileges built into the family structure and so did not care to examine it too closely. While they were not averse to freeing themselves from their traditional obligations in the family, they had no intention of giving up their prerogatives. To support a woman, promise permanence or fidelity, or take responsibility for the children one fathered might be bourgeois, but to expect the same woman to cook and clean, take care of the kids, and fuck on command was only natural. Despite an overlay of radical Freudian rhetoric, their sexual ethos was more or less standard liberal permissiveness; they were not interested in getting rid of the roles of wife and whore, only in "liberating" women to play either as the occasion demanded.

It remained for the women's liberation movement to begin to understand the family in a political way. Radical feminists exposed the hypocrisy of a "cultural revolution" based on sexual inequality, attributed that inequality to the historic, institutionalized power of men as a group over women as a group, and called for a mass movement to end it. Feminism became the only contemporary political movement to make an organized effort to change, rather than simply drop out of the patriarchal family.

Feminist consciousness-raising and analysis produced a mass of information about the family as an instrument of female oppression. But on those aspects of family chauvinism that did not directly involve the subordination of women, the movement had little to say. (There were individual exceptions, notably Shulamith Firestone in *The Dialectic of Sex*.) Radical feminists tended to be skeptical of the counterculture's vision of a communal utopia. Many defended the nuclear family, arguing that it was not marriage, only traditional marital sex roles that oppressed women; at the other extreme were factions that challenged the value of heterosexuality and even sex itself.

In a sense, radical feminism defined itself in opposition to the psychological explanations of behavior so prevalent on the left. Most early women's liberationists had come out of a left-counterculture milieu where they were under heavy pressure to go along with the men's notion of sexual freedom. As soon as feminism surfaced, the left began to resist it by arguing that the conventional pattern of male-female relationships was the result of capitalist conditioning, that men were not oppressors but fellow victims. As feminists pointed out, this argument ignored the advantages men's privileged status conferred, their reluctance to give up those advantages, and the day-to-day social and economic constraints that kept women in their place. In effect it absolved men of all responsibility for their actions and implied that women could remedy their condition simply by straightening out their heads.

Vital as it was to combat the left's mushy, self-serving psychologism, radical feminists have tended to fall into the opposite error of dismissing psychology altogether. This bias has been particularly limiting when applied to the crucial subject of sex. Feminists have been inclined to blame women's sexual problems solely on men's exploitative behavior and lack of consideration for women's needs, whether emotional or specifically erotic. The criticism is accurate so far as it goes. But it is impossible to understand female —or for that matter male—sexuality without acknowledging the impact of growing up in a culture that despite its surface permissiveness is deeply antisexual. A distorted, negative view of sex is basic to patriarchal psychology: since girls learn to regard their genitals as a badge of inferiority, boys to equate theirs with dominance and aggression, sexual pleasure gets tangled up with sadistic and masochistic feelings and hostility between the sexes. At the same time, both sexes have a powerful emotional investment in traditionally masculine and feminine behavior because they associate it with their sexual identities and with sex itself.

Just as a real sexual revolution must be feminist, a genuinely radical feminism must include a critique of sexual repression and the family structure that perpetuates it. Yet the two questions remain distinct in most people's mind—a distinction that contributes to the backlash, since it allows people to succumb to family chauvinist attitudes without confronting their antifeminist implications. As it so often does, the right has a clearer grasp of the problem than its opposition, which is one reason "pro-family" reactionaries have been more politically effective than feminists who protest that they're not against the family, they just want women to have equality within it. The issue of family chauvinism is at the core of the conflict between feminist and antifeminist women, as well as the antagonism that smolders even in sophisticated feminist circles between wives who feel that single women do not support them or understand their problems and single women who feel that wives are collaborating with the system. While feminists have rightly emphasized the common oppression of married and single women and the ways men have pitted us against each other, this kind of analysis ignores the fact that the family has its own imperatives: just as women can ally with men to defend the interests of a class or race, they can share their husbands' family chauvinism. Women in a patriarchy have every reason to distrust male sexuality and fear their own. Under present conditions heterosexuality really is dangerous for women, not only because it involves the risk of pregnancy and of exploitation and marginality, but because it is emotionally bound up with the idea of submission. And so long as women are economically dependent on their husbands, they cannot afford to countenance the idea that men have a right to anything so unpredictable as passion. As a result, women are as likely as men—if not more so—to see the family as our only alternative to unbridled lust and rapine.

To regard marriage and singleness simply as "options," or even as situations equally favorable to men and oppressive to women, misses the point. The institution of the family and the people who enforce its rules and uphold its values define the lives of both married and single people, just as capitalism defines the lives of workers and dropouts alike. The family system divides us up into insiders and outsiders; as insiders, married people are more likely to identify with the established order, and when they do, they are not simply expressing a personal preference but taking a political stand. The issue, finally, is whether we have the right to hope for a freer, more humane way of connecting with each other. Defenders of the family seem to think that we have already gone too far, that the problem of this painful and confusing time is too much freedom. I think there's no such thing as too much freedom—only too little nerve.

1979

Postscript: The Backlash

According to Irving

There is no more conspicuous evidence of postsixties confusion than the enormous success, both critical and popular (over 2,500,000 paperback copies in print), of *The World According to Garp*. Though *Garp* has its virtues as a novel, I think it owes its status as a phenomenon to its point of view: John Irving attempts to square an emancipated, profeminist stance with a profoundly conservative defense of the family, and because he is such a good storyteller he almost pulls it off. The novel evokes the positive side of family life with vivid conviction, and Garp's unorthodox household—he stays home with the kids and writes; his wife, Helen, is a college professor—is both credible and appealing. But ultimately the author's conservatism takes over the book. Both he and his protagonist are Victorians (or Freudians) at heart, bemused by what they see as the foolishness of sex, distrustful of its anarchic potential. For Garp the paradigmatic act of violence and evil is rape, which he uneasily connects with his own lust, judging his predatory, impersonal seduction of a teen-age babysitter a "rapelike situation." Directly or not, sex—particularly infidelity, the paradigmatic betrayal of the family tie—causes most of the trouble in the novel. Though Irving is committed to the central importance of the family as a source of human values, he does not hold with the myth of the family as a haven in a violent world: the world is us, our dangerous sexuality. This attitude is bound up with the most traditional kind of sexism. Irving regards lust as men's besetting sin, and implies that women—at least the right sort of women—are more admirable than men because they are less subject to this weakness. (The two women in the book who are preoccupied with sex are portrayed with utter condescension—one is a pathetic, stupid adolescent; the other a slob, a failed wife, and an incompetent mother.) Nor does Irving's horror of rape reflect feminist consciousness; from a feminist perspective rape is not, as the novel renders it, an expression of bestial impulses unfettered by civilized morality, but an assertion of power and woman-hatred, a patriarchal perversion.

In the book's climactic episode, Helen Garp's affair with a student leads to a gruesome accident in which one of the Garp children dies, another loses an eye, and Helen bites off her lover's penis. Helen's infidelity is nearly as exploitative as her husband's (though her motives have less to do with lust than with anger at Garp); she begins sleeping with Michael Milton in part because he is too much of a lightweight to take seriously. When Garp finds out, Helen calls Michael and summarily dumps him. He is distraught. Helen, who takes for granted her right to make all the rules, is annoyed that he won't just slink off without a fuss. Instead, he insists on coming to see her, with disastrous results. Though he ends up worse off than any of the surviving Garps, he gets no discernible sympathy, either from Helen or from the author, who turns him into a mean joke, everyhusband's fantasy of the perfect revenge. Except for a few offhand and/or nasty references to his condition, he disappears from the book; he and his feelings are irrelevant, outside the purview of the Garps' anguish for each other. Irving makes it hard for the reader to care about Michael Milton; he is an unattractive character, and the situation is ludicrous. But in giving Milton such a horrifying fate (at least it horrified me), Irving overplays his hand. Unless you get off on the idea of single men being castrated for fucking married women, the Garps' reaction seems callous (particularly since it was Garp's jealousy and carelessness that caused the accident) and the author's special pleading becomes intrusive. *Garp* would have been a more honest novel had Irving been willing to present the boy's mutilation as tragic—like the death of little Walt Garp—instead of comic. After all, what better metaphor for the traditionalist's belief in the wages of sexual sin? Or for the way people who break the rules are cut off from the connections the family offers?

Garp also caters to the privatism of the seventies by arguing insistently for the virtues of an individual moral outlook, as opposed (in the author's mind) to a political one. For Irving feminism as a positive force is embodied in individuals—in the Garps' disregard for conventional marital roles, or in the way Garp's mother, Jenny, leads her eccentric life exactly as she pleases. The collective approach to feminism is represented by the Ellen Jamesians, a group of violent, self-mutilating fanatics. That Jenny's version of independence involves renouncing sex is indicative of Irving's hang-ups; he fails to comprehend that it is when women want independence *and* sex that they run into trouble. The Garps' domestic arrangement is more congenial to my own fantasies. Still, I can't help thinking about a couple I know that tried to switch roles. The wife loved it; the husband hated it. He had an affair with a woman who was also home during the day, went to live with her, and got a job. She stayed home with her kid and his.

September 1979

Toward a National Man Policy

As if the United States didn't have enough problems, it seems that we are suffering from a serious man shortage. At first, most women assumed the situation was temporary, a side effect of unavoidable dislocations in the country's psychic economy. There was a lot of private grumbling, but no calls for action. As recently as last month, the optimists were urging, "Let's wait and see what happens. These things are cyclical. Men always wilt in humid weather." But lately the atmosphere has begun to change. More and more I hear ominous talk of a "man crisis" and allegations that the government and the media have been covering it up.

At a party the other night I ran into a friend, a militant feminist, who demanded to know what I thought should be done.

"Well, I'm skeptical about this crisis talk," I said. "Are you sure it isn't just you and me and a few of our friends going through a lean period?"

"Oh, come on!" said my friend scornfully. "That's just what they want us to believe—that it's *our* problem. But I've been comparing notes, and everyone has the same story. 'I haven't slept with anyone in six months.' 'I haven't had a serious love affair in two years.' Something very fishy is going on."

Toward a National Man Policy

By this time a few dozen women, attracted by the conversation, had crowded around us. The two or three men at the party were nowhere in sight. Women kept interrupting each other in their eagerness to contribute their horror stories.

"The agencies these days are unbelievable. The last time out, all I asked for was someone who would do half the housework. They laughed in my face! One broker said to me, 'Haven't you heard, honey? This is a time of lowered expectations.' "

"My cousin from Iowa went to one of those rip-off referral services. They sent her to a married man, a fourteen-year-old kid, and a few guys whose names they had obviously lifted from the divorce announcements in the newspaper. My cousin could have done that herself, for nothing."

"Divorce announcements! What a waste of time! Either the man's wife kicked him out, for good reasons, or he left her for someone else."

"Has anyone tried obituaries?"

"A cop I know tipped me off that this guy's wife had just died in a car crash. But it was on the Upper East Side, and by the time I got there, the line was around the block. And there was a sign that said 'No Odd Women.' "

A depressed silence fell. Finally my friend said belligerently, "Well, are we going to let them get away with this? Or are we going to fight?"

"There's no easy short-range solution," said a soft-spoken woman wearing an antinuclear button. "It's an environmental problem. They die faster than we do, and pollution is making it worse."

"Pollution has nothing to do with it," said my friend. "This shortage has been deliberately contrived for political reasons."

"The Arabs are buying up our men," another woman suggested, "so they can dictate our Middle East policy."

My friend rolled her eyes.

"That's xenophobic bullshit. The fact is, men are holding themselves off the market in retaliation for feminism. Look at the re-

173

sults. We sit around worrying that it's our fault. We fight over each other's husbands. We start having lower expectations."

"I agree," said a woman I recognized as a lesbian activist, "but it's also a strategy for attacking gay rights. Already you hear the propaganda—'What a shame, with all these men turning gay, heterosexual women can't find mates.' Let me tell you, this isn't just a straight women's issue. They're going to use it as an excuse to crack down on *all* homosexuals, even though lesbians don't use up any men at all."

The woman next to me was squirming and making irritated noises. I had last seen her at a demonstration, carrying a sign that said "Two, Three, Many Ayatollahs."

"You bourgeois feminists always miss the point," she said finally. "It's not men who are behind this so-called shortage, it's the ruling class. The 'man crisis' is nothing more and nothing less than the newest method of population control for the poor. If there's a shortage of men, who'll get first crack at them? Not poor or black or Hispanic women, you can be sure of that."

"Well, one thing is clear," said the antinuclear woman. "We have to start thinking in terms of alternatives. We can be sexually self-sufficient—after all, we do have each other."

"That's all very nice and ecological," my friend grumbled, "but it lets the men off the hook. And anyone who calls me a bourgeois feminist had better smile."

"Anyway," said Two Three Many, smiling, "I think we can all agree that there's only one solution. Short of revolution, that is. First we have to nationalize the men. Then, if it's really necessary, we can ration them."

"That'll be the day," my friend said. "Did you read about the president's press conference? A woman reporter asked him if there was anything to these rumors of a man crisis. He pooh-poohed the whole thing. Said there was no man shortage a little feminine charm wouldn't cure."

We groaned. I was getting angry. The discussion had convinced me we had a real struggle on our hands.

"But the reporter kept pushing," my friend continued. "She wanted to know, if the shortage got worse, how would the president handle it? He told her that of course, his first concern was to preserve the integrity of the American family. Therefore, in the event of a genuine man crisis he would propose a remedy that had already been tried and found workable by upstanding, God-fearing, family-oriented people."

"What's that?" I said.

"Polygamy."

September 1979

The Trial of Arline Hunt

I

Jewel's is one of a cluster of singles bars on Union Street near San Francisco's fashionable Pacific Heights district. The canopy over the door is stamped with the bar's motto, "Where Incredible Friendships Begin." At the entrance a sign warns that "blue jeans, T-shirts, collarless jerseys, tank shirts, transvestites, etc." are "taboos." The doorman wears a suit. Inside, the middle-brow, stained-glass-and-wood-paneling decor seems a perfunctory attempt to disguise the stark functionalism of the place, which is dominated by two bars, one sitdown and one standup, surrounded by lots of space. Unlike Hal's Pub across the street, Jewel's serves no food, not even coffee. A few small tables are tucked in the corners like afterthoughts. A slick rock band plays but there is rarely much room to dance. Jewel's attracts a mixed crowd—salesmen, secretaries, students, some freaks, a few blacks, an occasional young executive. The "taboos" are not strictly enforced but most patrons dress neatly, the women in pantsuits, the men

All names, places, dates, and other identifying details have been changed to protect the anonymity of participants in the case discussed.

in neo-mod suits or sport jackets or turtlenecks and styled hair. There are always more men and they set the tone, a compound of sexual bravado and joking belligerence. On a busy night Jewel's is so crowded that forced proximity becomes a kind of intimacy. Men overflow into the street, cruising the women who walk by.

September 18, 1974—a Wednesday—was not a busy night. It was raining and Jewel's was almost empty when two young women from the neighborhood came in and sat down at the bar. Arline Hunt and her roommate and best friend, Bobbie Richards, were both office workers in their early twenties. Arline was small and slim and had dark hair and a puckish, wry little smile. She wore a navy knit shirt with a collar and long sleeves, navy bell-bottoms, clunky shoes, a long silver chain and dangling earrings. From a distance she gave an impression of sophistication; up close her candid, friendly face suggested a college freshman. Bobbie, dressed in jeans and a sweater, looked like a fair, even younger version of Arline. They often dropped in for a few drinks at one or another of the bars on Union Street. That night they ordered beers and chatted with the bartender.

An hour or so later, a man walked in and sat next to Arline. Fred Dumond, the thirty-two-year-old owner of an agency for temporary typists, was a familiar figure on the dating bar strip. Fred was well put together, if a bit packaged-looking—a shortish but muscular body, hair styled in a shag cut, brown leather jacket over turtleneck jersey—and he projected a kind of self-confidence some would call glib. He had a reputation for being a ladies' man; the word people used was "swinger" or sometimes, less kindly, "operator." He ordered a bottle of Schlitz and started a conversation with Bobbie while Arline was in the ladies' room. When Arline came back, Fred began to focus on her with a caustic banter that made her laugh. He joked about the way people's profiles revealed their characters—take Barbra Streisand's, for instance. He talked about a car he wanted to buy and made sarcastic jokes about his split with his wife. Arline asked him questions. They all drank more beer. Fred kept bantering and Arline continued to be amused. Around 10:30, Bobbie had to leave; she was expecting a phone call from her boyfriend. Arline got up to go with her but Bobbie told her to stay if she felt like it. Fred urged her to have another drink; he would take her home. She decided to stay awhile and told Bobbie, "I'll be home in half an hour."

It took Bobbie twenty minutes to walk back to the apartment she shared with Arline and a third woman, Joanne Kovacs. They were all close friends from high school in the semirural town of Shelton, California. Their apartment was cheerful and unpretentious, with Arline's charcoal drawings on the walls and *Cosmo* and *Mademoiselle* on the coffeetable and beer in the refrigerator and a cat named Minestrone and Bobbie's tropical fish tank.

Bobbie received her phone call and went to bed. She was not, she recalls, at all worried about Arline. "It never occurred to me that there might be anything wrong. Fred seemed like a nice guy, friendly, even though I wasn't too impressed with him. He wasn't really our type of person. He made me think of a high-school greaser who had grown up and gotten neat clothes and a haircut. I didn't get the feeling that Arline was interested in him or that he was coming on strong to her. She was just enjoying a nice conversation. She likes to draw people out, to joke around with people. She is a very compassionate person and he was telling her about his problems. Later she told me, 'He looked sad, I thought he was lonely.' It was nothing unusual for her."

But then, around 3:00 a.m., the telephone rang again, waking Bobbie up. It was Arline. "Bobbie," she said, "I have just been raped." Bobbie heard a man's voice in the background yell, "That's a hell of a thing to say!" She heard Arline reply, "That's a hell of a thing to do!"

"I could tell she was really upset. I was really frightened—you know how you always have visions of murder. I said, 'Arline, where are you?' She said, 'Somewhere on Geary.' I asked her, 'Are you okay?' She whispered, 'I don't know, I'm scared, Bobbie, I think he's sick.' I know her, I knew she was petrified. I told her, which was asinine, 'Try to find out where you are.' So she said to him, 'What's this address?' and the phone went bang. From the way the guy hung up I thought, If Arline gets out of there alive, she's lucky. I woke Joanne and told her Arline was in trouble and then I called the police. They said they'd do what they could, but Geary was an awfully long road."

Bobbie and Joanne turned out the lights and sat by the kitchen window with a flashlight. They thought Fred might take Arline home; if they spotted him, they would call the police again. They sat and waited.

Number 2211 Geary Boulevard is part of a huge, bleak beehive of a luxury apartment complex owned by the Christian Science Church. Fred Dumond lived on the twelfth floor in apartment 1209. His next door neighbors, in apartment 1210, were John and Maureen Hollis, a solidly middle-American married couple in their fifties, the parents of grown children. Both of them worked as administrators in the church.

On September 18 the Hollises went to bed, as usual, at 10:00 p.m. Around 2:30 they woke up to the sounds of a woman screaming, which they later described as "terrifying" and "blood-curdling." "It was screaming at the top of the voice saying, 'Help me, please help me,'" said John Hollis. "I jumped out of bed," his wife recalled. "The phone was on my side of the bed and I called security and I said, 'I think there's a murder being committed.'" At first, dazed and sleepy, she couldn't tell where the sounds were coming from; they simply filled the room. But then she was sure: they were coming from next door, through the common wall that separated the bedroom of apartment 1209 from her own. She could also hear bumping noises and a man's voice. "I couldn't stand it. I went into the living room and I could still hear them in there. I was just terrified."

The screams continued—they went on, intermittently, for fifteen or twenty minutes altogether—and when there was no response from the building's security office, John Hollis made a second urgent call. Then he got dressed and went outside to see if there were lights in the windows of any of the apartments near his. He stood in front of the building and peered upward. There was a light in the bedroom of apartment 1209. He turned and saw a young woman standing about ten feet away.

"I've been raped," she said.

He took her to the security office, where the guards finally called the police.

When patrolman Martin Atkins and his partner, Robert Mitchell, arrived at 2211 Geary, Arline was laughing hysterically. "It's a nervous reaction," she apologized. "You can check with my psychiatrist." The two policemen questioned her, called for another radio car to take her to Pacific Hospital, and went up to 1209 to arrest the suspect. Patrolman Atkins knocked several times. When he got no response, the security man opened the door. They walked past a bathroom to the left of the front door and a kitchen on the right, into the living room, and then into the bedroom, which was off to the left of the living room, right next to the bathroom. Fred was lying in bed, apparently asleep, dressed in jockey shorts. There was a splatter of what looked like bloodstains on the sheet. Patrolman Mitchell shook him awake. Atkins told him he was under arrest for rape and advised him of his rights. Fred Dumond said, "You've got to be kidding."

Pacific Hospital boasts a model program for the treatment and counseling of rape victims. The project, initiated by a psychiatric nurse and a sociologist in 1972, has been an education for all concerned. "The emergency staff used to be into the whole phenomenon of blaming the victim," says Joan Christiansen, assistant nursing director in charge of emergency services. "She was either drinking, or being seductive, or walking around at 3:00 a.m. Since we've had the program there has been a total change in attitude.

Rape is a *crisis*. Different women react differently—some are upset, some calm, some in a state of shock—but every victim's life is disrupted in four ways: physically, emotionally, socially, sexually." At Pacific, nurses trained in counseling skills try to ease these disruptions by helping the rape victim to express her feelings and cope with specific problems, such as whether to press charges.

When Arline Hunt arrived in Pacific's emergency room, a nurse met her and saw her through the hospital routine. After receiving her consent, a gynecology resident examined her genitals for injuries, took smears for sperm and for a gonorrhea culture, gave her a prophylactic shot of penicillin and morning-after pills. The nurse told her to be sure and get a follow-up examination, since rape victims often get vaginal and urinary infections.

At 5:00 a.m., a counselor came and listened to Arline's story. Her report described Arline as "attractive, neatly dressed, cooperative, coherent, responding, pretty verbal." After the interview Arline tried to call her roommates, forgot her own telephone number, and had to look it up. By the time the police took her home she didn't feel like talking at all. Her period had started earlier that day and she was bleeding heavily. She hadn't had a chance to clean up at the hospital—the doctor had explained that washing might destroy evidence—and she felt, as she put it later, "filthy and disgusting." There was only one thing she wanted to do: take a shower.

I I

. . . *A few years ago, I signed up with a computer dating service. Dozens of men I knew absolutely nothing about had my address and phone number. They came to my apartment to pick me up, I went to theirs for drinks or dinner. It didn't occur to me till years later how dangerous this was. Anything could have happened. . . .*

. . . We met in a bar. Like it or not, it's one of the few ways to meet men in this city. I liked him; there weren't any suspicious vibes. He did make a couple of jokes about my tits, but I put it down to normal male obnoxiousness. He drove me home and I let him in because he said he had to use the bathroom. . . .

. . . As I was unlocking the hall door, a man came up behind me. I tried to slam the door on him, but couldn't. I was so embarrassed about acting paranoid that I apologized. I could have gone to a ground floor apartment and rung the bell or yelled, but I was afraid of being hysterical and paranoid and making a scene for nothing. So I just started walking casually upstairs. He followed me and pulled a knife. . . .

. . . While he was raping me I started getting the strangest feeling that all this was somehow familiar. I realized that it wasn't so different from times I'd fucked guys I didn't really want to fuck because I couldn't think of a graceful way to refuse. . . .

—FRAGMENTS FROM A CONSCIOUSNESS-RAISING SESSION ON RAPE

When Arline talks about September 18 her voice takes on a sardonic edge, as if she were describing not only her own horror but the folly of the human condition.

"We stayed for a couple of hours after Bobbie left, maybe more. I liked him. He was funny; he was making me laugh. And he seemed to need someone to talk to. But I didn't want to go out with him. He asked me and I said no, it's been nice talking to you but this is it. I was trying to explain without being too blunt. He wasn't my type. He was bragging about his money and that stuff doesn't impress me.

"A friend of his came in and bought us a few beers. Then I said

I had to leave. I got my coat and umbrella and gave him my pocketbook so I could put my coat on. We went outside and he hailed a cab—I assumed he was going to take me home. I asked him for my pocketbook. He said, 'Wait a minute.' We got in and he gave the cabdriver his address. I said, 'Hey, I've got to go home, I've got to work tomorrow,' and I told the driver to go to my place. Fred said, 'No, we'll work this out later.' He gave his address again, and I gave mine again. The cabdriver just kept going to 2211 Geary. I thought well, this guy is being childish. He's playing a little game. We got out in front of his building and I said, 'Can I have it back now?' and he went inside, and I followed him up in the elevator. I couldn't leave without my pocketbook—it had my money, my keys, my identification, my Valium. Just everything I needed. And he was just ignoring me. I figured he'll have his fun, he'll have his little joke, and when he gets tired of it he'll give me my pocketbook. I wasn't scared at all. It didn't occur to me. I meet a lot of guys who play these dumb games and it's annoying but they're not rapists. You can't go around suspecting everybody.

"I followed him into his apartment and he slammed the door and stood in front of it. I said, 'Okay, stop playing games, can I please have my pocketbook so I can get a cab and go home?' And he said, 'You are not going anywhere.' I said, 'What do you mean?' All of a sudden it was like he was a totally different person. The change in him was incredible. He said, 'You are not going anywhere. Go in the bedroom and take your clothes off.' I thought, I can't take this seriously. I felt sick. Sick and weak. I said, 'I promise I won't tell anybody about this if you'll just let me leave right now.'

"He pulled me into the bathroom and pushed me down on the side of the tub and went to the toilet and urinated. I was disgusted. I stood up and he pushed me down again. I picked up my umbrella and tried to use it against him, but he just pulled it away from me and started laughing. I still had my coat on. He pushed me into the bedroom and made a phone call to some guy. I don't remember what they said. Then I started to feel really faint. I didn't want to lie down, or it would be all over. So I asked him for a glass of water. He said, 'All right, but don't try anything.' He went into the kitchen and I ran over to the phone and dialed the operator. [The kitchen was between the bedroom and the door.] But he got back too quickly and hung up the phone and said, 'Don't you do that again.' And then he pushed me over to the bed.

"He pushed me down on the bed and I got back up again and he pushed me down again. I started screaming at the top of my lungs and he was saying, 'Shut up, they are making me do this.' And I said 'Who?' and he said, 'I can't tell you, but if you go out of here, they are going to get you anyway.' And so I started to scream again because at this point I didn't know what was happening and I didn't care. I just wanted somebody to hear me or something to happen. Then he started pulling down my pants—they were stretchy with an elastic waist—and I was fighting him but finally he pulled them off, and my underpants. I tried to push my fingers in his neck, and I tried to get him in the groin but it didn't work. He stuck his fingers into my throat so I couldn't scream.

"I saw there was no point resisting. I was afraid of what he might do. I knew he was crazy. He had a violent temper, he kept yelling at me to shut up. And he was strong. I was afraid he would try to strangle me with my necklace or rip my earrings out, so I took them off. I took my top off.

"I told him I had my period and he said, 'I don't care,' and ripped out my Tampax and threw it on the floor. He pinned my hands above my head. Then he got on top of me and had sexual intercourse and stuck his finger in the back part of me.

"After he stopped, I got off the bed. I saw my Tampax on the floor and I picked it up and said, 'You're disgusting!' and threw it down again. He was still lying in bed. I dialed the operator and said, 'There's been a rape at this number.' He grabbed the receiver and slammed it down. Then I called Bobbie. I felt almost fearless at that point.

"I got dressed and got my pocketbook and umbrella out of the bathroom and ran out. He was yelling at me that I was stupid, I was the stupidest woman he'd ever seen. I ran down twelve flights of stairs."

A woman who grows up in a big city learns early that her purse is a third arm, *never* to be relinquished, least of all to a man she has just met at a bar. Perhaps Arline Hunt had not been in San Francisco long enough to abandon the sheltered, upper-middle-class mentality of Shelton for urban war-zone smarts. Perhaps, on the other hand, something in her simply refused to live that way.

"I can't ask myself why did I do this or that. Why did I give him my pocketbook, why didn't I scream in the cab. Because I know I wouldn't have done anything different—I don't mean now, knowing what I know, but then. I guess," she says—that sardonic tone again—"I'm trusting, naive, dumb or whatever."

A friend and occasional lover, an advertising writer named Gary, put it another way. "There's something almost Zen about Arline: whatever will be will be, don't expect much and don't demand anything, just go along with whatever's happening. Arline never asks, 'What are we doing tonight?' She just comes in and sits down and asks for a beer. I would say Arline has a deflated opinion of herself, but she doesn't get bent out of shape. She likes to get fucked up and have a good time."

When Arline went off to her parents' alma mater, a small college in Kansas—ending up there because she hadn't felt like shopping around for schools—she expected to hate it. But she met some good people and had good times. She smoked grass, and took speed to stay up all night writing her C papers, and experimented with acid, which made her laugh and laugh, magnifying the laughter to freaky proportions. After two years she quit and went home.

When she moved to San Franscisco in 1973 it was without any great enthusiasm. She had been living with her parents for the last year, working at dull clerical jobs, and she was anxious to get away. The city itself did not excite her, but in the city she would have her friends.

People, relationships—what else really mattered? She hated her job as a clerk in a textbook company. She thought about finding something she would really like doing, perhaps something connected with art—she had been painting and drawing since childhood. Gary urged her to promote herself, to put together a portfolio and try to get a job designing greeting cards or place mats, but she never did.

So what it came down to was people and a good time. People who were sincere and not out for what they could get. People, she never failed to emphasize, who had an absurd sense of humor and could make her laugh.

Not that Arline's life was all fun and games. For one thing, there was Graham. Graham was Arline's first lover. They met when she was sixteen; he was out of high school and engaged. She thought he was an aggressive bastard and didn't understand what was driving her to sleep with him. She hated it: it was uncomfortable, she was just doing it to please him, and she felt guilty besides.

All through college Arline went out with lots of men, but she didn't have sex again until the summer she returned to Shelton. She fell in love with a young Englishman and agreed to marry him, but by the following winter she had changed her mind. Shortly afterward she ran into Graham at a party. He was married by then, with two kids.

"I still thought he was obnoxious," she recalls. "I don't know why I went out with him, but I did—I had to give a fake name to my parents. I got used to him. He was always the hard-ass guy, but in another way he wasn't, not really."

The relationship turned into an intense love affair. For the first time Arline really enjoyed sex. She was also miserable, crazy, dependent. They talked about running away and living together; then Graham began avoiding her. When she confronted him, he admitted that he couldn't leave his children. After that there were many goodbyes that didn't stick. Once, soon after Arline had moved to San Francisco, he came down for a disastrous visit. "I had said I would see him, but no sex. He completely forced it; it was scary. He was always too aggressive and demanding. My roommates didn't approve of him coming. I kept telling them not to worry, nothing was going to happen. So when he forced me I couldn't scream. I didn't want anyone to know. I just cried." As usual she forgave him and the affair dragged on.

It was around the same time that the trouble at work began. The company provided a small lunchroom where most of the employees—the office staff and the men who worked in the shipping department—ate at noon. One day Arline was sitting at a table playing cards with a group of people when she saw one of the shippers staring at her. "I was frozen, I couldn't look up. I had to stop playing. My body was uncontrollable. After that I tried sitting with my back to them. It just kept growing, a horrible feeling of anxiety. I was afraid to light a cigarette 'cause my hands were shaking. I started eating in the room I work in but it's glassed in and the shippers work outside and they would just naturally look in. Before, there were always times when I would be nervous but it never affected me in such a physical way. Maybe part of it is living in the city."

In August 1974, Arline began seeing a psychiatrist. Along with once-a-week therapy he prescribed Valium. At the time of her encounter with Fred Dumond she was taking five milligrams once or twice a day.

III

On September 19, at nine in the morning, Arline went to court to swear out her complaint. Bobbie went with her. They hadn't slept. Arline was still in shock and spacey from pills, and she and Bobbie had noticed for the first time a bruise on each of her wrists. Trying to answer questions, she broke down. James Delaney, the assistant district attorney who would be handling her case, told her, to her relief—she was afraid of seeing Fred in court—that she didn't need to hang around for the arraignment. At home she kept trying to erase the night, to pretend it never happened. "It was too weird, too sickening. I couldn't remember things . . . even now it's almost like it happened to someone else. But it was *there*."

Arline's parents were on vacation; when they came back the following week she called her mother. Arline says she never really considered not telling her parents, though she was apprehensive about their reaction. Her father, a biologist, and her mother, a housewife constantly involved with community projects, were high-energy achievers and Arline felt they disapproved of her for not using her abilities. They were also conservative and religious and emotionally reserved, all of which made communication difficult. Her mother would have none of Arline's attempt to explain that in her world Fred's behavior was not so extraordinary as to arouse suspicion. "How could you not know something was happening? Why didn't you tell the taxi driver this man had your pocketbook?" It was Arline's first exposure to an attitude that would soon become familiar.

On October 10 Arline had to appear for a probable cause hearing, at which a judge would decide whether the prosecution had enough of a case to present to a grand jury. The decision went in Arline's favor, but the hearing was traumatic. Fred Dumond attended but did not testify. He watched impassively as his lawyer, Burton C. Scott of the prestigious local firm of Frazier, Frazier and Santini, a man with a reputation for toughness and a glass eye that made his stare frightening, introduced Arline to the art of cross-examination.

"He was trying to catch me on every detail, twisting everything I said. In a situation like that you're not thinking, 'I'm gonna get raped, I'd better plan my strategy for the trial.' You're just thinking about wanting to get out of there. Times and sequences aren't on your mind.

"I was freaking out, one of the policemen was telling me to calm down. The lawyer brought up my psychiatrist and my pills. I may have my problems, but I'm not crazy. Then he asked me how I knew I was penetrated. I said, 'I could feel it.' He said, 'Oh, so you've felt that sensation before.' The D.A. objected to that one."

Bobbie also testified briefly. "It was brutal. The defense lawyer was trying to confuse Arline, make her feel stupid. He scared her to death. And all these old men up for other cases were standing around, watching and laughing, and Arline having to say, 'Well, if you want to be explicit, he put his penis inside me.' "

Arline considered dropping the case, but decided she had to go through with it: "I couldn't see letting him get away with it. I couldn't see just letting a sick person like that out on the street." She felt a rage at the thought that Dumond might get off. Her friends, trying to prepare her for the worst, were warning her how difficult it was to get rape convictions. Bobbie had seen the TV documentary *A Case of Rape*: the rapist had been acquitted and the victim and her husband had ended up getting divorced. "At first I couldn't face that possibility. The unfairness of it. I didn't know what I'd do. After a while I resigned myself. I knew the way things were run, he'd probably be acquitted. I already felt defeated." Gary told her she ought to look on the whole thing as a learning experience about the real world.

The case went to the grand jury, and Arline had to tell her story once more. Months passed; the trial was postponed twice, aggravating her anxiety and depression. She got scared walking around the neighborhood. She lost weight. Her psychiatrist doubled her dose of Valium. The atmosphere in the apartment was funereal; nothing much was funny these days. At this low point she decided to call her brother in Los Angeles and tell him the whole story.

He hadn't heard it before. Arline's parents had, after the initial shock, been sympathetic and concerned; they supported, even admired, her decision to prosecute. Yet they were obviously still touchy about the subject, for they hadn't said a word to anyone, including their three other children. Arline did not have much contact with her only brother, who was older and married, but she identified with him because he too had refused to do the expected:

after going to graduate school in physics, he had decided he didn't like it and was driving a school bus. His wife was a student and a feminist. At her suggestion Arline got in touch with the Women's Law Commune in Berkeley; a lawyer there promised to check on the DA's investigation to make sure all leads were being pursued.

In February, Arline met a computer programmer named David at a bar called Storey's, and they started going out. "My feelings about sex hadn't changed," she says. "I knew Dumond was really sick, that all men weren't like that. One thing I was secure in was his sickness." But she was upset when David made skeptical noises about her story, when he too wanted to know, come on now, really, *why* did you go up there in the first place. . . .

Three days before the trial, Arline and Bobbie had dinner at Hal's Pub. Bobbie, facing the door, saw two men walk in. "Arline," she said, "put your head down on the table and don't look up. Dumond and his friend are here." They both put their heads down. When they looked up again a few minutes later, the men were gone.

IV

> Q: *Would you describe your clothing, Miss Hunt? You describe having underpants on under your slacks. Did you have anything on underneath your sweater?*
> A: No.
> Q: *You had no bra on, did you?*
> A: No.

> Q: *Have you ever been raped before?*
> A: No, I haven't.

> Q: *Did you ever scratch this man?*
> A: I tried to put my finger in his throat.

Q: *Did you ever scratch this man?*
A: No.
Q: *How long were you fighting him?*
A: I don't know.
Q: *According to your testimony there was a struggle the whole time, was there not?*
A: My fingernails are not long enough to be able to harm anybody.
Q: *Did you ever bite him?*
A: No.
Q: *Did you ever land a kick?*
A: Did I what?
Q: *Did you land a kick, did you ever really kick him?*
A: I tried to.
Q: *And during this whole time you were not able to inflict an injury on him, is that so?*
A: He was stronger than I was, and I couldn't.
Q: *During this struggle, Miss Hunt, were you injured? Did you get any cuts—*
A: I got bruises on my wrists where he held them above my head.
Q: *Did you show them to the doctor at the hospital?*
A: No, because I didn't notice them until the next day, and other people did notice them.

Q: *Did you see him put his penis inside?*
A: No, I didn't see it.
Q: *And didn't you tell the district attorney when he asked you on direct examination that you don't think that he had a climax?*
(Delaney objects and is overruled.)
A: I didn't know. I didn't say I didn't think.
Q: *All right. You didn't know. So would it be fair to say you didn't feel what you might have felt was a climax, would that be a fair statement?*

A: I don't know what he had. I don't know if he had a climax or not.

Q: *When were you finally able to get out of that apartment?*
A: I don't know the time.
Q: *What time did you call your girlfriend Bobbie from the apartment?*
A: I told you I thought it was probably around 3:00, 2:30 or 3:00, something like that.
Q: *Would it refresh your memory if I told you that you said earlier that it was somewhere around 3:30?*
A: I don't know the exact time. I told you that before.
Q: *If it was somewhere around 3:00, is it your testimony from the time you got there at about 1:00 until about 3:00, you were on the bed struggling, two hours?*
A: I don't know how long it was.
Q: *How long did it take him to urinate in the bathroom?*
A: Do you think I had a watch on and I was looking at it? (Delaney objects and is overruled.)
Q: *Was it more than five minutes?*
A: I don't know.

(Before the judge in a closed hearing):
Q: *Have you ever tried to injure yourself?*
A: No, I haven't.
Q: *Have you ever tried to commit suicide?*
A: No, I haven't.
Q: *You hesitated. Is there any reason why you hesitated, Miss Hunt?*
A: Only because I think this is a little bit personal and doesn't pertain to what's going on.
—EXCERPTS FROM THE CROSS-EXAMINATION OF ARLINE HUNT

Jim Delaney knew that *People* v. *Dumond* would be a stinker. Arline Hunt had gone to a man's apartment from a dating bar, and

192

her pocketbook story (witnessed only by an anonymous cabbie the police had been unable to find) was hard to believe if you didn't know her. It also helped to know that rapes originating in these dating bars were becoming more and more common, becoming a pattern. Women were starting to be more aware of the risks, but there would always be people who took chances; a recent rash of hitchhiking murders in the Bay Area had not stopped thousands of women from hitchhiking.

It was also damaging that Arline had taken off her shirt and jewelry—though Delaney's wife had told him that having an earring torn out was one of her own big fears ever since it had happened to a friend of hers taking off a sweater. Finally, the doctor who examined Arline hadn't found any sperm, nor had he noticed her bruises, which weren't, in any case, impressive injuries.

Still, Delaney wasn't entirely pessimistic. The Hollises had agreed to testify. John was actually flying in from Chicago, where he was working on a temporary assignment. Maureen was not happy to be living alone at 2211 Geary, with Fred Dumond still next door; she worried that if she testified he might try to get even in some way. But she felt it was her duty to come forward. Besides being ultrarespectable, they were simply nice, obviously morally concerned people—ideal witnesses from a credibility standpoint. Delaney hoped they could convince a jury that Arline had been screaming for twenty minutes in the next apartment.

The trial of Fred Louis Dumond for rape, including a lesser charge of assault with intent to rape, began on March 3, 1975. The presiding judge was Andrew P. Blackburn, a highly respected jurist with a reputation—even among liberals who disliked his hard-nosed law-and-order stance—for meticulous fairness. Philip Pacetta, another attorney from Frazier, Frazier, had taken over the defense from Scott, who had a prior commitment. The three-woman nine-man jury was predominantly white, middle-aged, and working-class.

Arline and Bobbie arrived together. They were, according to Gary, "a mess—emaciated, untogether, out of control of the situation." For the fourth time Arline faced having to re-create the

193

details of September 18. "Usually I could just not think about it. Going through it all, again and again—that was the worst part." At the grand jury hearing a jury member had said, "Just tell the story—you don't have to relive it."

Delaney put Arline on the stand first. Her direct testimony went quickly; most of the day and part of the next were devoted to cross-examination. Pacetta was a younger, less formidable man than Scott, not so inclined to verbal brutality, and Judge Blackburn kept him more or less under control. The prosecution won a crucial point when Blackburn refused to admit Arline's psychiatrist and tranquilizers as evidence of mental instability; after allowing Pacetta to pursue the question *voir dire* (without the jury present), he ruled that it was prejudicial and irrelevant: "I find that no issue arises by reason of the young lady drinking beer and taking Valium at the same time such as would affect her memory or her ability to recall events or would cause her to imagine things that never took place. . . . I find in the second place that the lady has never had any history of imagining things." Still, the interrogation was an ordeal.

"I felt the lawyer was trying to make a fool of me. He wanted exact times, situations, positions, over and over again. I would forget things and he would trip me up. He would bring up discrepancies from the minutes of the probable cause hearing. Most of these things were irrelevant little details, but to the jury it would look like I was lying. There was a rip in my pants; I hadn't noticed it till after probable cause. The lawyer tried to make me say I'd testified that they weren't ripped. I just hadn't noticed it. He kept trying to make me admit to lies: 'Isn't it a fact that you were kissing?' He even brought up seeing Dumond in Hal's Pub. As if we were there to meet him. As if we had a date."

Bobbie sat in the courtroom, living Arline's misery. Two old men sitting next to her were snoring. She could hear others making cracks about Arline, snickering when she had to talk about her period, agreeing that, boy, she had sure screwed up her story now. "She was on trial," Bobbie said flatly. "If you hated the guy and

wanted to murder him, you wouldn't want to go through it—
except for principle. She would get confused. *What time? What
time?* It was six months ago and there were obviously things she
wanted to block out. She was on the verge of breaking down half
the time."

Arline was finally dismissed and the remaining prosecution witnesses took up the rest of the second day. Delaney had some small
successes: He got Officer Atkins to testify that he had noticed
Arline's bruises and mentioned them to Delaney at the September
19 complaint hearing; and he established that the hospital's negative sperm report was inconclusive. The examining physician
testified that menstrual blood could flush out sperm and that because of Arline's flow he had been unable to see whether seminal
fluid was present or not. He had simply taken his sample from the
area where it was most likely to accumulate. Delaney asked if his
findings meant that Arline's vagina contained no sperm. He an-
swered, "No. . . . I can only say that in the sample I took, there
was no sperm."

But the crucial witness was John Hollis. He recounted what he
had heard and done and made as good an appearance as Delaney
had hoped. On cross-examination, however, there was a brief
skirmish that would prove significant:

Q: *And isn't it a fact, Mr. Hollis, that on this particular night you
told the security guard that you thought the noises were
coming from the eleventh floor?*
A: No, I don't recall that I said they were coming from the
eleventh floor. I said since sound does travel, that was the reason I went out to see if there was any question, but the light
was on in the room next to my bedroom.

The following morning, the defense began by calling the super-
visor of security for 2211 Geary Boulevard. Pacetta had him read
into the record an entry from the security office log for September
19: "2:35 . . . received call from tenant in apartment 1210 complain-

ing about a loud noise and screaming coming from the 11th floor (he thinks)." Next, Fred's friend took the stand and testified that at Jewel's "Arline and Fred were talking, and all of a sudden she put her arms around him and pulled him close to her and whispered something." The third witness was Fred Dumond.

There was some disagreement among courtroom staffers, journalists, and other observers about Dumond's effectiveness as a witness. Some were impressed with his suntanned good looks, his sophisticated, expensive suit, and his calm confidence. Others thought he was a bit too smooth and sure of himself, that he was, as one veteran trial watcher put it, "a real con man." There were rumors about Dumond's behavior with women he had interviewed at his agency. He had two felony convictions—one for receiving stolen TV sets, the other for stealing from an employer—that Delaney was permitted to introduce for the purpose of impeaching his credibility. Even his lawyer didn't like him; Fred had been upset about Pacetta's taking over his case and relations between them had been strained. Months after the trial, Pacetta would comment that Fred had presented himself as "shallow" and "a swinger." In fact, Pacetta argued, it was just this image that made him credible: Why would a ladies' man like him have to rape anybody?

Fred's account contradicted Arline's in nearly every particular. She said he hadn't bought any of her drinks; he claimed he had. He swore that she never gave him her pocketbook. They were not arguing in the cab but kissing. At his apartment they petted on the couch in the living room, then moved to the bedroom, kissing, fondling, undressing. At one point Arline went to the bathroom, and he heard the toilet flush. After she came back, he put his fingers in her vagina and noticed that she was menstruating. (Obviously what she had flushed was her Tampax.) He was disgusted and asked her to leave. She got angry and upset. They argued; there was some "fairly loud" but not "excessively loud" yelling. Arline called her roommate and accused him of rape. He got furious and hung up the phone. He said, "Get the hell out of my house—you are a nut." She yelled at him some more, then left.

Delaney's cross-examination worried one point and another, but he was unable to ruffle Dumond's cool. He began their last exchange by asking, "Did you hear her scream at all?"

A: Scream, no.
Q: *Did you hear anybody scream?*
A: I don't recall hearing—hearing screaming at that point.
Q: *Arline never screamed?*
A: She was talking in a rather hysterical voice, but she wasn't screaming, no.
Q: *Did you hear her scream "Help me, help me, God help me?"*
A: No. I didn't. She never said that.

Dumond stepped down and, after a last minor witness, the defense rested.

On the fourth and last day of the trial Delaney introduced a rebuttal witness: Maureen Hollis. She testified that when she first awakened, she had thought the sounds might be coming from the eleventh floor. But after a few minutes, she had been quite certain they came from next door. She described them as "bloodcurdling screams and shrieks."

Then came closing arguments. In his summation Pacetta used the phrase "dating bar" fourteen times. He reminded the jury that Arline had been having a good time at Jewel's; that she had not protested to the cabdriver or anyone else that Fred had her pocketbook; that he had not forced her to go home with him; that she had taken off some of her clothing; that she had not seen the defendant penetrate or felt him climax; that no sperm was found; that the security report specified the eleventh floor. He suggested that Arline's testimony was confused and inconsistent, that she had spent more time at Fred's than her story accounted for. If Fred was going to rape her, Pacetta wondered, would he take her to his own home? Let her call her roommate? Bring her a glass of water? Go to sleep afterward? In short, did this attractive, well-dressed young man look like a rapist?

Delaney argued that Arline had no reason to be afraid of Fred before he slammed the door; that she had taken off her things out of fear; that she didn't have to *see* the penetration to know it happened; that she wasn't concentrating on the defendant's climax but on her own anguish; that the sperm report wasn't definitive; that no one had kept track of time that night; that it could have been almost 2:00 before they got to the apartment; that no one, let alone a terrified woman who had just been raped, could remember everything; did the jurors recall every detail of, say, their last accident? On the contrary, it was the defendant's memory ("we did this for fifteen minutes, this for twenty") that was too good to be believed. Why, if Arline was lying, would she make up something as far out as the story about watching him urinate? Or admit taking off clothes? In fact, why would she subject herself to all this—a complaint session, a probable cause hearing, and now this trial? Who was more believable: this woman who had nothing to gain except the mortification of testifying about these indignities committed upon her, or this man with a criminal record, on trial for rape—this man who professed to be so repelled by Arline's bleeding, yet went to sleep on the bloodstained sheets? But all this aside, one thing could not be explained away: the screaming the Hollises had heard. Not mere loud argument, but "terrifying," "bloodcurdling" screams.

One argument Delaney didn't make had the courtroom habitues shaking their heads. Was it likely that this man-of-the-world, who had so many women falling all over him that he didn't have to rape anybody, would get so upset about a girl having her period? Whatever had happened up there, that, they agreed, sounded far-fetched. Later, Phil Pacetta would argue, with the characteristic ironic undertone that made his out-of-court defenses of Dumond sound more like insults, "He had wined her and dined her, investing all that time in a potential score—and at the last minute he finds out she's bleeding. Why should he get involved with a woman who's bleeding all over the place? He felt that *she* was out to rape *him!*"

At Delaney's suggestion Arline stayed away from the courtroom the day Fred testified. "I'm glad I wasn't there. I would have freaked out when he told that story. When I heard what it was, I thought, he's got to be kidding. I was really happy because I figured he didn't have much of a chance. I called my mother and asked her if she would believe what he said. She said, 'I'm prejudiced but it sounds fishy to me.'

"I couldn't tell much about the jury. There was one older woman who kept giving me scrutinizing looks; I didn't know if she was just concentrating or what. But I honestly thought that they couldn't believe his story."

The jury went out at 3:00 p.m. and deliberated for four hours. Since the court session was over for the day, the judge ordered the verdict sealed. In the morning the foreman announced it: "Not guilty." Judge Blackburn told the jurors to be seated and asked the clerk to poll them. This was a routine procedure on a guilty verdict; it was rarely done for an acquittal. Something was up. One by one, the jurors confirmed their verdict: not guilty. Judge Blackburn directed the clerk to affirm the verdict. Then, with barely controlled anger, he began:

"It is almost impossible in this county to get a conviction of rape. . . . I am reluctantly coming to the conclusion, whether it is the permissive society or what we are living in, at least as far as jurors are concerned, rape is no longer a crime. And when we have a trial, instead of trying the defendant, you make the poor girl the defendant. . . . You have seen television programs, girls don't report rape for the humiliation involved in it, the degradation they go through in the trial. . . . They are made the defendant, and they walk out of this courtroom with one thought in their mind: in our courts there is no justice for the victims of rape. And I can't say that I disagree with them.

"How many countless rapes are committed and never hit the courtroom because of the way jurors treat rape victims. I don't know, but it has gotten to be almost a national scandal. . . . And if you jurors believe the girls who are victims of this kind of violent sexual assault aren't entitled to the protection of our juries, just like the defendants are, then it is a sick society.

"Now I am coming to this case. You had two responsible citizens of this state, irreproachable of integrity and principles, who testified before you that they heard screaming there for twenty minutes. Can it be, ladies and gentlemen, that you believed the screaming, terrified girl, with bloodcurdling calls, consented to the advances of this defendant? Can you disbelieve those people? And can you believe a defendant who stood with two convictions, one that he was a thief and the other that he dealt in stolen property? . . . Believe him and disbelieve them? Well, that's what you have done. . . .

"I wish I could say to you that you performed your jury service in the highest traditions of this state, and I can't."

He ended by summarily dismissing them from jury duty for the rest of their terms.

V

The day the verdict came down, Arline was at work. When she didn't hear from Jim Delaney, she called his office. She had to pry the information out of him. Did they come to a decision? Yes. What was it? Well, it's gonna be in the paper tomorrow. What does that mean? What do you think? Not guilty. Arline began to cry. Then Delaney told her about the judge's speech.

Blackburn's rebuke transformed *People* v. *Dumond* from a routine rape case—a "swearing contest," in courthouse parlance—to a controversial one. Local feminists were delighted; most defense lawyers were outraged at what they regarded as an attempt to intimidate juries. An exception was Philip Pacetta, who not only defended Blackburn's right to speak but when asked if he agreed with the judge's comments said: "The record speaks for itself."

The jurors themselves were, for the most part, disturbed and angry. One woman juror called Blackburn's action "a rape of the jury system" and wrote a letter of protest to the chief justice of the California Supreme Court demanding that Blackburn apologize to the jurors in open court. A male juror declared, "To be blunt, I think the judge is nuts."

To Arline, Blackburn's statement was a boost. It showed that at least she wasn't a joke, soothed her fears that people were laughing at her and thinking she was a liar. It made her feel a little less defeated. Then she read an article in an underground paper that quoted one juror as saying, "I thought just the way the others did. She was as guilty as he was. If she hangs around a place like that, she deserves everything she gets." The casual cruelty of the remark—"someone's torn ego using me as a punching bag"—was only part of what outraged her. If she "deserved what she got," that implied that she "got" something, which meant that this juror hadn't believed Fred Dumond when he denied having sex with her: "Some fine upstanding citizen, to condone perjury and then sit in judgment of me!" That perception, as the comments of other jurors would confirm, was essentially accurate. Whatever one thought of the propriety of Blackburn's outburst (or, for that matter, of the verdict itself), his target was well chosen.

In some ways Arline Hunt had been more fortunate than most rape complainants. The police had treated her considerately—although, according to a source at the courthouse, they were privately incredulous at her story—and so had Pacific Hospital. The Women's Law Commune agreed that the D.A. had conducted an excellent investigation. Opinions on Delaney's role in court were mixed. "Delaney is a type," said a local journalist. "A San Francisco old boy, hale and hearty. I wouldn't call him any kind of hero. I doubt that he really cared about the case before Blackburn made it into a big thing." Gary complained that Delaney smiled too much. "He wasn't as distressed as he should have been. I didn't feel that Arline had a good relationship with him. She was a docile client and he was none too aggressive." Delaney himself worried that he was not aggressive enough in cross-examining Fred. "He was such a smooth bastard: I was in a dilemma as to whether there was anything I could do to break his story or whether badgering would just solidify it." But there were other people—Arline was one—who felt he had tried very hard to win.

The trial itself, unpleasant as it was, could have been much worse. Arline was not, for example, subjected to an inquisition on her sexual experience. And another judge might have allowed the defense to bring up her psychiatric treatment. Except for Pacetta's emphasis on dating bars and bralessness, the trial had probably been as fair as the adversary system—with its built-in potential for harassing witnesses and confusing the jury with side issues—allowed.

The basic problem was that the jury reflected the nature of the jury pool, which in San Francisco as elsewhere is mainly drawn from the most conservative segment of the population. Transients are grossly underrepresented, young people and the conspicuously educated almost always challenged. Moreover, most states make it easier for women to be excused from serving, though the effect of such policies on rape trials is not as obvious as it might appear: not only are most female jurors conservative, elderly housewives who tend to disapprove of sexually active single women, but many women seem to feel a defensive need to blame the rape victim in order to reassure themselves that "it could never happen to me." In any case, the three women on Fred Dumond's jury—all of them over fifty—were as actively in favor of acquittal as most of the men. During a recess a court official overheard two of the women jurors talking in the corridor; they agreed that by going to a bar and not wearing a bra, Arline Hunt was "asking for it." And one woman, acting as a technical adviser to the male jurors, assured them that it was impossible to remove a Tampax by force—a patent absurdity.

What was decisive, for the majority of jurors, was simply that Arline had gone to a man's apartment—no one took the pocketbook story seriously—and was therefore fair game. They had surprisingly little trouble rationalizing the screams: "You hear screaming—maybe it's serious, maybe not. She was half in the bag.

Sometimes you entice a person and then get scared." "The screaming didn't carry any weight—I think the words were put in [the
witness's] mouth. There weren't any marks on her." "Women
scream for many reasons." "It came from the eleventh floor." "It
was overdramatized, there wasn't enough evidence. No blood in
the hall or anything like that." Few of the jurors seemed to care
much whether Fred's story was true and some were explicitly
skeptical; the man who had called Blackburn "nuts" said flatly,
"He didn't impress me. I couldn't say I believed him any more
than I believed her."

Two of the men fought for conviction, but Donald Peterson, a
thirty-two-year-old laborer and bartender, was the only juror who
would admit to doubts about the verdict. "I was for conviction,"
Peterson said, "but it looked to me like we weren't going to con-
vict. And there was a little doubt—no physical evidence, gaps in
time, the stuff about the Tampax. Assault I could have gone with,
but to put a guy away for fifteen years for rape . . . I felt sorry for
her. She ran into a dude who wouldn't take no for an answer. The
women were impressed with him but to me he looked like a real
rat bastard. I meet a lot of guys like him where I work, and if he
took out my sister, I'd be waiting up. Yeah, I believe she really
screamed. But that kid would have had to have her arms broken
before *they* would believe her. Except for one guy, who was trying to tell them, 'You're trying the girl, not the guy.' I had second
thoughts then. I still do."

Shortly after the trial, Fred Dumond dissolved his business, was
evicted from his apartment—probably at the instigation of the
Hollises—and disappeared. At Arline Hunt's apartment something
like normality began to reassert itself. Then in early June, Arline
quit her job. She had been feeling much better—or so Bobbie had
thought—but now her depression deepened again. She felt that a
man she was seeing was putting her off, that a girlfriend was
rejecting her. One day she was talking on the phone to her married
sister in Michigan and began to feel that her sister wanted to hang
up. When she got off the phone she was crying. While Bobbie was

in the bathroom, she took every pill in the house, then told Bobbie what she had done. She spent a month in the private psychiatric hospital with which her doctor is affiliated. After her release, she began looking for another job.

1975

Abortion: Is a Woman a Person?

If propaganda is as central to politics as I think, the opponents of legal abortion have been winning a psychological victory as important as their tangible gains. Two years ago, abortion was almost always discussed in feminist terms—as a political issue affecting the condition of women. Since then, the grounds of the debate have shifted drastically; more and more, the right-to-life movement has succeeded in getting the public and the media to see abortion as an abstract moral issue having solely to do with the rights of fetuses. Though every poll shows that most Americans favor legal abortion, it is evident that many are confused and disarmed, if not convinced, by the antiabortionists' absolutist fervor. No one likes to be accused of advocating murder. Yet the "pro-life" position is based on a crucial fallacy—that the question of fetal rights can be isolated from the question of women's rights.

Recently, Garry Wills wrote a piece suggesting that liberals who defended the snail-darter's right to life and opposed the killing in Vietnam should condemn abortion as murder. I found this

This piece combines two columns written for *The Village Voice*.

notion breathtaking in its illogic. Environmentalists were protesting not the "murder" of individual snail-darters but the practice of wiping out entire species of organisms to gain a short-term economic benefit; most people who opposed our involvement in Vietnam did so because they believed the United States was waging an aggressive, unjust and/or futile war. There was no inconsistency in holding such positions and defending abortion on the grounds that women's welfare should take precedence over fetal life. To claim that three very different issues, each with its own complicated social and political context, all came down to a simple matter of preserving life was to say that all killing was alike and equally indefensible regardless of circumstance. (Why, I wondered, had Wills left out the destruction of hapless bacteria by penicillin?) But aside from the general mushiness of the argument, I was struck by one peculiar fact: Wills had written an entire article about abortion without mentioning women, feminism, sex, or pregnancy.

Since the feminist argument for abortion rights still carries a good deal of moral and political weight, part of the antiabortionists' strategy has been to make an end run around it. Although the mainstream of the right-to-life movement is openly opposed to women's liberation, it has chosen to make its stand on the abstract "pro-life" argument. That emphasis has been reinforced by the movement's tiny left wing, which opposes abortion on pacifist grounds and includes women who call themselves "feminists for life." A minority among pacifists as well as right-to-lifers, this group nevertheless serves the crucial function of making opposition to abortion respectable among liberals, leftists, and moderates disinclined to sympathize with a right-wing crusade. Unlike most right-to-lifers, who are vulnerable to charges that their reverence for life does not apply to convicted criminals or Vietnamese peasants, antiabortion leftists are in a position to appeal to social conscience—to make analogies, however facile, between abortion and napalm. They disclaim any opposition to women's rights, insisting rather that the end cannot justify the means—murder is murder.

Abortion: Is a Woman a Person?

Well, isn't there a genuine moral issue here? If abortion *is* murder, how can a woman have the right to it? Feminists are often accused of evading this question, but in fact an evasion is built into the question itself. Most people understand "Is abortion murder?" to mean "Is the fetus a person?" But fetal personhood is ultimately as inarguable as the existence of God; either you believe in it or you don't. Putting the debate on this plane inevitably leads to the nonconclusion that it is a matter of one person's conscience against another's. From there, the discussion generally moves on to broader issues: whether laws defining the fetus as a person violate the separation of church and state; or conversely, whether people who believe an act is murder have not only the right but the obligation to prevent it. Unfortunately, amid all this lofty philosophizing, the concrete, human reality of the pregnant woman's dilemma gets lost, and with it an essential ingredient of the moral question.

Murder, as commonly defined, is killing that is unjustified, willful, and malicious. Most people would agree, for example, that killing in defense of one's life or safety is not murder. And most would accept a concept of self-defense that includes the right to fight a defensive war or revolution in behalf of one's independence or freedom from oppression. Even pacifists make moral distinctions between defensive violence, however deplorable, and murder; no thoughtful pacifist would equate Hitler's murder of the Jews with the Warsaw Ghetto rebels' killing of Nazi troops. The point is that it's impossible to judge whether an act is murder simply by looking at the act, without considering its context. Which is to say that it makes no sense to discuss whether abortion is murder without considering why women have abortions and what it means to force women to bear children they don't want.

We live in a society that defines child rearing as the mother's job; a society in which most women are denied access to work that pays enough to support a family, child-care facilities they can afford, or any relief from the constant, daily burdens of motherhood; a society that forces mothers into dependence on marriage

207

or welfare and often into permanent poverty; a society that is actively hostile to women's ambitions for a better life. Under these conditions the unwillingly pregnant woman faces a terrifying loss of control over her fate. Even if she chooses to give up the baby, unwanted pregnancy is in itself a serious trauma. There is no way a pregnant woman can passively let the fetus live; she must create and nurture it with her own body, in a symbiosis that is often difficult, sometimes dangerous, always uniquely intimate. However gratifying pregnancy may be to a woman who desires it, for the unwilling it is literally an invasion—the closest analogy is to the difference between lovemaking and rape. Nor is there such a thing as foolproof contraception. Clearly, abortion is by normal standards an act of self-defense.

Whenever I make this case to a right-to-lifer, the exchange that follows is always substantially the same:

RTL: If a woman chooses to have sex, she should be willing to take the consequences. We must all be responsible for our actions.

EW: Men have sex, without having to "take the consequences."

RTL: You can't help that—it's biology.

EW: You don't think a woman has as much right as a man to enjoy sex? Without living in fear that one slip will transform her life?

RTL: She has no right to selfish pleasure at the expense of the unborn.

It would seem, then, that the nitty-gritty issue in the abortion debate is not life but sex. If the fetus is sacrosanct, it follows that women must be continually vulnerable to the invasion of their bodies and loss of their freedom and independence—unless they are willing to resort to the only perfectly reliable contraceptive, abstinence. This is precisely the "solution" right-to-lifers suggest, usually with a touch of glee; as Representative Elwood Rudd once put it, "If a woman has a right to control her own body, let her exercise control before she gets pregnant." A common ploy is to compare fucking to overeating or overdrinking, the idea being that pregnancy is a just punishment, like obesity or cirrhosis.

In 1979 it is depressing to have to insist that sex is not an unnecessary, morally dubious self-indulgence but a basic human need, no less for women than for men. Of course, for heterosexual women giving up sex also means doing without the love and companionship of a mate. (Presumably, married women who have had all the children they want are supposed to divorce their husbands or convince them that celibacy is the only moral alternative.) "Freedom" bought at such a cost is hardly freedom at all and certainly not equality—no one tells men that if they aspire to some measure of control over their lives, they are welcome to neuter themselves and become social isolates. The don't-have-sex argument is really another version of the familiar antifeminist dictum that autonomy and femaleness—that is, female sexuality—are incompatible; if you choose the first, you lose the second. But to pose this choice is not only inhumane; it is as deeply disingenuous as "Let them eat cake." No one, least of all the antiabortion movement, expects or wants significant numbers of women to give up sex and marriage. Nor are most right-to-lifers willing to allow abortion for rape victims. When all the cant about "responsibility" is stripped away, what the right-to-life position comes down to is, if the effect of prohibiting abortion is to keep women slaves to their biology, so be it.

In their zeal to preserve fetal life at all costs, antiabortionists are ready to grant fetuses more legal protection than people. If a man attacks me and I kill him, I can plead self-defense without having to prove that I was in danger of being killed rather than injured, raped, or kidnapped. But in the annual congressional battle over what if any exceptions to make to the Medicaid abortion ban, the House of Representatives has bitterly opposed the funding of abortions for any reason but to save the pregnant woman's life. Some right-to-lifers argue that even the danger of death does not justify abortion; others have suggested "safeguards" like requiring two or more doctors to certify that the woman's life is at least 50 percent threatened. Antiabortionists are forever worrying that any exception to a total ban on abortion will be used as a "loophole": better that any number of women should ruin their health or even die than that one woman should get away with not having a child "merely" because she doesn't want one. Clearly this mentality does not reflect equal concern for all life. Rather, antiabortionists value the lives of fetuses above the lives and welfare of women, because at bottom they do not concede women the right to an active human existence that transcends their reproductive function. Years ago, in an interview with Paul Krassner in *The Realist*, Ken Kesey declared himself against abortion. When Krassner asked if his objection applied to victims of rape, Kesey replied—I may not be remembering the exact words, but I will never forget the substance —"Just because another man planted the seed, that's no reason to destroy the crop."* To this day I have not heard a more eloquent or chilling metaphor for the essential premise of the right-to-life movement: that a woman's excuse for being is her womb. It is an outrageous irony that antiabortionists are managing to pass off this profoundly immoral idea as a noble moral cause.

The conservatives who dominate the right-to-life movement have no real problem with the antifeminism inherent in their stand; their evasion of the issue is a matter of public relations. But the politics of antiabortion leftists are a study in self-contradiction: in attacking what they see as the violence of abortion, they condone and encourage violence against women. Forced childbearing does violence to a woman's body and spirit, and it contributes to other kinds of violence: deaths from illegal abortion; the systematic oppression of mothers and women in general; the poverty, neglect, and battering of unwanted children; sterilization abuse.

Radicals supposedly believe in attacking a problem at its roots. Yet surely it is obvious that restrictive laws do not keep women

---

* A reader later sent me a copy of the Kesey interview. The correct quotation is "You don't plow under the corn because the seed was planted with a neighbor's shovel."

from seeking abortions; they just create an illicit, dangerous industry. The only way to drastically reduce the number of abortions is to invent safer, more reliable contraceptives, ensure universal access to all birth control methods, eliminate sexual ignorance and guilt, and change the social and economic conditions that make motherhood a trap. Anyone who is truly committed to fostering life should be fighting for women's liberation instead of harassing and disrupting abortion clinics (hardly a nonviolent tactic, since it threatens the safety of patients). The "feminists for life" do talk a lot about ending the oppression that drives so many women to abortion; in practice, however, they are devoting all their energy to increasing it.

Despite its numerical insignificance, the antiabortion left epitomizes the hypocrisy of the right-to-life crusade. Its need to wrap misogyny in the rhetoric of social conscience and even feminism is actually a perverse tribute to the women's movement; it is no longer acceptable to declare openly that women deserve to suffer for the sin of Eve. I suppose that's progress—not that it does the victims of the Hyde Amendment much good.

March and April 1979

Abortion: Overruling

the Neo-Fascists

Judge John F. Dooling's 328-page decision striking down the
Hyde Amendment is heartening in a way that transcends its
strictly legal impact*: for the first time a federal judge has taken

* Judge Dooling held that for Congress to exclude payment for "health-
related" abortions from an otherwise comprehensive program of medical aid
to the poor violated indigent women's Fifth Amendment rights to privacy,
due process, and equal protection and the First Amendment's guarantee of
religious freedom. The decision has one major limitation: given the Supreme
Court's 1977 ruling that states may withhold Medicaid payments for "elective"
abortions, Dooling had no choice but to restrict the application of his opinion
to abortions that are, in the judgment of a pregnant woman's doctor, necessary in the light of all factors affecting the woman's health—her physical and
emotional state, her age, her economic, familial, and social situation. Though
this definition of a "medically necessary" abortion is as liberal as possible,
short of discarding the concept altogether, the distinction between necessary
and elective abortions is inherently sexist. Since forced childbearing violates
women's fundamental right to self-determination, the only person qualified
to judge whether an abortion is necessary is the pregnant woman herself.
When the radical feminist campaign to repeal the abortion laws began in
1969, our first target was the "reformers" who sat around splitting hairs over
how sick or poor or multiparous a woman had to be to deserve exemption

the offensive against the arguments and tactics of the right-to-life movement. The ruling does not contain a word of denunciatory rhetoric, yet simply by accumulating facts it damns the movement as cruel, dishonest, and fanatical, devoid of decent regard either for the health and welfare of women or for anyone's freedom of conscience.

Much of the opinion is devoted to an exhaustive, scarifying compendium of the destructive effects of unwanted pregnancy. This is in itself a compelling comment on the sadism of the "pro-life" crowd. But Dooling goes on to do a thorough demolition job on the Hyde Amendment's rigid requirements for Medicaid-funded abortions, focusing on the inherently ghoulish nature of the "life endangerment" and "severe and long-lasting physical damage" standards (the latter a concession in last year's version of the amendment—a rider to the annual HEW appropriations bill—that was deleted from this year's). Since it is rarely possible to tell, particularly in the first few months of a woman's pregnancy, whether a potentially life-threatening condition will actually kill her, or exactly how bad the damage to her health will be, the effect of such requirements is to force the woman to go on with her pregnancy until a full-blown emergency develops—a procedure totally repugnant to accepted medical practice and ethics. Dooling agrees that this is an intolerable bind and concludes that both criteria are so vague as to violate the Fifth Amendment's due-process clause. He further observes that the sixty-day reporting requirement in rape and incest cases functions to deny abortions to a large percentage of rape victims and to make the incest exception virtually meaningless (incest, the judge notes drily, tends to be secretive).

Throughout his opinion Dooling displays a refreshing impa-

---

from reproductive duty. In the past few years the idea that abortions without some special justification are merely "convenient"—as if unwanted pregnancy were an annoyance comparable to, say, standing in a long line at the supermarket—has been revived with a vengeance.

tience with right-to-life cant and double-talk. He demonstrates that the purpose of the Hyde Amendment was never to save the taxpayers money, keep the government neutral on a delicate moral issue, or distinguish between "necessary" and so-called "convenience" abortions. The amendment, says Dooling bluntly, was a ploy by antiabortion congressmen frustrated in their attempt to pass a constitutional amendment that would override the Supreme Court's 1973 proabortion decision; its purpose was quite simply to circumvent the Court's ruling and prevent as many abortions as possible. Dooling, a practicing Catholic, makes short work of the antiabortionsts' pretensions to being a spontaneous grass-roots movement that owes its political victories to sheer moral appeal. He confirms that right-to-life's main source of energy, organization, and direction has been the Catholic Church and describes in detail how the movement uses one-issue voting to put pressure on legislators, candidates, and the party organizations that nominate them—a tactic that gains it influence far out of proportion to its numbers. After quoting various Christian and Jewish theologians' differing opinions on abortion and the question of fetal personhood, Dooling argues that the antiabortionists' absolutist view is not based on any moral or religious consensus but reflects a sectarian position that "is not genuinely argued; it is adamantly asserted." He also documents the movement's utter contempt for its opponents (we are all, by definition, mass murderers) and the refusal of right-to-life organizations and activists to take a stand against violent attacks on abortion clinics. The Hyde Amendment, he concludes, is religiously motivated legislation that imposes a particular theological viewpoint, violating dissenters' First Amendment rights. (In response to this aspect of the decision Carolyn Gerster, the president of the National Right to Life Committee, declared that she couldn't imagine a religion that would condone abortion, "unless it were one that included child sacrifice." Gerster's imagination is limited. Major denominations that regard abortion as an individual moral decision include the Baptists, Methodists, Episcopalians, and Conservative and Reform Jews.

Abortion: Overruling the Neo-Fascists

Jews will find Gerster's choice of words especially chilling; the charge that Jews kill children for ritual purposes is an old anti-Semitic canard, a traditional excuse for pogroms.)

In every respect the Dooling decision confirms my own conviction that the antiabortion movement is the most dangerous political force in the country. I believe—and in saying this I intend no hyperbole whatsoever—that it is the cutting edge of neo-fascism, a threat not only to women's rights and to everyone's sexual freedom and privacy but to freedom of religion and civil liberties in general. Right-to-life propaganda leaves no doubt that abortion is only the immediate focus of a larger crusade to crush women's liberation, sexual "immorality," birth control, sex education, and all other manifestations of "Godless humanism"—that is, the separation of church and state—in favor of patriarchal authority, the traditional family, and "Christian values"—that is, Christianity at its most authoritarian, parochial, and bigoted. The movement's most vicious bit of rhetoric—its continual assertion that legal abortion has murdered more people than Hitler—cannot be dismissed as meaningless bombast. However absurd (antiabortionists' ideas about sex, women, and authority are actually quite similar to Hitler's; under the Nazis, abortion was a serious crime, in some circumstances punishable by death), this invocation of the Holocaust is clearly designed to justify whatever methods the movement chooses to adopt—after all, one doesn't quibble about democratic means when fighting genocidal maniacs. The comparison is also anti-Semitic; not only does it trivialize and co-opt the slaughter of the Jews, it does so in the name of the very "Christian values" chiefly responsible for anti-Jewish persecution. Anyway, it's only a matter of time till the right-to-lifers notice, if they haven't already, that Jews (except for the Orthodox) are more liberal on abortion and "Godless humanism" generally than any other religious or ethnic group.

If you think I'm exaggerating, look up the January 21 *New York Times* and read about the recent conference of antiabortion leaders. On contraception: "a form of moral insanity." On divorce: ". . . just as we are able to dispose of our spouses if we feel like it, so are we able to do away with our children if we feel like it." On politics: "One place the ordinary Christian can be effective to turn the tide is to begin by supporting and electing only pro-life candidates." On the firebombing of abortion clinics: "I don't cry real hard when I hear about one of their firetraps burning down." There was the obligatory reference to "the smell of the camps" and general agreement that the related evils of abortion, divorce, contraception, euthanasia, and genetic engineering are the logical product of secularism. You don't have to be Jewish, or female, or homosexual, or an atheist to get the message, but it helps.

Given the antiabortionists' single-mindedness and resultant political clout, it is all too possible that they will either push their constitutional amendment through Congress or get the required number of state legislatures to call a constitutional convention that might or might not have the power to tear apart the Bill of Rights. Since most Americans do not share either their attitude toward abortion or their general world view, a certain amount of alarm would seem to be in order. Yet so far the public has reacted to the right-to-life juggernaut, and to proabortion activists' organizing efforts, with an almost willful apathy. Nearly everyone I know supports legal abortion in principle, but except for hard-core feminists hardly anyone takes the issue seriously. Press coverage and analysis of the abortion debate range from nonexistent to condescending. (The *Times* ran its piece about the antiabortion conference on the style page.) When I buttonhole people and harangue them about abortion doing for the right what Vietnam did for the left, I don't even get arguments—just blank looks. On occasion even feminists have been obtuse about what we're facing —the most egregious example being NOW's attempt last year to meet with antiabortionists to discuss "common interests" and "depolarize" the issue. (The right-to-lifers responded by displaying two mysteriously obtained dead fetuses and denouncing "baby killers.")

Part of the problem is that at the moment abortion is still legal and still available to most women; it's always harder to get people to defend something they have than to demand something they lack. Another important factor is sexism; the antiabortion movement doesn't threaten men in an immediate, direct way, and abortion is regarded as a women's issue, which is to say trivial, sectarian, and "middle-class."

But something else is going on that's even more disturbing: a lot of people who intellectually abhor everything the antiabortionists stand for are emotionally intimidated by their argument. The right-to-lifers' most dangerous weapon is not their efficiency in the legislative arena but their ability to confuse and immobilize potential opponents by tapping the vast store of sexual guilt and anxiety that lies just below this society's veneer of sexual liberalism. Patriarchal culture, with its deeply antisexual ideology, has existed for some five thousand years; the radical idea that people have a right to sexual freedom and happiness has been a significant social force for little more than a century; in this country the changes we think of as the "sexual revolution" have all taken place within the past two decades. Most of us grew up with the old values. It is hardly surprising that even among sophisticated liberals people's emotions do not necessarily coincide with their enlightened ideas. And sophisticated liberals who nonetheless believe on some level that the desire for sex without "consequences" (i.e., children) is self-indulgent, and that the ability to control one's passion is a test of character, are likely to be apologetic about their support for abortion rights. There is now a sizable body of literature on the theme of "I'm for legal abortion, but. . . ." Many proabortion liberals and feminists indulge a poisonously sentimental and self-flagellating view of the right-to-lifers as upholders of principle and altruism and sacrifice—the idea being that the rest of us are merely pursuing our selfish interests. Even more people, I'm convinced, are handling their ambivalence by simply blocking out the whole subject.

The sort of Orwellian reversal whereby apostles of brutality and repression become morally admirable even in the eyes of their opponents drives me crazy. That a seventy-one-year-old male, Catholic judge, who probably disagrees with all my ideas about sexual freedom, should see this nonsense for what it is and come up with an effective refutation is the sort of irony that keeps me sane.

January 1980

Feminism, Moralism,

and Pornography

For women, life is an ongoing good cop–bad cop routine. The good cops are marriage, motherhood, and that courtly old gentleman, chivalry. Just cooperate, they say (crossing their fingers), and we'll go easy on you. You'll never have to earn a living or open a door. We'll even get you some romantic love. But you'd better not get stubborn, or you'll have to deal with our friend rape, and he's a real terror; we just can't control him.

Pornography often functions as a bad cop. If rape warns that without the protection of one man we are fair game for all, the hard-core pornographic image suggests that the alternative to being a wife is being a whore. As women become more "criminal," the cops call for nastier reinforcements; the proliferation of lurid, violent porn (symbolic rape) is a form of backlash. But one can be a solid citizen and still be shocked (naively or hypocritically) by police brutality. However widely condoned, rape is illegal. However loudly people proclaim that porn is as wholesome as granola, the essence of its appeal is that emotionally it remains taboo. It is

This is an expanded version of two columns written for *The Village Voice*.

from their very contempt for the rules that bad cops derive their power to terrorize (and the covert approbation of solid citizens who would love to break the rules themselves). The line between bad cop and outlaw is tenuous. Both rape and pornography reflect a male outlaw mentality that rejects the conventions of romance and insists, bluntly, that women are cunts. The crucial difference between the conservative's moral indignation at rape, or at *Hustler*, and the feminist's political outrage is the latter's understanding that the problem is not bad cops or outlaws but cops and the law.

Unfortunately, the current women's campaign against pornography seems determined to blur this difference. Feminist criticism of sexist and misogynist pornography is nothing new; porn is an obvious target insofar as it contributes to larger patterns of oppression—the reduction of the female body to a commodity (the paradigm being prostitution), the sexual intimidation that makes women regard the public streets as enemy territory (the paradigm being rape), sexist images and propaganda in general. But what is happening now is different. By playing games with the English language, antiporn activists are managing to rationalize as feminism a single-issue movement divorced from any larger political context and rooted in conservative moral assumptions that are all the more dangerous for being unacknowledged.

When I first heard there was a group called Women Against Pornography, I twitched. Could I define myself as Against Pornography? Not really. In itself, pornography—which, my dictionary and I agree, means any image or description intended or used to arouse sexual desire—does not strike me as the proper object of a political crusade. As the most cursory observation suggests, there are many varieties of porn, some pernicious, some more or less benign. About the only generalization one can make is that pornography is the return of the repressed, of feelings and fantasies driven underground by a culture that atomizes sexuality, defining love as a noble affair of the heart and mind, lust as a base animal urge centered in unmentionable organs. Prurience—the state of

mind I associate with pornography—implies a sense of sex as forbidden, secretive pleasure, isolated from any emotional or social
context. I imagine that in utopia, porn would wither away along
with the state, heroin, and Coca-Cola. At present, however, the
sexual impulses that pornography appeals to are part of virtually
everyone's psychology. For obvious political and cultural reasons
nearly all porn is sexist in that it is the product of a male imagination
and aimed at a male market; women are less likely to be consciously interested in pornography, or to indulge that interest, or
to find porn that turns them on. But anyone who thinks women
are simply indifferent to pornography has never watched a bunch
of adolescent girls pass around a trashy novel. Over the years I've
enjoyed various pieces of pornography—some of them of the
sleazy Forty-second Street paperback sort—and so have most
women I know. Fantasy, after all, is more flexible than reality, and
women have learned, as a matter of survival, to be adept at shaping
male fantasies to their own purposes. If feminists define pornography, per se, as the enemy, the result will be to make a lot of
women ashamed of their sexual feelings and afraid to be honest
about them. And the last thing women need is more sexual shame,
guilt, and hypocrisy—this time served up as feminism.

So why ignore qualitative distinctions and in effect condemn all
pornography as equally bad? WAP organizers answer—or finesse
—this question by redefining pornography. They maintain that
pornography is not really about sex but about violence against
women. Or, in a more colorful formulation, "Pornography is the
theory, rape is the practice." Part of the argument is that pornography causes violence; much is made of the fact that Charles Man-
son and David Berkowitz had porn collections. This is the sort of
inverted logic that presumes marijuana to be dangerous because
most heroin addicts started with it. It is men's hostility toward
women—combined with their power to express that hostility and
for the most part get away with it—that causes sexual violence.
Pornography that gives sadistic fantasies concrete shape—and, in
today's atmosphere, social legitimacy—may well encourage sug-

gestible men to act them out. But if *Hustler* were to vanish from the shelves tomorrow, I doubt that rape or wife-beating statistics would decline.

Even more problematic is the idea that pornography depicts violence rather than sex. Since porn is by definition overtly sexual, while most of it is not overtly violent, this equation requires some fancy explaining. The conference WAP held in September was in part devoted to this task. Robin Morgan and Gloria Steinem addressed it by attempting to distinguish pornography from erotica. According to this argument, erotica (whose etymological root is "eros," or sexual love) expresses an integrated sexuality based on mutual affection and desire between equals; pornography (which comes from another Greek root—"porne," meaning prostitute) reflects a dehumanized sexuality based on male domination and exploitation of women. The distinction sounds promising, but it doesn't hold up. The accepted meaning of erotica is literature or pictures with sexual themes; it may or may not serve the essentially utilitarian function of pornography. Because it is less specific, less suggestive of actual sexual activity, "erotica" is regularly used as a euphemism for "classy porn." Pornography expressed in literary language or expensive photography and consumed by the upper middle class is "erotica"; the cheap stuff, which can't pretend to any purpose but getting people off, is smut. The erotica-versus-porn approach evades the (embarrassing?) question of how porn is *used*. It endorses the portrayal of sex as we might like it to be and condemns the portrayal of sex as it too often is, whether in action or only in fantasy. But if pornography is to arouse, it must appeal to the feelings we have, not those that by some utopian standard we ought to have. Sex in this culture has been so deeply politicized that it is impossible to make clear-cut distinctions between "authentic" sexual impulses and those conditioned by patriarchy. Between, say, *Ulysses* at one end and *Snuff* at the other, erotica/pornography conveys all sorts of mixed messages that elicit complicated and private responses. In practice, attempts to sort out good erotica from bad porn inevitably come down to

"What turns me on is erotic; what turns you on is pornographic."

It would be clearer and more logical simply to acknowledge that some sexual images are offensive and some are not. But logic and clarity are irrelevant—or rather, inimical—to the underlying aim of the antiporners, which is to vent the emotions traditionally associated with the word "pornography." As I've suggested, there is a social and psychic link between pornography and rape. In terms of patriarchal morality both are expressions of male lust, which is presumed to be innately vicious, and offenses to the putative sexual innocence of "good" women. But feminists supposedly begin with different assumptions—that men's confusion of sexual desire with predatory aggression reflects a sexist system, not male biology; that there are no good (chaste) or bad (lustful) women, just women who are, like men, sexual beings. From this standpoint, to lump pornography with rape is dangerously simplistic. Rape is a violent physical assault. Pornography can be a psychic assault, both in its content and in its public intrusions on our attention, but for women as for men it can also be a source of erotic pleasure. A woman who is raped is a victim; a woman who enjoys pornography (even if that means enjoying a rape fantasy) is in a sense a rebel, insisting on an aspect of her sexuality that has been defined as a male preserve. Insofar as pornography glorifies male supremacy and sexual alienation, it is deeply reactionary. But in rejecting sexual repression and hypocrisy which have inflicted even more damage on women than on men—it expresses a radical impulse.

That this impulse still needs defending, even among feminists, is evident from the sexual attitudes that have surfaced in the antiporn movement. In the movement's rhetoric pornography is a code word for vicious male lust. To the objection that some women get off on porn, the standard reply is that this only shows how thoroughly women have been brainwashed by male values—though a WAP leaflet goes so far as to suggest that women who claim to like pornography are lying to avoid male opprobrium. (Note the good-girl-versus-bad-girl theme, reappearing as healthy-versus-sick, or honest-versus-devious; for "brainwashed" read "seduced.") And the view of sex that most often emerges from talk about "erotica" is as sentimental and euphemistic as the word itself: lovemaking should be beautiful, romantic, soft, nice, and devoid of messiness, vulgarity, impulses to power, or indeed aggression of any sort. Above all, the emphasis should be on *relationships*, not (yuck) *organs*. This goody-goody concept of eroticism is not feminist but feminine. It is precisely sex as an aggressive, unladylike activity, an expression of violent and unpretty emotion, an exercise of erotic power, and a specifically genital experience that has been taboo for women. Nor are we supposed to admit that we, too, have sadistic impulses, that our sexual fantasies may reflect forbidden urges to turn the tables and get revenge on men. (When a woman is aroused by a rape fantasy, is she perhaps identifying with the rapist as well as the victim?)

At the WAP conference lesbian separatists argued that pornography reflects patriarchal sexual relations; patriarchal sexual relations are based on male power backed by force; ergo, pornography is violent. This dubious syllogism, which could as easily be applied to romantic novels, reduces the whole issue to hopeless mush. If all manifestations of patriarchal sexuality are violent, then opposition to violence cannot explain why pornography (rather than romantic novels) should be singled out as a target. Besides, such reductionism allows women no basis for distinguishing between consensual heterosexuality and rape. But this is precisely its point; as a number of women at the conference put it, "In a patriarchy, all sex with men is pornographic." Of course, to attack pornography, and at the same time equate it with heterosexual sex, is implicitly to condemn not only women who like pornography, but women who sleep with men. This is familiar ground. The argument that straight women collaborate with the enemy has often been, among other things, a relatively polite way of saying that they consort with the beast. At the conference I couldn't help feeling that proponents of the separatist line were talking like the modern equivalents of women who, in an era when straightforward prudery was socially acceptable, joined convents to

escape men's rude sexual demands. It seemed to me that their revulsion against heterosexuality was serving as the thinnest of
covers for disgust with sex itself. In any case, sanitized feminine
sexuality, whether straight or gay, is as limited as the predatory
masculine kind and as central to women's oppression; a major
function of misogynist pornography is to scare us into embracing
it. As a further incentive, the good cops stand ready to assure us
that we are indeed morally superior to men, that in our sweetness
and nonviolence (read passivity and powerlessness) is our strength.

Women are understandably tempted to believe this comforting
myth. Self-righteousness has always been a feminine weapon, a
permissible way to make men feel bad. Ironically, it is socially
acceptable for women to display fierce aggression in their crusades
against male vice, which serve as an outlet for female anger without threatening male power. The temperance movement, which
made alcohol the symbol of male violence, did not improve the
position of women; substituting porn for demon rum won't work
either. One reason it won't is that it bolsters the good girl–bad girl
split. Overtly or by implication it isolates women who like porn or
"pornographic" sex or who work in the sex industry. WAP has
refused to take a position on prostitution, yet its activities—particularly its support for cleaning up Times Square—will affect prostitutes' lives. Prostitution raises its own set of complicated questions.
But it is clearly not in women's interest to pit "good" feminists
against "bad" whores (or topless dancers, or models for skin
magazines).

So far, the issue that has dominated public debate on the anti-
porn campaign is its potential threat to free speech. Here too the
movement's arguments have been full of contradictions. Susan
Brownmiller and other WAP organizers claim not to advocate
censorship and dismiss the civil liberties issue as a red herring
dragged in by men who don't want to face the fact that pornography oppresses women. Yet at the same time, WAP endorses the
Supreme Court's contention that obscenity is not protected speech,

a doctrine I—and most civil libertarians—regard as a clear infringement of First Amendment rights. Brownmiller insists that the First Amendment was designed to protect political dissent, not expressions of woman-hating violence. But to make such a distinction is to defeat the amendment's purpose, since it implicitly cedes to the government the right to define "political." (Has there ever been a government willing to admit that its opponents are anything more than antisocial troublemakers?) Anyway, it makes no sense to oppose pornography on the grounds that it's sexist propaganda, then turn around and argue that it's not political. Nor will libertarians be reassured by WAP's statement that "We want to change the definition of obscenity so that it focuses on violence, not sex." Whatever their focus, obscenity laws deny the right of free expression to those who transgress official standards of propriety— and personally, I don't find WAP's standards significantly less oppressive than Warren Burger's. Not that it matters, since WAP's fantasies about influencing the definition of obscenity are appallingly naive. The basic purpose of obscenity laws is and always has been to reinforce cultural taboos on sexuality and suppress feminism, homosexuality, and other forms of sexual dissidence. No pornographer has ever been punished for being a woman hater, but not too long ago information about female sexuality, contraception, and abortion was assumed to be obscene. In a male supremacist society the only obscenity law that will not be used against women is no law at all.

As an alternative to an outright ban on pornography, Brownmiller and others have advocated restricting its display. There is a plausible case to be made for the idea that antiwoman images displayed so prominently that they are impossible to avoid are coercive, a form of active harassment that oversteps the bounds of free speech. But aside from the evasion involved in simply equating pornography with misogyny or sexual sadism, there are no legal or logical grounds for treating sexist material any differently from (for example) racist or anti-Semitic propaganda; an equitable law would have to prohibit any kind of public defamation. And the very thought of such a sweeping law has to make anyone with an imagination nervous. Could Catholics claim they were being harassed by nasty depictions of the pope? Could Russian refugees argue that the display of Communist literature was a form of psychological torture? Would proabortion material be taken off the shelves on the grounds that it defamed the unborn? I'd rather not find out.

At the moment the First Amendment issue remains hypothetical; the movement has concentrated on raising the issue of pornography through demonstrations and other public actions. This is certainly a legitimate strategy. Still, I find myself more and more disturbed by the tenor of antipornography actions and the sort of consciousness they promote; increasingly their focus has shifted from rational feminist criticism of specific targets to generalized, demagogic moral outrage. Picketing an antiwoman movie, defacing an exploitative billboard, or boycotting a record company to protest its misogynist album covers conveys one kind of message, mass marches Against Pornography quite another. Similarly, there is a difference between telling the neighborhood news dealer why it pisses us off to have *Penthouse* shoved in our faces and choosing as a prime target every right-thinking politician's symbol of big-city sin, Times Square.

In contrast to the abortion rights movement, which is struggling against a tidal wave of energy from the other direction, the anti-porn campaign is respectable. It gets approving press and cooperation from the city, which has its own stake (promoting tourism, making the Clinton area safe for gentrification) in cleaning up Times Square. It has begun to attract women whose perspective on other matters is in no way feminist ("I'm anti-abortion," a participant in WAP's march on Times Square told a reporter, "but this is something I can get into"). Despite the insistence of WAP organizers that they support sexual freedom, their line appeals to the antisexual emotions that feed the backlash. Whether they know it or not, they are doing the good cops' dirty work.

October and November 1979

227

The Myth of the Powerful Jew

The Village Voice devoted considerable space to the crisis in black-Jewish relations touched off by the resignation of U.N. Ambassador Andrew Young in August 1979. In its August 26 issue the *Voice* published "Such Good Friends," by Joel Dreyfuss, who reiterated and elaborated on black leaders' criticism of the Jewish community. The following article, my response to Dreyfuss and other black critics, ran a week later. Since I wrote the piece on a four-day deadline, I've added a few points I would have included if I'd had an extra week or two to think.

"Anti-Semitism is the socialism of fools."
—AUGUST BEBEL, GERMAN SOCIALIST
AND LEADER OF THE SOCIAL DEMOCRATS IN
THE LATE NINETEENTH CENTURY

Obviously, the fury of black people at Andy Young's departure reflects a decade or more of increasing tensions between blacks and Jews. What is perhaps less obvious is how much the entire incident reflects deteriorating relations between Jews and non-Jews generally. Any useful discussion of black-Jewish conflict must begin by acknowledging two basic realities. One is that American Jews are white* and predominantly middle-class and so tend to have a white middle-class perspective on racial issues.

The other is that blacks are part of the gentile majority and so tend to share the misconceptions about Jews and the overt or unconscious anti-Jewish attitudes that permeate our culture. Unfortunately, neither group has been eager to accept its share of responsibility for the conflict. If Jews have often minimized their privileges and denied or rationalized their racism, blacks have regularly dismissed Jewish protest against anti-Semitism in the black community as at best oversensitivity, at worst racist paranoia. And in the end, guess who benefits from all the bitterness? Hint: the answer isn't blacks or Jews.

Blacks have repeatedly argued that black hostility toward Jews is simply the logical result of Jews' behavior, either as landlords, teachers, and other representatives of white authority in black neighborhoods or as political opponents of black goals. As a Jew who stands considerably left of the mainstream Jewish organizations, let alone neo-conservative intellectuals—and as a feminist who supports affirmative action for women as well as minorities—I don't think it's that simple. To attack a rip-off landlord with standard anti-Semitic rhetoric about greedy, exploitative Jews is to

* To be more precise, white Americans have generally classified Ashkenazim —Jews of European origin—as white, Jews have benefited from white privilege (though we have suffered from ethnic discrimination as non-Anglo Saxons), and it is probably accurate to say that most American Jews think of themselves as white. But as a number of readers—both Jewish and black— pointed out, the definition is questionable. Jews are a multiracial people and, as one correspondent put it, even among Ashkenazim "there are those of us who cannot fit the racial designation as white." (He described himself as dark-skinned and stereotypically Jewish-looking.) Several people suggested that while many Jews can pass as white, identifying with white people has been a way of internalizing our oppression, and that to be authentically Jewish we must embrace a nonwhite identity. I would say rather that since Jewishness is not a racial category—since, on the contrary, the definition of the Jews as one people is an offense to the very idea of pure races—to identify fully as Jews is to refuse to define ourselves in racial terms, to repudiate race as a way of categorizing people, and to oppose all institutions and practices that perpetuate racial hierarchies.

imply that the problem is the iniquity of Jews rather than the race and class of white landlords. (When blacks protest the behavior of white cops, who are rarely Jewish, they don't feel compelled to mention the officers' ethnic backgrounds.) Black criticism of Jewish politics invites the same objection. At worst Jews have been no more hostile to black power than the rest of the white population, though most people couldn't withdraw from the civil rights movement since they hadn't been involved in it in the first place. While the resistance of Jewish organizations to affirmative action has been to some extent based on fear of maximum quotas for Jews—and on the (illusory) hope that achievement and material security will protect us from anti-Semitism—it has more to do with the fact that most Jewish men share with most other white men the belief that affirmative action is illegitimate "reverse discrimination." In fighting community control, the Ocean Hill–Brownsville teachers were acting not as Jews but as white people whose livelihood was threatened. Besides, on all these issues a significant number of Jewish liberals and radicals has supported blacks and opposed the Jewish establishment. In general, though segments of the Jewish community have drifted to the right along with the rest of the country, Jews remain the most liberal group in the white population, far to the left of non-Jews in comparable economic and social circumstances. So why have blacks made such a point of singling out Jews for criticism?

As Joel Dreyfuss noted in last week's *Voice*, disillusionment is a factor; Jews have talked a better line and had a better record on race than other whites, and groups with a history of oppression are always supposed to be more sensitive to each other's aspirations, although, as James Baldwin put it, "if people did learn from history, history would be very different." The disillusionment is compounded when Jews invoke their status as an oppressed people to avoid confronting their racism (though blacks have committed the same evasion in reverse). It is also convenient and tempting to vent one's anger at a visible and relatively vulnerable minority. But the main impetus to black resentment of Jews *as Jews* seems to be that black people do not perceive Jews as vulnerable. Dreyfuss argues that the issue for blacks is Jewish power; he claims that "American Jews exert an economic, political, and intellectual influence on this country far out of proportion to their numbers" and repeats the familiar allegation that Jews dominate the media.

I would guess that this view is shared by a great many, if not most, non-Jewish whites as well as blacks. I think it is profoundly wrong. Jewish privilege is real; Jews certainly exert intellectual influence; but actual power is another matter. As business people, professionals, journalists, academics, Jews are in a position to further whatever interests they share (or think they share) with the rest of the white middle class or with the ruling elite. But the real test of power is whether Jews can protect specifically Jewish interests when they diverge from—or conflict with—the interests of non-Jews. If the United States government decides it is in America's economic and military interest to abandon Israel, do Jews have the power to prevent a change in policy? If there is a resurgence of anti-Semitism in this country, do Jews have the power to quell it and insure their survival? These questions are not hypothetical; America's Middle East policy is certainly changing, to the dismay of most Jews, and I experience more anti-Semitism (mostly from white people) than I did ten years ago.

If Jews have power, its sources are mysterious. Jews may own newspapers and movie studios, but the truly powerful own banks, factories, and oil. Jews have been virtually excluded from America's corporate and financial elite. There are few Jews at the highest levels of government or the military. As a tiny minority—3 percent of the population—Jews do not have the political clout of sheer numbers, except in a few heavily Jewish areas like New York. With the decline of the cities, Jewish influence has decreased; power to set national policy is now centered in the Southwest, hardly a Jewish stronghold, and the widespread anti–New York, antiurban sentiment that has fed the conservative backlash is aimed at Jews as well as blacks.

If Jews are "overrepresented" in certain privileged occupations, it is equally true that Jews' awareness of their vulnerable position and their identification with other oppressed groups have led them to get involved in liberal and radical movements "far out of proportion to their numbers." Yet Dreyfuss, so sensitive to Jewish influence in other areas, not only neglects to mention Jewish leftism but tries to write it out of history. In a bizarre attempt to blame the Jews for Roy Wilkins's and Whitney Young's break with Martin Luther King over the latter's opposition to the Vietnam War, Dreyfuss alleges that the rift "reflected [Wilkins's and Young's] dependence on Jewish support, since Jews strongly supported the U.S. presence in Vietnam." This charge is too absurd to deserve a response, but for the all too easily "forgotten" record, from the start Jews and Jewish organizations were virtually unanimous in their opposition to the war. Jews played a major role in the antiwar movement and the new left generally, and while George McGovern suffered the worst defeat in American electoral history, Jews voted for him 2 to 1. Such politics hardly reflect an uncritical identification with power. Nor do our increasingly conservative rulers share Dreyfuss's incognizance of Jews' leftist tendencies, though they are inclined to encode their distaste in euphemistic references to New Yorkers or intellectuals. Attacked from the left for being too well-off and from the right for being too left-wing, Jews lack even the contingent power of dependable political allies.

Jews are relatively well organized and vocal politically, but as with other well-organized minorities, their effectiveness has depended on the absence of any strong counterforce. It is ridiculous to imagine, as Dreyfuss apparently does, that the United States' Middle East policy is or ever has been dictated by Jews. Here he displays some confusion, since he also points out that Israel is "viewed in the Third World as a surrogate for Western interests" and faults Jews for once again choosing the wrong side. So which is it? Does America support Israel because of the Jews, or are Jews merely bolstering American imperialism? The reality is that until recently, Jewish pressure on behalf of Israel dovetailed neatly with the American government's political objectives. But Jews' stake in Israel and United States interests in the Middle East are by no means the same. Whatever our differences about the Israeli government, Palestinian rights, or American foreign policy, most Jews agree on the need for a Jewish state. The American government encouraged the establishment of Israel for power-political reasons (and perhaps as a way of dealing with the embarrassing problem of Jewish refugees no country was willing to absorb); it has continued to support Israel as a pro-Western, anti-Soviet ally in a strategically vital region. But in the past few years the U.S. has been reevaluating its stance, in line with changing political realities; as a result, Jewish lobbying has met increasing resistance. Despite supposed Jewish control of the media, coverage of the Middle East and the climate of public opinion have evolved more or less in accordance with government policy, growing steadily less sympathetic to Israel.

In general, the major media—including Jewish-owned institutions like the *New York Times*—reflect establishment politics, whether or not they coincide with Jewish interests or opinion. Evidently, either Jews are less dominant in the media than popular wisdom insists, or Jewish publishers and Hollywood producers put their class loyalties before their Jewishness. Dreyfuss complains that "Jewish dissidents in the Soviet Union enjoy a flood of publicity, but black dissidents in South Africa are ignored until they are killed." Can he seriously believe this bias reflects Jewish influence rather than government and corporate hostility to the U.S.S.R. and sympathy with the staunchly capitalist South African regime? He contrasts indifference to racism in television with the "uproar" that followed the casting of Vanessa Redgrave as a concentration camp victim. Yet the Jewish protest elicited no serious, thoughtful response, only condescending lectures about the evils of blacklisting and the right to criticize Israel. (I keep waiting for someone to notice that these days dumping on Israel is about as daring as defending the family, but no such luck.)

The danger of getting carried away with fantasies about Jewish power is manifest in Dreyfuss's assertion that "Jews have taken control of [New York City's] political apparatus. In the process of exercising their new powers they have neglected to appease the powerless. . . ." Just a minute. Who is this "they"? It certainly isn't me, or even the American Jewish Committee; it would seem, actually, to be one lone Jew, Ed Koch. (What about poor Abe Beame? He may not have been memorable, but he did exist.) In his zeal to pin blacks' troubles on the Jews, Dreyfuss not only makes a dubious leap from the particular to the general, he totally ignores the context of Koch's administration—draconian fiscal retrenchment imposed on the city from outside. Koch's brushing aside of minority concerns is indefensible (again, his whiteness, not his Jewishness, is the relevant category), but the people who really call the shots on New York are the president, Congress, and a bunch of bankers and realtors. I fail to see what Jews as a group are getting out of this depressing situation.

It is disingenuous of Dreyfuss to argue that "Jewish power in America has always been a difficult subject to address. . . . Their most effective tactic has been to attack any references to the power of Jews as 'anti-Semitic,' immediately blocking further discussion." Talk about blocking discussion! I can only pursue this one honestly if I'm permitted to say what I think, which is that the notion of Jewish power is a classic anti-Semitic myth. There are historical parallels to Jews' present position in America. In pre-Inquisition Spain, in Weimar Germany, Jews were a privileged and seemingly powerful group, a conspicuous cultural force. But their status did not protect them; on the contrary, charges of excessive Jewish power and influence in behalf of their own nefarious ends served as a rationale for persecution. Hence American Jews' feelings of insecurity, which—according to Dreyfuss—blacks find so mystifying.

Discrimination against Jews in America has not been comparable to the systematic, relentless bigotry inflicted on blacks. But in concluding that Jewish oppression can be defined as "exclusion similar in conception but vastly different in degree from the black experience," Dreyfuss makes a common mistake. Though there are obvious parallels between white racism and anti-Semitism—particularly racial anti-Semitism of the Nazi variety—the psychology of anti-Semitism, the way it functions in society, and the nature of the threat to the Jews are in certain respects unique. Unlike racism, anti-Semitism does not necessarily involve straightforward economic subjugation. Historically, Jews' distinctive class and cultural patterns, their visibility as representatives or symbols of authority (from the Harlem storekeeper on up the class ladder, but rarely at the very top), and their reputation as hustlers, achievers, intellectuals, and social activists have been the basis of anti-Semitic stereotypes used to justify attacks on Jews. Jews are simultaneously perceived as insiders and outsiders, capitalists and communists, upholders of high ethical and intellectual standards and shrewd purveyors of poisonous subversive ideas. The common theme of these disparate perceptions is that Jews have enormous power, whether to defend established authority or to undermine it. It is this double-edged myth of Jewish power that has made Jews such a useful all-purpose scapegoat for social discontent. The classic constituency for fascism is the conservative lower middle class, oppressed by the rich, threatened by the rebellious poor (particularly if the poor are foreign or another race); for this group Jews are a perfect target, since they represent the top and the bottom at once. Oppressed classes like the peasants in czarist Russia have traditionally directed their anger at the Jews just above them in the social hierarchy. Politically, the specter of the powerful Jew functions in much the same way as a foreign enemy: it invites warring classes, races, and political groups to submerge their conflicts and enjoy a heady sense of spurious unity.

The advantage to ruling classes of keeping Jews around as surrogate authority figures, outside agitators, and enemies of the people is obvious. But anti-Semitism can't be explained simply as a political tool; it is deeply irrational. The insane obsessiveness of Hitler's determination to wipe out the Jews even at the expense of his war effort was, in my view, not an aberrational form of anti-

Semitism but its logical extreme. I think anti-Semitism is bound up with people's anger not only at class oppression but at the whole structure of patriarchal civilization—at the authoritarian family and state, at a morality that exalts the mind, denigrates the body, and represses sexuality. It's no coincidence that a Jew, Sigmund Freud, was first to observe that "civilized" self-denial generates an enormous reservoir of unconscious rage. I believe it is this rage, along with misdirected anger at economic and political oppression, that erupts in the murder of Jews. In one sense, Jews *have* been immensely powerful: they created a potent myth—influential in both Christian and Islamic cultures—that explains patriarchal civilization and includes an elaborate set of rules for right living in it. And Jews themselves play a special role in this myth, as God the Father's chosen people, commanded to carry out an ethical and spiritual mission in behalf of the world—to obey God's laws and by doing so bring the Messiah, who will redeem and liberate us all. As the protagonists of this paradoxical vision, Jews are at once superego figures and symbols of revolution, who evoke all the ambivalent feelings that stem from the contradictions of patriarchy.

Just as the idealization of femininity is inseparable from male resentment of women, anti-Semitism is two-faced. It includes admiration of Jewish achievements, the idea that Jews are morally superior, guilt, and identification with the Jew-as-victim. The complementary attitudes inevitably follow: envy; the conviction that Jews are too powerful; a combination of special outrage and covert gloating whenever Jews are revealed to be, alas, morally imperfect (check out the reaction to any Jew judged guilty of unsaintly behavior, from Bernard Bergman to Menachem Begin); resentment at having to feel guilty about the Jews, it was thirty-five years ago, after all; a mixture of self-congratulation and defensiveness at daring to criticize Jews; anger at Jews who refuse to act like victims. (An article on the Vanessa Redgrave flap pointed to her acceptance of the inmate's role as evidence that anti-Zionism and anti-Semitism are not synonymous. On the contrary, Redgrave exemplifies a mentality that has flourished ever since 1967, when Israel became the prime metaphor for the powerful Jew: she hates Bad Jews—Zionists—and loves Good Jews—victims, preferably dead.) But the power of Jews as emotional symbols would mean little if they were not hugely outnumbered and so, in reality, powerless. It is the combination that makes anti-Semitism so appealing: to kill a gnat, imagining it's an elephant, is to feel powerful indeed.

I think people's feelings about Jews are largely unconscious, that discrimination and outbreaks of anti-Jewish persecution are only the most obvious symptoms of a chronic social disease that exists mainly under the surface. This is why anti-Semitism flares up so readily in times of social crisis; it is why Jews feel permanently insecure; it accounts for the gap in communication between Jews who feel that gentiles are oblivious to the threat of anti-Semitism and gentiles who think that Jews are always looking for anti-Semites under the bed. Anti-Semitism involves dark impulses that most people would rather not recognize in themselves, impulses connected with our deepest guilts and anxieties. Even people who are sophisticated about the politics of race and sex tend to cling to a simplistic view of anti-Semitism as plain old discrimination, punctuated from time to time with persecution by evil lunatics—in either case, nothing to do with *them.* There is enormous resistance, even among Jews, to analyzing anti-Semitism as a serious, ongoing social force or to recognizing the anti-Jewish subtext in superficially reasonable political arguments. A lot of Jewish alienation has to do with the subterranean character of anti-Semitism. Suppose your friends and colleagues were always having fits of selective amnesia, during which they insisted that what you clearly remembered was your imagination. Eventually you would begin to question your reality: What's going on? Am I crazy? Is she doing this to me on purpose? By means of a similar process, Jewish "paranoia" about anti-Semitism often becomes paranoia in fact.

Black people who scapegoat Jews for white racism and exaggerate Jewish power are collaborating in a familiar and scary game.

That black leaders should blame Jews for Andy Young's resignation is not surprising, but the evidence doesn't bear them out.
Jews, who can add two and two like anyone else, could not fail to
note that Young's meeting with Zehdi Terzi was consistent with
the noises the administration has been making for some months. It
is Carter's policy Jews care about, not Young—a point Jewish
spokespeople have taken care to emphasize. If Carter starts talking
to the PLO, Young's dismissal won't gain him any Jewish support;
if he doesn't, Young's retention wouldn't have lost him any. (And
what about black support? Carter's decision to get rid of Young
may well have cost him reelection.) Besides, Jewish organizations
are hardly unaware of black-Jewish tensions. As subsequent events
have shown, it was not in their interest for Young to resign, and
most of them pointedly refrained from suggesting it. Did Carter
act to appease the Israeli government? I doubt it—I think the
Israelis understand that Carter is their problem, not Young—but if
he did, it was in behalf of American diplomacy, not the Jews.

I don't know why Carter let Young resign instead of slapping
him on the wrist. Maybe it was just what it looked like—that in
arranging to talk with Terzi and then lying about it, Young took
his individualism a step too far and convinced the president he
couldn't be trusted. Maybe not. The affair still has its loose ends,
particularly the question of whether, as Murray Kempton plaus-
ibly suggested, Young is taking the rap for a meeting that was
actually the State Department's idea. But there is disturbing irony
in the fact that (Jewish-dominated media notwithstanding) blacks
have succeeded in defining the issue as Jewish power. Given the
energy crisis and the general economic malaise, Americans may be
more than normally receptive to the idea that Jews have been
controlling our foreign policy. If Carter plans to move significantly closer to the PLO (and anyone who thinks such a move
would reflect solicitude for the Palestinians, as opposed to solicitude for oil, is less cynical than I), it can't hurt him to have anti-
Jewish sentiment floating around.

Behind the furor over Young lurks the larger issue of how relations between Jews and blacks, Jews and gentiles, blacks and whites affect and are affected by the Israeli-Palestinian conflict. Dreyfuss draws clear battle lines: Jews, white racists, and imperialists for Israel; blacks for the Palestinians, as victims of racist colonialism. But he leaves something important out of this picture —or cartoon—and that something is anti-Semitism (a semantically unfortunate term since Arabs are also Semites). Middle East politics would be a lot less confusing and agonizing if anti-Zionism and anti-Semitism were, as so many people want to believe, entirely separate issues. Which is to say that things would be a lot simpler if the Israelis weren't Jews. But if anti-Semitism is, as I have argued, a systemic and pervasive pathology endemic to Christian and Islamic cultures (and, I would imagine, easily communicable to any patriarchy), then anti-Semitism is as much a factor in the Middle East as oil, the military importance of the region, the Palestinians' demand for a homeland, and anti-Arab racism. Anti-Semitism is an actual or potential influence on the conduct of the United States, the Soviet Union, Europe, the United Nations, the Arab countries, and the Palestinians themselves. (Overt anti-Semitism has never been as widespread or severe in the Islamic world as in the Christian West. But since World War II, the Arabs have been using explicitly anti-Jewish propaganda, borrowed from Europe, as a weapon against Israel, and anti-Semitic policies have resulted in a massive exodus of Jewish refugees from Arab countries; "oriental" Jews, largely from the Middle East and North Africa, are now a majority of the Israeli population.) Fear of genocidal anti-Semitism is a determining influence on Israeli policy, far more decisive, I believe, than expansionism, racism, or the fanaticism of religious nationalists. Without anti-Semitism there would still be a power struggle between the West and the Third World, but the Israeli-Palestinian conflict would not exist, since there would be no political Zionism and no Jewish state.

Anti-Zionism, in the modern political sense, is the argument that a Jewish state in Palestine inherently violates the rights of the Palestinian people. It regards Zionism as a racist, imperialist movement in which the European Jewish bourgeoisie (Jewish power, again) acted in concert with the colonial powers to displace the indigenous Arabs, furthering white Western domination of the Middle East. It assumes that religious belief is the movement's ideological rationale, and so the PLO calls for the abolition of the Israeli state in favor of a "democratic, secular" Palestine. The essential problem with this argument is that it ignores or denies the reality of the Jewish condition. First of all, to get around the fact that the Jews also have historic ties to Palestine, that they are not simply aliens and interlopers, anti-Zionists tend to define Jewishness purely in terms of religion and dismiss as mythology the idea that Jews around the world are one people. Thus Yasir Arafat's insistence that there is no contradiction between defining Palestine as an Arab state and guaranteeing equal rights for "Arabs of the Jewish faith." But Jews have always regarded themselves, and been regarded by others, as an organic entity, in some sense a nation; a traditional excuse for anti-Semitism has been that Jews have divided loyalties. Jews from Arab countries consider themselves Jews, not Arabs of the Jewish faith. Nor is political Zionism basically a religious movement. Orthodox Jews who believe in the biblical prophecies are Zionists by definition, but they did not conceive of Zion in political terms—indeed, many opposed the establishment of a Jewish state as sacrilegious. The movement for statehood came from "emancipated" Jews who believed that Jews would always be oppressed so long as they were homeless and forced into marginality in gentile societies. Zionism is a national liberation movement,* and despite the rise of religious nationalism and a powerful religious establishment that (like the Catholic

---

* This term does not quite fit, though it comes closer than any other; as usual, the Jewish experience confounds standard categories. "National liberation" is generally understood to involve an indigenous people's struggle to free themselves from foreign domination. Zionism, as a movement to gather a dispersed, oppressed people and recreate an independent territorial national entity, had no real historical or conceptual precedent, though it was heavily influenced by European nationalism.

Church elsewhere) has imposed some religious laws on an unwilling majority, Israel is essentially a secular state.

As for the charge that Zionism is an imperialist plot, it does not simply misdefine the Jews but makes them disappear. Imperialism involves migrating or extending one's influence from one's own country to another. But Jews in the nineteenth century had no country; they were aliens everywhere. Though anti-Zionists are fond of referring to Western Jews as "Europeans," the Europeans themselves took a rather different view of the matter. In any case, the relationship between Zionists and the Western nations has always been tense and ambiguous; they have served each other's needs, but their needs are very different. The Zionists ended up having to fight Britain as well as the Arabs. And the Jews who settled in Palestine after World War II were neither ambitious capitalists nor Zionist ideologues; they were traumatized refugees who were unwelcome anywhere else. Some years ago, I asked a woman who supported the PLO if she thought Jews had no right to national aspirations. Not at all, she assured me, so long as their nation wasn't on someone else's land. Which set me to musing about possibilities. The Sahara Desert? The Amazon Jungle? Imagine what would have happened if the Zionists had accepted Britain's offer of a homeland in Uganda. There is enormous and painful irony in the fact that the only conceivable way for Jews to lay claim to a piece of land was for one group of nations to force us on another. But the aspect of this irony that anti-Zionists consistently refuse to face is what it says about the world's attitude toward Jews. In a way, what the PLO and the Arab nations are demanding is their equal right to treat Jews the way nations have always treated us—that is, to deny us the right to exist on our own terms, rather than on sufferance.

As far as I'm concerned, the only solution to the Israeli-Palestinian impasse that makes moral sense is two independent states. Whatever one's intellectual position on Zionism—that is, the idea that all Jews should settle in Israel—Israel's existence as an alternative has clearly reduced Jewish vulnerability and, I believe, is a psychological deterrent to anti-Semites. The abolition of Israel and the incorporation of a Jewish minority in an Arab-dominated Palestine would at best put all Jews back in a pre-Holocaust situation, and for the Israelis the reality could be far worse. It is questionable whether all Israelis would be allowed to remain as equal citizens; the PLO's charter, which defines as Palestinians only Jews who lived in Palestine before "the Zionist invasion," is not reassuring on this point. And is the mutual hatred of all these years expected to just evaporate? But practically speaking, these questions are irrelevant, because the Israelis will defend their state until they are massacred or driven out. In which case the world will no doubt blame them for being stubborn.

Another difficulty with the idea that anti-Zionism has nothing to do with anti-Semitism is that the great majority of Jews perceive the two issues as inseparable. One might argue, with equal logic, "I'm not a racist, I'm just against forced integration," or "I love women, it's feminists I can't stand." Vanessa Redgrave may think that Zionism is "a brutal racist ideology" and "the opposite of Judaism," but she will find precious few Jews who agree with her. This puts her in the peculiar position of implying that except for an enlightened minority, Jews are brutal racists, and that she knows what Judaism is better than we do. Which is why her ritual tributes to Jews' heroic record of struggle, and so on, are not only empty but obnoxious. As most Jews see it, the Israelis' right to national self-determination would be taken for granted if they weren't Jewish. The Palestinians have the same right, of course. What makes the Middle East situation so excruciating is the spectacle of two displaced, oppressed peoples, each of them victimized by more powerful nations, trying to kill each other. But at this point in history, absolute justice for the Palestinians would mean absolute injustice for the Jews.

My guess is that most *Voice* readers have no quarrel with this last point. Anti-Zionist thinking predominates in most of the world, but here it has been mostly confined to the sectarian left. Nearly everyone agrees, in principle, on Israel's right to exist. Yet

I feel that non-Jews in America—particularly my peers, middle-class liberals and radicals, the vanguard of "enlightened" opinion—do their own milder version of making the Jews disappear. In theory, they acknowledge that Jews are oppressed. In practice, they see Israel much as Dreyfuss sees the Jews—as a powerful nation beating up on the have-nots. They assume that Israeli chauvinism, expansionism, and refusal to admit the justice of the Palestinian cause are primarily or entirely to blame for preventing a settlement. But a two-state compromise can work only if the international community supports and enforces it, and the international atmosphere is overwhelmingly hostile to Israel. Most countries endorse the PLO's claim to all of Palestine; if it weren't for the United States, Israel would be long gone. And now American support is eroding.

In this situation the Israelis are damned if they do and damned if they don't. If they resist a Palestinian state, they stand condemned as oppressors and obstructionists and give their only major ally an excuse for withdrawing support. If they agree, the Palestinians with their own state as a base will be in an infinitely better position to pursue their claim to what they deeply believe is theirs, and the Israelis have no good reason to believe that anyone will lift a finger to defend them. Is it any wonder that they resist what has got to look like suicide by installments? Why should they trust the PLO to accept a state as more than a temporary expedient? Why should they trust the United States, when no country has ever proved trustworthy in its dealings with Jews? The American ruling class is profoundly anti-Semitic; it is not going to protect Israel for humanitarian reasons, any more than it was willing to provide a haven for Jewish refugees during World War II or "waste" a few planes to bomb Auschwitz. Under the circumstances the self-righteous, simplistic condemnation of Israel that currently passes as a "balanced view" is, in my opinion, anti-Jewish. Many aspects of Israeli government policy, including its alliances with reactionary regimes, disturb me enough to make me wonder if in its determination to survive Israel will lose its reason for being. But at least I can recognize desperation when I see it; at least I can understand—no, share—the bitterness that says, "To hell with morality and world opinion! World opinion never did a thing for the Jews!"

The Israelis are in the classic Jewish bind. To the Palestinians and the Third World they are white oppressors, but to their fellow white oppressors they are Jews. If they are surrogates for the West, it is largely in having to pay for Western sins. For once, the West may end up paying as well; Dreyfuss is probably right, "History is on the side of the 'have-nots,' here and abroad." But no matter whose side history is on, Jews have always been expendable. And so long as we are expendable, to talk of "Jewish power" is obscene.

August 1979

My Podhoretz Problem—

and His

Mention Norman Podhoretz to a radical, or even a liberal, and chances are the response will be something like "*That asshole! I can't take him seriously!*" Chances are also that the vehemence of the dismissal will belie its content. The left's reaction to *Breaking Ranks: A Political Memoir* has been no exception; the general tone was captured best by Nicholas von Hoffman in *New York*, going on at vituperative length about how boring and inconsequential Podhoretz is. Anyone so hated by people who insist he doesn't matter must be hitting a nerve. And in fact, Podhoretz hits nerves all the time, with what he says and what he blurts, who he is and who he purports to be. He gets under radicals' skin in the way a William Buckley never can because he could so easily be one of us; he comes from the same impolite, urban middle-class milieu, long on brains and (relatively) short on wealth, inclined to bloody fights rather than elegant debates, imbued with left-wing assumptions. Like many leftists, Podhoretz is Jewish; also like many leftists, Jewish or not, he has relied on verbal braininess as his chief means of getting on in the world. He purports to be, among other things, an intellectual. Yet despite his occupation and his manifest engagement with ideas, he has always impressed me as far more visceral than cerebral. The power of his writing to anger or, conversely, to evoke the superior eye-roll depends largely on its subtext. On some level Podhoretz is usually raising a basic question: is real freedom desirable, or even possible? For the past decade his answer has been an aggressive and passionate no. Since his message often comes packaged in frenetic exaggeration and dubious logic, he is an easy target. But because radicals are not nearly so sure of their own answer as they pretend, he makes them nervous.

Though radicals would prefer to dismiss it as the reflex piggery of a self-satisfied elite, neo-conservatism is a politics of reaction in the literal as well as the political sense—a response to the failures and weaknesses of the left. The major figures in the neo-conservative camp, most of them self-proclaimed liberals, many of them ex-socialists, developed their formative ideas in the wake of the old left's worst trauma—its confrontation with socialism according to Stalin. As a distinctive politics, neo-conservatism crystallized at the end of the sixties, about the time the new left collapsed into sectarian dogmatism and nihilistic violence. Like the rest of the crew, Podhoretz keeps bringing up the embarrassing fact that Marxist revolutions have produced not free societies where workers control their lives but dictatorships that deny both political and personal liberty. He insists that capitalism, with all its imperfections, is the only alternative to tyranny. Yet for all his democratic rhetoric, he is hardly a libertarian. What appalls him about the sixties and post-sixties left is not just its Marxism but its cultural and above all its sexual radicalism. It is in fact this animus, or anyway its intensity, that most clearly marks him as conservative rather than liberal. As Peter Steinfels points out in his book, *The Neoconservatives* (a fine piece of analysis, of the non-eye-rolling, know-your-enemy genre), there is a muddle in the neo-conservatives' logic—the free market they defend erodes the authority of the family, religion, and government, creating the "adversary culture" they deplore. But this contradiction masks a deeper one.

Why is it that as soon as people have any real choice in the matter, they start rejecting authority? Could it be that they are asserting a fundamental and legitimate need for freedom? That's what I think; Podhoretz takes for granted that authority is necessary to civilized life. Stripped to basics, our argument is not unlike the one I've always had with my father, now retired from his anomalous (for a Jewish liberal) career as a New York City cop. His experience convinced him that people are basically antisocial and will do anything they can get away with. That, finally, is the quarrel conservatives (whatever they call themselves) have with radicals, who supposedly believe that we are, or can be, capable of building a society that functions without police.

The irony is that by this standard, most radicals aren't. Though I don't know any radicals who admit to liking police, the left has been at best ambivalent about freedom. Most leftists cling to the assumption that economic inequality is the root cause of oppression, though a class analysis alone clearly cannot account for the perversion of socialism, or the persecution of Jews, or the oppression of women. During the seventies the left has moved steadily to the right on cultural issues. Leftists regularly disparage concern for feminism, gay rights, sexual liberation, and personal freedom as frivolous or even reactionary. They may blame rampant "narcissism" on capitalism, while Podhoretz blames it on radicalism, but the effect is the same. Part of this unholy alliance between the neo-conservatives and their enemies comes down to plain sexism—men defending their right to police women. But there's something else. Authoritarian culture is all we know. Somewhere in most of us—if not in all of us—is the fear that freedom can only mean trouble.

Radicals tend to hide that fear; Podhoretz acts it out in public, more loudly and nakedly than anyone else. Foolish as he often is, he hits my nerves. When I fight with neo-conservatives in my head, it's Podhoretz I have in mind, not Irving Kristol. And in one way or another I've been fighting with him ever since the late sixties, when *Commentary* published a piece of mine after much editorial wrangling over whether its subject, Bob Dylan, could possibly be as important as I thought. In certain ways I empathize with Podhoretz; I'm Jewish and ambitious, and just as he used his intellectual skills to get out of Brownsville, I've used mine to stay out of the kitchen. The differences—that I am a woman, have never been poor, belong to another generation (younger both chronologically and culturally)—are more crucial, and so we've ended up on opposite sides. Still, when I argue with him, I'm also arguing with myself; over the years my father told a lot of gruesome stories.

Similarly, Podhoretz's revulsion against radicalism is the measure of his attraction to it. In the early seventies, when I retreated from the wars to a small town, I spent a lot of time in the library, reading *Commentary*'s attacks on the movement. This was not just an exercise in masochism. *Commentary* seemed to be the only place I could find something I badly needed—a sustained, impassioned discussion of What Went Wrong. The magazine was as obsessed with the subject as I was, no easy feat. Nearly a decade later, Podhoretz is still obsessed. *Breaking Ranks* is not a neoconservative manifesto, except by the way. The prologue describes it as "my odyssey to radicalism . . . the whole story of how and why I went from being a liberal to being a radical and then finally to being an enemy of radicalism in all its forms and varieties." Just as Satan takes over *Paradise Lost*, this more modest epic is dominated by its villains—the hydra of Stalinism, the sirens of the "new sensibility," the "voices like snakes and beetles and rats" (in Norman Mailer's words) that shredded Podhoretz's confessional book, *Making It*.

That Podhoretz is fascinated by radicals I knew, but it startled me to read that he sees himself as an ex-radical who "played a not inconsiderable part" in launching the movement. During the sixties I thought of him as a liberal with a certain sympathy but a greater skepticism toward the left, and it never occurred to me that he might think otherwise. "When I wrote *Making It*," he claims, "I still considered myself a member, and even in some sense a leader, of the radical movement." That sentence drove me back to *Mak-*

ing It to see if I'd missed something. I hadn't. The book is full of insights about the American class system, but it never suggests that the iron law of capitalism, screw or be screwed, might be other than eternal truth. In *Breaking Ranks*, Podhoretz most often uses the word "radical" to mean "extreme" or "bold" or to describe any position outside the liberal and/or Cold War consensus. He comes closest to a coherent viewpoint in discussing his enthusiasm for Paul Goodman's ideas, and I find it particularly interesting that it was cultural radicalism—Goodman, Norman Mailer, Norman O. Brown—he responded to. But though I'm willing to take his word that Goodman in some sense converted him, the conversion never sounds quite real. At the start of his odyssey he is defending marriage and middle-class life against the beats' "refusing to grow up and settle down"; suddenly he is fed up with the fifties gospel of maturity and resignation, eager for change, talking about the "pathologies of American life." The best he can do for an explanation (characteristically, he offers it in behalf of the entire culture as well as himself) is to cite Robert Nisbet's crack that boredom is the most neglected force in history. But the answer begs the question—boredom is already a form of rebellion. What was Podhoretz rebelling against? Had our national pathologies infected *his* life? Did his endorsement of Goodman's sexual radicalism reflect any change in his sanguine view of marriage? He doesn't say; perhaps he doesn't know.

Nevertheless, Podhoretz claims to speak with the authority of the disaffected insider. *Commentary*'s antimovement broadside was effective, he argues, because "We knew the radical world of the '60s at first hand and in all its aspects." In other words, since Podhoretz was born too late to slay Stalinist dragons in the thirties, he is determined to cast himself in an updated version of that role. But what he actually knows at first hand is the much narrower world of liberal and radical intellectuals. His solipsistic notion that *Commentary* and the *New York Review* were at the center of the sixties universe leads him to rewrite history. Unfortunately for his pretensions to leadership, he was born too early. He has never understood the most distinctive aspect of sixties radicalism—the generational culture that created it.

Podhoretz scoffs at the idea that what happened in the sixties was a rebellion of youth; the conflict, he argues, was "a political one cutting across all age groups on an axis of social class and ethnicity." Well, yes—the white left and counterculture consisted mostly of upper-middle-class WASPs and Jews, some of whom were rumored to be over thirty. But the energy for the revolt, and much of its content, came from the specific, collective experience of the generation born between (approximately) 1940 and 1950. We were, as the Port Huron Statement put it, "bred in at least modest comfort"; since we never had to worry about survival, we were naive enough to be daring (and smug). We absorbed mass culture—advertising, neon, comic books, TV, the endless array of consumer goods—before we were old enough to think about it. The expanding economy transformed us from adolescents—an age group—into teen-agers—a market, which then became a culture based on self-conscious protest against adult authority, especially in regard to sex. And rock-and-roll expressed it all. Name any target of the radical movement—corporate liberalism, the old left, the bureaucratic university, the family, conventional sexual morality, rationalism (not the same as rationality, though the distinction was often fudged)—and behind it was the specter of "mature" respectability. It wasn't a matter of refusing to grow up and settle down but of refusing to equate one with the other. Among older people, feelings about the movement split sharply along class and ethnic lines, but countercultural attitudes and styles gradually spread to young people throughout the class structure. (Oddly, Podhoretz refers to the fact that McGovern "barely carried a majority of young voters" as if it supported his argument; given how McGovern did with the rest of the electorate, it seems a clear refutation.) Nor was sixties youth culture synonymous with radicalism; in many ways it was just a newer and more sophisticated adaptation to the system. Which is why, despite the conservatism of recent years, American culture has changed irrevocably.

Podhoretz recognizes this; he observes (as usual overstating the case) that if the movement is dead, "it died as much because it won as because it lost. Its attitudes and ideas are now everywhere." But he doesn't hear what he's saying. He argues that the "new culture" was nothing new, but merely the latest version of what Lionel Trilling had called the "adversary culture"—the anti-bourgeois, antiliberal, anti-American attitudes, of both the left and the right, that intellectuals had absorbed from modern literature. The only thing that made the counterculture different was "its unprecedented size and influence." This is like saying that the Atlantic Ocean is no different from Walden Pond, except that it has more water. That the counterculture was a mass phenomenon, rather than a tiny band of dissidents, changed the whole meaning of bohemia. Most counterculturists identified to some degree with the attitudes and ideas of the "adversary" tradition. yet the fact that bohemianism had become such an attractive choice (with all the money floating around in the sixties, it involved little if any real sacrifice) tended to undermine those attitudes, and the sheer numbers of people involved inevitably diluted the ideas. An important reason for the counterculture's relative indifference to intellectual and literary values—one of Podhoretz's big complaints—was that so many of its members were not intellectual or literary. The cultural lingua franca for sixties dissidents was not literature but a mass art—pop music. And it was precisely this aspect of the counterculture, its expansion way beyond a small intellectual elite, that made radicals hope they could actually change the society, as opposed to tossing spitballs at it from the sidelines.

With this hope in mind a substantial faction of the counterculture dissented from the literary antibourgeois perspective. As many of us saw it, literary culture reflected certain class values—basically, those of the European aristocracy—and disdain for mass culture was rooted in class snobbery. We rejected the idea that mass art was either inherently corrupt or inherently inferior to "high" art. Rather, it had its own set of aesthetic principles that derived from its American bourgeois origins. At its best, we felt, it had radical implications; it expressed the libertarian, democratic impulses that capitalism encouraged but could not satisfy. What we loved most about rock was the way it made disparate groups connect—hippies, bikers, artists, high school kids, college kids, soldiers, even (sometimes) whites and blacks.

As this view implies, we argued that capitalism had its positive side, that American society was not just a vast sinkhole of oppression, and that radicals who despised America were indulging the most reactionary sort of class bias—an argument that, ironically, had much in common with the thesis of *Making It*. Certainly the new culturists I hung around with were more sympathetic to the book than Podhoretz's peers, including his friends. (According to *Breaking Ranks*, the private reaction to *Making It* was even worse than the public one; Trilling actually urged him not to publish it.) Like Podhoretz, we admired Mailer's *Advertisements for Myself* and were impatient with prissy moralizing about the bitch goddess. Besides, Podhoretz's governing idea, that *Making It* should embody its subject—should be, in his words, "a Mailer-like bid for literary distinction, fame, and money, all in one package"— appealed to our sense of how mass culture worked. But because of our interest in the aesthetics of celebrity, we could have told him something about why his bid did not come off: Mailer was a genius at the art of image making, while Podhoretz had much less feel for it than the average two-year-old.

When *Making It* came out, Richard Goldstein, who was then editing a counterculture magazine called *US*, conceived the idea of running a Classic Comic version of the book and asked me to write the scenario. The project never got done, but I still have my scenario—a mix of satire and affection, aimed less at Podhoretz's ideas than at his exasperating yet endearingly vulnerable egotism and (re his quarrel with James Baldwin, "My Negro Problem," and so on) filled with crass jokes about Jews and blacks that don't sound so funny anymore. I guess you could call it a bid for truth, catharsis, and laughs, all in one package. It was this sort of spirit that informed radicals' fascination with pop culture, which

Podhoretz can only see as a plot against literature and intellectual standards and as further evidence of the low level of radical thought. While he accuses the movement of contempt for nuance, he doesn't hesitate to mangle distinctions himself. He ignores or plays down the differences between the counterculture, the organized radical left, and the reformist new politics movement, assumes that *New York Review* writers represent all three tendencies, then ignores the differences among the writers themselves. In the apparent belief that radical intellectuals (and by extension all radicals) have one head, which can be cut off with a single but thorough stroke, he castigates us for two directly opposing sins. First, he charges that while we pretended to be disinterested idealists, and therefore uniquely qualified to run the country, what we really wanted was power. At the same time, those of us who did criticize radicals for confusing their class biases with highminded literary values are accused of subordinating art to ideology.

This is not to deny that the movement had an antiintellectual current, whose central theme was that intellectuals are an elite, hence inherently or at least presumptively reactionary. A lot of radical writers, including me, were bothered by the contradictions in our role. Here we were, trying to create a movement that would abolish class hierarchy, yet we were middle-class, had elite literary educations and the privilege of access to the media, and often used that privilege to criticize the movement. If part of our uneasiness was honorable—a rejection of the lie that we were disinterested idealists—part of it was nothing more than the unadmitted desire to escape our marginality. Like left-wing Jews who take refuge in universalism, we wanted to blend in with "the people." (A breast-beating antiwriting remark of mine, which Podhoretz quotes—without attribution, much to my relief—was provoked by an editor's attempt to compliment my writing by distinguishing it from what he saw as mindless activism.)

That desire was futile and wrong-headed; every movement needs critics, class-biased or no. But Podhoretz ought to be less self-righteous on this point, since he so obviously wants to escape his own marginality by blending in with the establishment. He argues that intellectuals should support American capitalism because communism proscribes intellectual freedom and the left is hostile to it; that Jews should support the system because Israel's security depends on American protection and because the left has promoted anti-Zionism, anti-Semitism, and egalitarian notions that threaten Jews' relatively privileged status. But capitalism needs critics too, and Podhoretz's view of Jewish interests ignores a basic dynamic of anti-Semitism: in "protecting" Jews, ruling classes set us up as substitute targets for the anger of the oppressed. I don't think Podhoretz admits to himself that neither Jews nor intellectuals can ever really make it, no matter how privileged they may be. On the contrary, from his rhetoric one would think that radical intellectuals are (or for a time were) immensely powerful and that his own decision to embrace the system was a brave rebellion. This view depends heavily on the premise that the Upper West Side is the world. But it allows Podhoretz to reconcile his personal contradictions, to retain a sense of himself as an iconoclast while succumbing to his need to identify with authority.

For me the most interesting questions posed by *Breaking Ranks* have to do with the psychology of backlash. Why did Podhoretz feel called upon not merely to reject the left, but to make a career of repudiating radicalism itself, "in all its forms and varieties"? He is not much more forthcoming on this subject than on why he became a radicaloid in the first place; he refers to some sort of religious illumination that clarified his thinking, but with frustrating and unaccustomed reticence omits the details. Otherwise he offers platitudes: sixties radicals confused politics with religion; they blamed all problems on the state instead of the human condition or their own failings; their pursuit of unattainable messianic aims inevitably led to nihilism. Radicalism, he concludes, is a "spiritual plague" motivated by self-hatred posing as selfless idealism. As a healthy alternative, he proposes the frank pursuit of one's material interests; like Adam Smith and Charles Wilson, he is confident that this approach best serves the common good.

If Podhoretz were simply arguing that the sixties left tended to substitute millennial fantasies for concrete political goals, or that it craved instant solutions to enormously difficult problems, we would have no argument. But what he really wants is to remove large areas of human behavior from political scrutiny and contention. Any interest that is not narrowly economic is to be regarded as "spiritual," therefore to be pursued privately if at all. This distinction allows Podhoretz to dismiss the issues cultural radicals raise by defining them as nonissues and calling the people who raise them nasty names. His urge to abandon rational argument for invective, which prowls through the pages of *Breaking Ranks* like a restless guard dog, finally breaks loose in the epilogue. The chief targets here are women's liberation and the gay rights movement, which Podhoretz sees as the inheritors of sixties radicalism and proof that the plague has not yet run its course. Advocates of these causes are "women who do not wish to be women" and "men who do not wish to be men." Like the beats before us, we want to avoid growing up and taking on the responsibilities of parenthood. Our self-hating rejection of our biological natures has destroyed our will to reproduce; the birth rate falls while the abortion rate rises. Our "identification of sterility with vitality" links us to—what else?—"the new narcissism of the Me Decade."

Other objections aside, this tirade is a tangle of inconsistencies. It would appear, after all, that feminists and militant gays have been doing what Podhoretz, in another context, endorses—pursuing their interests. True, these interests are not just economic, but they are not nebulously spiritual, either. Faced with such indubitably secular demands as women's insistence that men share child care, or homosexuals' desire to be openly gay without fear of punishment, Podhoretz suddenly discovers the need to transcend individual selfishness—an imperative he seems to equate with having children, as if there were no other way to connect with the race. At the same time he argues that our demands really reflect the most profound sort of self-rejection. (Not for us the crude strategy of disguising self-hatred as idealism; we have hit on the far more diabolical scheme of disguising it as self-interest.) He does not try to show that we are wrong, that the present system of relations between the sexes is indeed the inevitable and desirable expression of sexual differences. Nor does it occur to him that this very system—which sets up an excruciating conflict between the demands of motherhood and the rewards of a full life outside the home—might have something to do with the falling birth rate. He simply condemns our benightedness as if it were obvious to all right-thinking people. (This attitude is characteristic of neo-conservative writing on sexual politics. Even when Midge Decter devoted an entire book to the subject, she constructed her argument by asserting certain traditional ideas about men and women as self-evident fact, then analyzing feminists' motives for denying reality.) Refusal to grapple with basic questions about sex seems an odd stance for an intellectual—unless, of course, he's afraid of the answers.

In a way Podhoretz is right—there is a spiritual issue at stake in cultural politics, and it does have to do with self-hatred versus self-acceptance. But it's a bit more complicated than he thinks. Self-hatred can masquerade as radicalism; I know, for instance, that somewhere in my rebellion against the prescribed feminine role lurked a secret hope of escaping femaleness altogether. That sort of self-hating hope comes from accepting the oppressor's world view; it is really the very opposite of radicalism. Yet in the rebellion was a deeper self-love, a refusal to submit to a false and limiting definition of who and what I was. Antifeminist women play out their own version of this conflict. What could be more self-hating, for a woman, than to oppose legal abortion or a constitutional ban on sex discrimination? And yet there is a self-affirming impulse in such protest; it says, in effect, "If this is what being a woman means, I'm going to be the best woman you ever saw!"

The trouble with the conservative brand of self-acceptance is that it is alienated: it requires identifying with an externally imposed definition of oneself, which means not only lying on Procrustes' bed but kissing his ass. I think Podhoretz is trapped by an external definition, by the role of the poor Jewish kid whose advancement and, in a sense, survival depends on getting straight A's and impressing everyone in sight. In *Making It* he wrote eloquently about the acculturation process, but he has never really faced how deep it goes or how unjust it is. Reading *Breaking Ranks*, I was struck by how relentlessly he sees himself through other people's eyes, through their praises and betrayals. As a result, the tone of the book is somewhat sour, for there have been fewer praises and more betrayals than Podhoretz feels he deserves. The dirty little secret *Making It* didn't tell (because the author didn't know it?) was that Podhoretz's hunger for approval is more central to his character than his hunger for money, power, or fame.

Podhoretz doesn't understand why his New York intellectual "family," whose approval he probably wants most, punished him for celebrating success, while they let Norman Mailer get away with it. His theory is that he is more honest, that unlike Mailer he refuses to undercut his unpalatable truths with "the reassuring gesture, the wink of complicity." With some justice he accuses Mailer of playing the fool, "free to speak the truth to the king, but only because, being a fool, he need not be taken seriously." Yet the key to Podhoretz's problem is not in Mailer's foolery but in his own earnestness. *Advertisements for Myself* said that by God, we want it all and ought to grab it. *Making It* said that if we learn the rules of the game and play it very well, they'll let us have a taste. Mailer is id, Podhoretz superego; Mailer plays the macho outlaw, Podhoretz the respectable husband; Mailer lusts for gold, Podhoretz for gold stars. If Mailer is, as Podhoretz calls him, "the bad boy of American letters," Podhoretz is the good boy forever lecturing the bad boys that if they continue playing hooky they will come to grief. Naturally, the bad boys kick the shit out of him (with an extra kick or two because they're afraid he's right); they don't realize that when he lectures he is trying to convince himself. There is more than a little Mailer in Podhoretz (as there is more than a little Podhoretz in Mailer). But he won't face down the gorgon of authoritarian culture and ask what manner of beast it is, why we should do its will. Instead, he announces his return from an odyssey that barely had a chance to begin.

December 1979

Part Three

Next Year in

Jerusalem

Next Year in Jerusalem

In the spring of 1975 my brother Michael, then twenty-four, was on his way home from his third trip through Asia when he arrived in Israel, planning to stay a few weeks before heading back to New York. On April 28 he wrote to our parents: "I've been staying at, of all things, an Orthodox Jewish yeshiva—when I got to Jerusalem I went to visit the Wailing Wall and got invited they hang around there looking for unsuspecting tourists to proselytize. It's sort of a Jewish Jesus-freak type outfit—dedicated to bringing real Judaism to backsliding Jews. I haven't been especially impressed by the message, but it's been a really interesting week." On June 4 he wrote me, "I've had my lack of faith shaken."

I appreciated the ironic turn of phrase. Then its meaning hit. I read on: "I've read and talked about it enough to realize that the arguments for the existence of G-d (a spelling which shows how superstitious I'm becoming)—and the Jewish version of it at that —are very plausible and intellectually if not emotionally convincing. . . . It's frightening, because while I can convince myself of the possibility and even probability of the religion, I don't like it—its 613 commandments, its puritanism, its political conservatism, its Jews-first philosophy. On the other hand, if it is the truth, not to follow it means turning your back on the truth." He was postponing his return till the end of July.

I called my parents. My mother thought I was being an alarmist —Mike couldn't be serious about religion; it was too removed from the way he'd been brought up. "He's spelling God 'G-d,' " I said. There is a religious law that you cannot destroy paper on which you have spelled out "God."

Two weeks later they got another letter: "I haven't written because I'm having trouble describing what's happening. I feel more and more that I'm trapped into a religion whose truth I can't deny. . . . I've never given much thought to the existence of G-d—my LSD experiences had (same as with Ellen) left me with the idea that there was 'something' there, but I never thought it was knowable or explainable (& if it was explainable certainly more in terms of mystical experience & Buddhism than the 'G-d of our Fathers' of Judaism). But my time here has really forced me to come to terms with what that 'something' might be. . . . I'm not Jesus-freaking out—I haven't come to this through any blinding moment of illumination or desire to be part of a group—it's been an intellectual process (which I've been fighting emotionally all the way), and I'd like nothing better than to reject it—I just don't think I'll be able to.

"The final shock in this letter is that I may not leave here at the end of July. If I accept this as the truth, I have to take time to learn about it."

The "truth" Mike proposed to accept was Judaism in its most extreme, absolutist form: the God of the Old Testament exists; He has chosen the Jewish people to carry out His will; the Torah (the Five Books of Moses and the Oral Law elaborating on them) is literally the word of God, revealed to the Jews at Mount Sinai; the creation, the miracles in Egypt, and other biblical events actually happened; the Torah's laws, which are based on 613 *mitzvos* (commandments) and govern every aspect of one's existence, must be obeyed in every detail; they are eternal, unchangeable; Conservative, Reform, and other revisionist versions of Judaism simply reflect the regrettable human tendency to shirk difficult obligations.

My parents had the same first impulse: "Let's go to Israel and bring him home." My father was already out of his chair and about to leave the house to go buy plane tickets when they looked at each other and decided they were overreacting. My own reaction was a kind of primal dread. In my universe, intelligent, sensible people who had grown up in secular homes in the second half of the twentieth century did not embrace biblical fundamentalism —let alone arrive at it through an "intellectual process." My brother was highly intelligent, had always seemed sensible. What was going on?

My father is a retired police lieutenant; my mother is a housewife. They married during the Depression and now live in a house with a paid-up mortgage in a modestly middle-class section of Queens, New York. They are college-educated, literary-minded, and politically liberal. I am the oldest of their three children; my sister, a graduate student in linguistics, is in the middle; Mike is the youngest. Mike and I were born in December, nine years apart almost to the day. The coincidence of birthdays is one of many similarities. If the prospect of Mike's becoming an Orthodox Jew was frightening, it was not simply because he was my brother, someone I loved. I felt an almost mystical identification with Mike. Our baby pictures were identical, and though Mike was now taller and thinner than I, we had the same fair skin, curly brown hair, and astigmatic, sleepy green eyes. We were (not that I really believed in that stuff—still—) cliché Sagittarians: analytical, preoccupied with words and ideas. We were inclined to repress feelings; our intellectual confidence coexisted with emotional insecurity and a tendency to depression.

I was fascinated with the notion that Mike was what I might

have become had I been a man, the last born instead of the first, a child of the seventies rather than the sixties. I wondered how much the differences between us had to do with our circumstances rather than our basic natures. For there were differences, of course. Mike was much more reserved than I; he rarely talked about his feelings, his problems, or his relationships. I was more worldly, more willing to compete in and compromise with a hostile system. My friendships were central to my life; he was, or seemed to be, a loner.

The qualities we shared were more pronounced in Mike, the opposing tendencies more hidden. Next to him I always felt a bit irrational and uncool. Picture a recurrent family scene: my father and I are sitting in the kitchen, having a passionate political argument. My brother is listening, not saying a word. Suddenly I put myself in his place, become self-conscious. I hear all the half-truths and rhetorical exaggerations that in the emotion of the moment I have allowed to pass my lips. I realize, with chagrin, that my father and I have had, and my brother has listened to, the same argument at least half a dozen times before. I am sure Mike thinks we are ridiculous.

I was disturbed and mystified by what I saw as my brother's swing from a skepticism more rigorous than my own to an equally extreme credulity. How could anyone familiar with the work of a certain Viennese Jew possibly believe in God the Father? What puzzled me even more was Mike's insistence that he was being reluctantly convinced by irresistible arguments. It seemed to me that his critical intelligence could only be in the way.

On acid I had, as Mike observed, experienced the *something* that Westerners have most commonly called "God"—the source of all truth, beauty, goodness. Unlike Mike, I had felt that I knew what it was. "So this is what it's all about," I had marveled. "It's so simple, so obvious. And I've known it all the time. I just didn't know I knew." But when I came down it was less obvious. The ecstasy—a word that didn't quite convey a feeling as natural as a spring thaw, as comfortable as coming home—gradually slipped away. "All God is," I would try to explain, "is reality—the simple, wonderful reality behind the abstract concepts and ingrained habits of perception that keep us from ever really experiencing it." And I would sound hopelessly abstract even to myself. Soon, whatever clouded the doors of perception in ordinary life began to invade my acid trips as well. I tried to fight that process—doggedly pursuing the right mood, the right situation—and only made things worse; finally, frustrated and demoralized, I stopped tripping. The entire experience had a permanent, profound effect on the way I saw myself and the world. I knew that connecting with Reality—I couldn't call it God; to me that word meant an old man with a white beard—was the crucial business of life, the key to freedom, sanity, happiness. I knew that if I could make the connection I would think: "How silly of me to have forgotten!" But I didn't know how to proceed.

This problem was not, of course, peculiar to me. It had been plaguing spiritual seekers for thousands of years. Many had tried, far more eloquently than I, to express what they agreed was inexpressible. Recognizing the inadequacy of intellectual analysis, religions tried to evoke the crucial connection through myths, rituals, rules of conduct. But in the end religion, like language, tried to express the truth in concrete form and so inevitably distorted it. If all religions were inspired by a common Reality, each reflected the particular cultural, political, and psychological limitations of the people who invented and practiced it. Which posed another problem. If you understood that your religion was only an imperfect approach to the truth, you remained outside it, an observer, a critic. If, on the other hand, you truly believed—worshiped an omnipotent God, accepted Jesus as your savior, surrendered to a guru—you were confusing a set of metaphors for reality with Reality itself. And that put you back on square one. Or did it?

On my second acid trip I had had a joyous vision of the birth of Christ. In one part of my mind I had become an early Christian, experiencing the ecstasy of grace, redemption, the washing away of sin. But on a deeper level I had remained aloof, thinking, "Remember, you are a Jew." For the first time I had had a wistful inkling of what it must be like to be committed to a powerful myth. Maybe if you had faith that Jesus would save you, He would. Maybe the point was simply to stop listening to that observer-critic inside my head, to surrender my will, to have faith, and what I had faith in didn't matter any more than whether I took a train or a bus to my destination.

"Suppose you had faith in Hitler?" my observer-critic, that irrepressible crank, could not help objecting. Still, part of what had messed up my acid trips was doubt, whispering like the serpent: What if the straight world is right, and what you think is Reality is a seductive hallucination? I couldn't assent to the experience without reservation, following wherever it led; it might lead to insanity. So I tried to compromise. I wanted to tap the ecstasy whenever I wanted and be "normal" the rest of the time. It was, I suppose, the same impulse that makes sinners go to church on Sunday, with much the same result.

I was aware of the link between my skepticism and my Jewishness. It was, after all, the Jew who was the perennial doubter, the archetypal outsider, longing for redemption while dismissing the claims of would-be redeemers as so much snake oil. But what did any of this have to do with the kind of Jewishness my brother was talking about?

Mike had grown up into the economic and cultural slough of the seventies. Though he had always been an excellent student, he had never liked school; he had found college as boring and meaningless as high school and elementary school before that. Since graduating from the University of Michigan in 1970, with a B.A. in Chinese, he had spent nearly half his time traveling. Recurrent asthma had kept him from being drafted. Between trips he would come back to New York and drive a cab to make money for the next trip. He had never had a job he liked. During his last stay in New York he had begun writing articles about Asia, and he had gone back with the idea of doing more. He had had a few pieces in newspapers, but no major breakthrough, and one major disappointment: an article he'd worked hard on was first accepted by a magazine, then sent back.

Mike was also depressed about Cambodia and Vietnam. In 1973 he had spent almost two months in Cambodia and had come away convinced that as much as the people hated the corrupt Lon Nol government, they did not want the Americans to leave and permit a Communist takeover. As Mike saw it, they wanted to be left alone to farm, while the Khmer Rouge made them take sides and shot those who chose incorrectly; they were religious Buddhists, while the Communists were antireligious and would make young men work instead of becoming monks; in short, they wanted to return to their traditional, prewar way of life, which the Communists would permanently destroy. Those premises had led Mike to what seemed an unavoidable conclusion: the Americans should not withdraw. For someone who had shared the American left's assumptions about the war, it was a disturbing reversal. If he had been wrong about Cambodia, he thought, perhaps he had been wrong about Vietnam. This past fall, a return trip to Cambodia and two weeks in Vietnam had reinforced his doubts.

When Mike arrived in Jerusalem, he had been traveling for seven months. He was going home to uncertain writing prospects, another cab job or something similar, no close friends, isolation in a political atmosphere that took for granted the assumptions he had discarded, and a general ambience of postcounterculture aimlessness. It took no great insight to suspect that what traditional Judaism offered—absolute values to which Mike could dedicate his life; a new and exciting subject to study; a close-knit religious community; a stable, secure social structure—was considerably more attractive. Anyway, I didn't believe that people ever made profound spiritual changes for purely intellectual reasons; there had to be feelings Mike wasn't acknowledging. Not that this proved anything about the validity of Judaism. A believer could argue that Mike had been drifting because he hadn't found God, that his unhappiness was, in fact, God's way of leading him to the truth. Still, I worried that he was succumbing to an authoritarian illusion in an attempt to solve (or escape from) his problems.

In answer to my request for more details Mike sent a seven-page, single-spaced typed letter. I chewed it over, making notes in the margin. Much of it was devoted to debunking evolution. The marvelous complexity and interdependence of everything in the universe—so the argument ran—show planning and purpose and could not have come about through the random process of natural selection. Plants and animals are perfectly constructed machines; the brain has been compared to a computer. When you see a computer, your obvious conclusion is that someone built it according to a plan. ("Rampant anthropomorphism!" I scribbled.) Every detail of creation is purposeful. For example, ready-to-eat fruits (like apples) have tempting, bright colors; vegetables that require cooking (like potatoes) are drab. ("What about toadstools?") No one has ever seen a mutation that changed one species into another. How does evolution explain something like a poisonous snake, whose survival advantage depends on a combination of traits, each useless alone? Did its poison come first, and did it then wait around millions of years for the ability to inject—or vice versa? And why did creation stop; why aren't new things constantly coming into being? ("Human chauvinism!" I wrote. "Who says creation stopped—new life forms take eons—we can't even see plants grow.")

As for the God-given nature of the Torah, when you study it in Hebrew, along with the commentaries that have been written on virtually every word, it is hard to believe that such depth and complexity could have been achieved by human beings; Judaism is such a restrictive religion that the Jews would never have accepted it if the entire people hadn't witnessed the revelation; biblical prophecies predict the Jewish exile, the return to Israel, and other historical events. The prophecies were impressive, I had to admit: "Ye will be torn away from the land whither thou goest . . . and G-d will scatter you among the nations. . . . thou wilt find no ease and there will be no resting place for the sole of thy foot. . . . And then G-d thy G-d will return . . . and gather thee together. . . ." And so on. I began to get a headache.

Finally, my brother came to the subject I had been anticipating and dreading: women. Orthodox Judaism enshrined as divine law a male supremacist ideology I had been struggling against, in one way or another, all my life. It was a patriarchal religion that decreed separate functions for the sexes—man to learn, administer religious law, and exercise public authority; woman to sanctify the home. For Mike to accept it would be (*face it!*) a betrayal. Already I had had the bitter thought: "You want to go back in time, find a community where mama will still take care of you. You're just like the rest." Under the anger was fear that my sense of special connection with my brother was an illusion. *If I were a man . . . if he were a woman . . .* there was an unbridgeable gap in that *if.*

From a secular viewpoint, Mike conceded, Judaism gave men the better deal, but from a religious viewpoint it wasn't so clear. For one thing, God-fearing men, though they had the power to oppress women, would not do so. And if our purpose on earth was not to do interesting work or have a good time but to come close to God, then women had certain advantages: they had fewer commandments to perform, fewer opportunities to sin, and by having children could approach God more easily.

"Power to oppress is oppressive," I wrote in the margin. "Power corrupts the saintliest man. Exemption from responsibilities is implicit insult." Yet I realized that, after all, my objections were beside the point. This God, if He really existed, had chosen to create a hierarchy of sexes. Doubtless He had some purpose in mind, some spiritual test, perhaps a lesson in conquering pride. It might seem unfair, but it had to be for the best in the end . . . and I could never believe in such a God, never, it violated my surest sense of what Reality was about. When you connected there were no hierarchies, divisions, roles; all that was part of the husk that fell away. "I am the vanguard of the revolution!" I had shouted, high on acid, climbing up a mountain trail followed by two men who were truly my equals, our battle-of-the-sexes fright masks discarded somewhere down the road. There would be misunderstandings later, but that was another story.

No, I couldn't believe in the Jewish God. He had been invented by men seeking a rationale for their privileges. He had been invented by people seeking to reduce an ineffable Reality to terms they could understand—to a quasi-human "creator" with a "plan" and a "purpose," standing outside the universe and making it the way a carpenter made a table.

In August my parents visited Mike in Jerusalem. He was still living and studying at Yeshivat Aish HaTorah. A yeshiva is a school where Jews study Torah; this one also functioned as a small religious community. It occupied modest quarters—a communal study room, a few classrooms, a library, an office for the rabbi— in the Jewish section of the Old City; several nearby apartments served as dormitories. Aish HaTorah (the name means "Fire of the Torah") is an English-speaking yeshiva headed by Noach Weinberg, a rabbi from New York. Most of its students—there were around twenty-five at the time—were young Americans; most had been tourists passing through. Mike was taking courses in Chomesh (the Five Books of Moses), the Mishna (the written codification of the Oral Law), *halacha* (Jewish law), biblical Hebrew, and "48 Ways to Gain Knowledge" (talks by the rabbi on Jewish ideas about learning). His weekday schedule began at 7 in the morning, with an hour of prayer before breakfast. Ordinarily, he had classes and study hours from 9 to 1, then lunch and twenty minutes of afternoon prayer, classes and study from 3 to 7:30, dinner, evening prayer from 8:30 to 9, and more classes till 10. He usually studied till around 11:30. During mother and dad's visit he was taking some time off in the afternoon and evening.

My parents had both, in their individual ways, been struggling to come to terms with Mike's "conversion." My mother considered herself in some sense religious; she believed in God, even believed that the Torah might be God-given. But she couldn't see that God required us to observe all those regulations. Wasn't it enough to be a good person? Characteristically, she focused on practical concerns. Was Mike happy? Would religion give him what he badly needed—something satisfying to do with his life?

My father was the son of an Orthodox rabbi, but for all his adult life he had equated rationalism and religious tolerance with enlightenment. Clarence Darrow, defending Scopes and evolution against Bryan and the fundamentalist know-nothings, had been his intellectual hero. To have a child of his reject those values was a painful shock. But he had been forced by his respect for Mike's mind—and no doubt by the logic of his own belief in tolerance—to reexamine his attitudes. He went to Jerusalem prepared to listen.

The trip was reassuring. Mike seemed happier, more relaxed, more sure of himself. He was enjoying his studies. "He was different," my father told me. "There was a step up in emotional vibration. I'd never seen him so enthusiastic before." I remained skeptical; Mike's enthusiasm might be some sort of manic facade. I was still working on my reply to his long letter, debating whether to mention my qualms about his motives. From one point of view Mike was doing something incredibly brave, even heroic: in quest of truth as he saw it he was breaking with the values and assumptions of his family, his peers, American society, and the entire post-Enlightenment West. For me to bring up psychology would be to add whatever clout I had to the enormous pressure of conventional wisdom that Mike was probably having trouble enough resisting. And then there was my old religious question: even if Judaism confused its central metaphor with absolute truth, would it work for Mike if he believed? Judaism, I reminded myself, was a spir-

271

itual discipline that had been practiced for over three thousand years; psychotherapy had existed for less than a hundred, with inconclusive results.

For three years I had been seeing a Reichian therapist. I was seeking relief from specific emotional problems, but my larger spiritual problem lurked in the back of my mind. What, after all, were emotional problems but forms of—or metaphors for—disconnection? The Reichian method is based on the premise that muscular tensions hold back repressed emotions which the therapist can elicit by attacking the bodily "armor" directly, bypassing the treacherous intellect. I believed this approach worked; it had helped me a lot. Yet I could claim no miracles, only that I had come—slowly, undramatically—to feel better, see more clearly. For all I knew, my brother would get further with Judaism.

Still—suppose Mike was really being trapped, not by arguments but by his emotions? Suppose by bringing up my worries I could help him—by which I meant save him. For despite my theoretical conviction that we all had to seek the truth in our own way, I hoped, with guilty passion, that Mike would get off this particular path, would wake up one morning, ask, "What am I doing here?" and come home. I decided to say what I had to say. For me, Freud was far closer than Darwin to the heart of the matter.

THE MIRROR

In America most of the time I was unhappy and bored. I couldn't find what I wanted to do or people I wanted to be with. You were supposed to be very hip and inside I wasn't. I didn't identify with hip people or enjoy being around them. I couldn't figure out where I fit in. Traveling was my escape. I would go through a lot of rottenness and boredom for the sake of some periods of happiness—experiences that really took me out of myself, like trekking in the Himalayas.

When I came to Israel from Jordan I was very tired out and I wanted to go home. I didn't have much money left. There was a girl I really wanted to go back and see though I had no reason to believe she would want to see me. I was really homesick. But I felt a responsibility to see something new. I went with the guy from the yeshiva looking for an interesting experience. Reb Noach gave me the usual pitch: "Stay here a week, if you haven't seen a yeshiva you haven't seen Israel." We had a big political argument —I said things looked bad for Israel and the only reasonable thing to do was give back the occupied land and make peace. We had a talk about the moral imperative proof of God. Reb Noach asked where I got my concept of good. I said, "From my parents."

That week I realized Judaism was much more interesting than I'd thought. When I read Jewish philosophy I realized my mind was Jewish. I felt that for the first time I had found people who thought the way I did, who were really logical and consistent. But the idea of God was very alien to me. Then I read a pamphlet about Torah and science. I started reading the arguments about evolution. Suddenly I had a flash: "This whole theory is ridiculous!" It had a tremendous effect. I felt that my mind had been playing tricks on me. I'd been accepting this theory without really looking into it—just like Cambodia. Logically, you knock down the theory of evolution and you're stuck with—God created the world.

I left to do some traveling and went to Safed. I was sitting down looking at a map and two English guys, students of this Hasid who was up from Tel Aviv for the weekend, invited me to meet him. I went and we started talking. He had pure charisma. I related to Reb Noach as a good person, but this Hasid was someone with power. He said that people go all around the world looking into this and this and they know it's not true—then they're hit with Judaism and they leave because they're afraid it's true. It had a big effect on me because of my realization about evolution and because I'd been asking myself why I was leaving. I knew I was scared to stay and check it out.

The English guys kept telling me there were no coincidences, it wasn't an accident that I was there at the same time the Hasid happened to be visiting. I started getting scared—was all this really true? I felt lousy about myself. I had always prided myself on being open-minded. Now I had no logical reason for leaving, just an emotional desire to go home. I felt totally wiped out.

When I got back to the yeshiva I started reading Torah with the Hersch commentaries. There was a daily Chomesh [Five Books] class. I was learning some Hebrew and could feel the power of the Torah much more than in translation. And the prophecies— I kept trying to find arguments against the prophecies and couldn't come up with any.

After two or three weeks I was in doubt—what was I going to do? One day I was reading the prophecies at the end of Dvarim [Deuteronomy] and I had this cold shiver—I realized that I really believed all this. My first reaction was to compromise—I would go home, read, then decide. Or I would take a few years and travel and then come back. Finally I realized my whole life would have to change.

The first time I went to Southeast Asia I had a lot of asthma trouble. I'd almost feel like I was having a heart attack. Sometimes my pills wouldn't work and I was afraid they would just stop working. When I got into religion I realized—how can I expect a pill to work? God controls what goes on. Your life can be snuffed out at any moment. That had a strong part in keeping me here. It wasn't that I started believing in God to conquer a fear of death. Intellectually believing doesn't do that anyway. But I realized I couldn't compromise and say two years from now I'll come back, because there's no assurance of anything.

I went and canceled my plane ticket. It was painful. I was afraid my family would reject me, think I was crazy. My mind was telling me one thing. My emotions still wanted to go home.

Around Thanksgiving, Mike came to New York for a month. Seeing him was a relief. His skullcap and newly grown beard made him look less boyish, but he was still wearing jeans. I felt no

distance between us, no sense that he was in any way not himself. I
hugged him, wondering if the Orthodox prohibition against men
touching women they weren't married to applied to sisters.

Mike stayed with our parents. So that he could observe the
dietary laws, mother bought him his own dishes and silverware
and pots, boiled her cooking utensils and took them to a *mikva*
(ritual bath), cleaned the oven and left it on at the hottest setting
for two hours, served him kosher food, cooked him meat and dairy
dishes separately in the new pots. Mike prayed three times a day,
said blessings over his food and grace after meals, washed his hands
on rising in the morning and before eating bread. Since the complicated Sabbath laws could be fully observed only in an Orthodox
environment, he spent weekends with religious families.

He had been home several weeks when we had The Talk. We
had already had a number of talks, but it was this one that sank in.
We were having lunch at a kosher cafeteria on Forty-seventh
Street, patronized largely by Hasidim and other ultra-Orthodox
Jews in the diamond business. It was crowded with men in traditional black suits. I was insisting that it was impossible to prove the
existence or the nature of God. The ultimate Reality was by definition ungraspable by reason; Mike's belief had to be based on
intuition, not logic.

"It's both," Mike said. "First, you have to have an intuition that
logic is real—that logic tells you something about the way the
world is. Then if an idea is illogical—if it's inconsistent with what
you know—you intuitively know it's wrong. Like the complexity
of the world is inconsistent with the idea that it all happened at
random, by natural selection."

"Not necessarily. In an infinite universe, even the most unlikely
combination of events can happen—"

"It's possible. But it's not *probable*. And when you take all the
proofs together—the depth of Torah, the prophecies—maybe you
can explain any one of them away, but you can't explain them *all*
as coincidence. It just gets too improbable. Reasoning can tell you
what's most probable, and when you have an overwhelming probability, your intuition tells you it has to be true."

"Well, my intuition tells me the world wasn't created in six days."

Mike explained that the length of the six days of creation was open to question, since the sun wasn't created till the fourth day; that there was no problem with the idea of a biological evolution guided by God rather than natural selection, or of humanlike beings existing before Adam, so long as you accepted Adam as the first true man in the spiritual sense—made "in the image of God." I was struck by the way he argued. He sounded like me in the early days of feminism, talking to women who were unconvinced. It had been one of those rare times when I felt both sure of my ground and sure it was in the other person's interest to see things my way. That confidence had made me a good organizer; now, on the receiving end, I felt defensive.

I wasn't sure why. I did not find Mike's antievolution argument persuasive, but I was not, in any case, a dogmatic evolutionist. On acid I had had the strong impression that it was somehow in the nature of Reality to ceaselessly order itself into complex patterns; even before that, I had been inclined to believe there was some unknown organizing principle in the universe. Once I had confessed to a friend, "I don't think the universe is absurd." "You don't?" she said. "No. I think it's basically logical." There was a pause. "Maybe," my friend said, "you *need* to see logic in it." Maybe, maybe not. Either way, there was no need to assume a God with a personality, a will, or a purpose.

"But it's possible," Mike said. "You have to admit it's logically possible."

"It's based on a naive analogy. A chair is made by a person, so the world has to be made by a superperson."

"You're assuming the secular view of reality—that we created God, not the other way around. The Jewish perspective is like a mirror image. It's not God who's like a human being; it's human beings who are made in God's image. Our way of making things is *something like* God's way. We don't get the idea of God from having parents—our relationship with our parents is meant to give us an idea of how to relate to God."

"Reality isn't a being with a personality," I said. "It's just—Reality."

"You had a mystical experience that showed you there's a spiritual reality. Judaism says that on top of this experience, which all religions share, we have a revelation that tells us what that reality is, what it wants from us."

"The idea that it *wants* something contradicts my experience," I insisted.

"Not your experience. Just your interpretation of it."

"But I didn't interpret it. I just had it. That's what made it unique."

"Of course you interpreted it. You've grown up with a whole view of reality that says we're free, we can do what we want. So naturally you see God as something impersonal, instead of a God who says, 'You have to do what I want, not what you want.' "

I shook my head, but I felt the presence of the serpent. Had I experienced Reality or just another deceptive metaphor?

"I don't do whatever I want," I said. "I try to do what's right."

"But you decide what's right."

"Not *me*, not my ego. The part of me that's attuned to Reality decides. Reality defines what good is." Pretty mushy, my observer-critic remarked.

"All right. But in practice you don't really believe that you're required to live a certain way. Except for obvious things, like not killing. Judaism says God gave us a law, this is what it is, we have to obey it."

"I believe," I began, aware that I was entering a mine field of rhetoric, "I feel I *know*, from my—experience"—*or was it just an interpretation*—"that when we're in touch with Reality, what's right and what we really want are the same. To love and be loved, to have a just, decent society. To figure out how to make that truth work in practice—to struggle toward it—that's what life is about. Freedom isn't doing whatever we please; it's a basic ethical value. It means taking responsibility for the struggle. Not looking to some authority to get us off the hook."

"But it doesn't work. Look at what's happening in the world;

look at what Western 'enlightenment' has accomplished. Total chaos, and it's getting worse."

It was the classic conservative line. Your utopian dreams are unrealistic, against human nature. Look at the evidence. Bloody wars; repressive governments; nuclear threat; ecological destruction. And what revolution—be honest, now—what revolution has really succeeded by your standards? I was on familiar terms with this litany. Though I considered myself a radical, had been a leftist and feminist activist, I struggled perpetually (again) with doubts. And if I believed, finally, in my obligation to defy a pessimism that amounted to self-fulfilling prophecy—what was that but a leap of faith?

"In a Torah community," Mike was saying, "there's no crime, the family isn't falling apart. People are serious about being good people because they're living for God, not just themselves."

"Intuitively, I can't see it," I said. "This cosmic dictator idea of God. I just don't see it."

"But you have to ask why. There are powerful emotional reasons for not seeing it. You'd have to admit that God controls your life, that you're not free. You'd have to submit to a lot of restrictions you don't like. You'd have to *change*. No one wants to change."

True.

"You have an incredibly complex and organized universe. Everything in it works together perfectly. The most obvious explanation is that a creator planned it that way. Everyone intuitively saw that—everyone believed in God—until evolution gave them an excuse not to. Or take the prophecies. You can explain them as a bunch of improbable coincidences, but why resist the obvious answer—that they come from God, who knows the future?"

"It was the Bible predicting the return that gave the Zionists the idea in the first place," I objected.

"But it would never have happened if it weren't for the Nazis," Mike said. "Another coincidence?"

I had no answer. The prophecies had bothered me from the start. And Mike had a point: why was it so important to me to explain them away? During my first session with my Reichian shrink he had poked my jaw muscles and asked drily, "Do you ever lose an argument?" With a shock I saw that I wasn't winning this one. Mike's premises were not only far more sophisticated than I had thought; they were the basis of a formidably comprehensive, coherent world view. All along Mike had been asking me questions I couldn't answer. How did I explain the creation of the world? How did I explain the strange history of the Jews—their unremitting persecution and unlikely survival; their conspicuous role in world affairs? How did I explain the Torah itself, with its extraordinary verbal intricacy, the meanings upon meanings the rabbis had found in phrases, words, even letters; the consistency with which their analyses hung together after the fifteen hundred years or more that they had spent hunting down contradictions? I knew that "comprehensive and coherent" did not necessarily mean "true." "I don't know" was an honorable answer. But it did not win arguments.

I was suffering from acute mental vertigo. What a phony I was—glibly assuring Mike that his transformation had to be based on intuition rather than mere argument, while all along my confidence in my own intuition had rested on the assumption that I had the better arguments. The last thing I wanted was to be left with only fragile, fallible intuition as a shield against a system of ideas that neatly reversed everything I believed. Like a mirror image.

I understood now what Mike had meant when he said he felt trapped, understood how his skepticism could turn against itself. My own skepticism told me that however sure I was of my perceptions, I could be wrong. Therefore, since I could not prove Judaism was false, I had to admit that it could be true. And the thought of admitting any such thing threw me into a panic. Which of course was the best possible evidence for Mike's suggestion that I rejected Judaism simply because I did not care to accept it. I wanted nothing so much as to forget the whole question, and for that very reason I was bound by all my standards of intellectual honesty and courage to pursue it.

I was overwhelmed with superstitious paranoia. This was exactly how Mike had been drawn in, Mike who was so much like me. Mike was the one person in the world who could have gotten me to listen seriously to this argument. And he had stopped off in Israel mainly because of me: I had been there earlier that year, with a group of journalists, and had written him that it was interesting. From his point of view none of this was coincidental.

During the next few days my panic intensified. The one aspect of my life that I had never seriously doubted was my obligation to make my own choices and my own mistakes and, if need be, suffer the consequences. Since the only certainty was that the way to Reality was uncertain, I had no alternative. Now I saw that this certainty was as uncertain as any other. And so for the first time I faced a choice that was truly absolute, that included no tacit right to be wrong—the spiritual equivalent of a life-or-death decision in war. If the Jewish God existed and I willfully rejected Him, I would be making the ultimate, irretrievable mistake. Contrary to the common impression, Jewish theology included a system of reward and punishment that operated in both this life and the next. The eternal punishment for rejecting Torah was called *karait*—"cutting off"—which meant, I assumed, what I would call total alienation from Reality. Only it was much more vivid and terrifying when you envisioned it as a punishment rather than an impersonal consequence, as losing the love, incurring the wrath of the ultimate parent.

And if I gave up my precious freedom, a renunciation that felt like death, for what I saw as an alien, joyless, shackled existence—and it turned out that the serpent had betrayed me again, that there was no God of Wrath or God of Love after all? And how could I ever know for sure? It seemed to me that whatever I did I was in trouble.

I had shed another layer of innocence. I would never again feel smug about Patty Hearst, Rennie Davis, the legions of postacid freaks who had joined mystical cults. I understood. It could happen to me. For the first time I wished I had never taken drugs, never seen beyond the scientific rationalism that might be narrow but was surely safe. I envied my father's faith in evolution. I envied everyone around me, going peacefully about their lives, taking for granted—if they thought about it at all—that Mike's brand of religion was eccentric fanaticism, nothing to do with them. I especially envied non-Jews. The 613 *mitzvos* were reserved for the Chosen People. Others had only to obey certain basic moral laws—mostly obvious things, like not killing.

I had frustrating conversations with friends who found it hard to believe that someone so sensible and intelligent could be wondering if she ought to become an Orthodox Jew.

"Maybe it's right for him; that doesn't mean it's right for you."

"If it's true, then it has to be right for me."

"You couldn't live that way."

"That's not the point. The point is, is it true?"

"Maybe it's true for him."

"You don't understand. Judaism claims to be absolute truth. Either it's true for everybody, or it's not true at all."

"Nobody has a monopoly on the truth."

"That's the secular point of view. From the Jewish point of view there *is* an absolute truth, I *can* know it, I just don't want to accept it."

"Well, why should you accept it if you don't want to?"

"Because if it's true, then all my ideas are wrong, I'm living the wrong way, I'm totally blowing it."

"Who's to say there's only one way to live?"

"*But don't you see?* You say, 'We're free to decide how to live.' Religious Jews say, 'No, you're not free.' So you say, 'We're free to reject that argument.' It's circular reasoning!"

"Why are you getting so upset?"

Then I talked to a woman who understood. She had grown up Catholic and lost her faith. It seemed that losing your faith and losing your lack of faith had much in common. At some point you were suspended between two competing, self-consistent realities, knowing you had to go back or forward, with no one to help you and no net. And once you were out there, you realized that skeptic and believer were mirror images, reflecting a vision of logic in the universe.

Judaism teaches that God's rewards and punishments operate on the principle of *mida k'neged mida*—"measure for measure." For example, a friend of Mike's had asked to borrow 100 Israeli pounds; Mike had lent the money, but grudgingly; shortly afterward he had 100 pounds stolen from his wallet, though there was more money in it. He had no doubt that the two events were related.

During my panic I had become obsessed with the thought that this principle might explain a central irony in my own life. I had come of age at a time when sexual liberation did not yet mean groupies and massage parlors, when it was still a potent metaphor for liberation in general. At the core of my feminism was rage at the suppression of female sexuality and a romantic vision of sexual freedom as joyous, unreserved acceptance of my body, my femaleness, my partner in love. Though I hated the way this vision had been perverted, co-opted, and turned against women, I believed no less in the vision itself.

The irony, of course, was the contrast between ideal and reality. Part of that reality was historical: feminism had transformed women's consciousness without, as yet, transforming society, leaving a gap between what many of us demanded of a relationship and what most men were willing to give. Yet there were ways of making the best of this situation, while I tended to make the worst of it. At thirty-four, with a marriage and two quasi-marriages behind me, I felt, all too often, like an awkward teen-ager. My distrust of men fed a prickliness that provoked rejection that confirmed my distrust; worse, I was still afflicted, on some level, with the adolescent notion—no doubt the result of all those real and symbolic fights in the back seat—that to give in to sexual pleasure was to lose a power struggle. In general I thought of myself as fairly sane, but my conflicts about sex and men felt out of control—and thinking in those terms was undoubtedly part of the problem. For the sexual dilemma was the same as the spiritual one: to try harder was not only useless but self-defeating.

I had come to see my predicament as a sort of cosmic mockery, deflating my utopian pretensions. But from the Jewish standpoint, what could be a neater measure-for-measure punishment for refusing my ordained role as wife and mother? The symmetry was perfect: feminist consciousness had inspired both my sexual aspirations and the defensiveness that undermined them. It was the message one might expect from a cranky, conservative-Freudian God, out to show me that feminism was the problem rather than the solution, that all this emancipation claptrap violated my true nature and would deny me the feminine fulfillment I really craved.

Another mirror image, more powerful than the rest, it exposed my most private pain and doubt. I knew then that I had to go to Israel and confront my terror at its source—to put myself in my brother's place and see if I reached the same conclusions. I also knew that I had to write about the process. I was not sure these imperatives were compatible. When I decided not only to write about my trip but to write about it on assignment—which meant committing myself to come home and deliver a manuscript—I felt a bit like Ulysses tying himself to the mast. The difference, of course, was that I could cut myself loose if I chose. And in its perverse way, my very need to hedge was evidence of my good faith. At least it would have to do.

FIRST ENCOUNTERS

I left New York on March 22, 1976, on an overnight flight packed with Jewish tour groups. Here and there I saw religious men in beards and yarmulkes (skullcaps). At dawn they began getting up to form a *minyan* (ten-man quorum) for morning prayer. The Israeli flight attendants gave them dirty looks for blocking the aisles.

We arrived around noon. I wandered outside, past clumps of armed teen-age soldiers, looking for Mike. I was beginning to wonder if we had missed each other when a tall, thin boy wearing a yarmulke approached me.

"Are you Ellen?"

Chaim was a student at my brother's yeshiva; he had come to meet me because Mike had a bad cold. He explained that we would stop first at Rabbi and Rebbetsen Weinberg's, where I would leave my bags, then go find Mike. We took a cab into Jerusalem, talking sketchily about the experiences that had brought each of us here, and caught the bus for Kiryat Zanz, a religious neighborhood nestled in a rocky hillside. In contrast to the gorgeous landscape, the rows of identical low apartment buildings were dreary, housing-project modern. Block 5 Building 2 housed the Weinbergs and their nine children.

The *rebbetsen* invited us into an apartment that conveyed a sense of busy warmth. It was crammed with books and artifacts— menorahs, vases of flowers, bright fabrics, pictures of wise men, a colored-glass chandelier.

Denah Weinberg is a striking woman. Slim, fair, blue-eyed, in her late thirties, she looks like a picture-postcard of the ideal Jewish matriarch—one part strength and competence, one part motherliness, one part a modest, almost austere beauty accentuated by the kerchief that covers her head. (When an Orthodox woman marries, her hair becomes private, seen only by her husband.) I immediately craved her approval without quite knowing why. We sat in the kitchen chatting about my brother while children wandered in and out. I mentioned that I wanted to find out more about women's role in Judaism.

"Good!" the *rebbetsen* said. "People misunderstand it."

"Suppose I don't want children," I began, "or anyway no more than one or two. . . ."

Mrs. Weinberg's reply threw me. "If someone gave you money, would you turn it down?"

"I don't get the comparison." Money buys freedom; children take it away: the instant I had the thought it seemed unbearably crass.

"Children are a blessing," said the *rebbetsen* firmly. The conversation had taken a depressing turn. I could no more imagine having nine children than contemplate climbing Mount Everest.

"I don't want to devote all my time to children," I said. "I want to write."

"You can do both. A Jewish woman shouldn't spend all her time with her children. We can do much more."

"If I had a bunch of kids I wouldn't have any time and energy to spare."

"The Almighty wants us to use our talents. He wouldn't punish you by not letting you write. You'd find the time."

Well, maybe so. I wasted so much time, after all. No doubt a disciplined person could raise half a dozen kids in the time I spent daydreaming, reading junk, sleeping late. But I would never be that person; I knew my limitations. Or was that just an excuse for laziness?

The *rebbetsen* kissed me good-bye, and Chaim and I took a bus to the walled Old City. The Jewish Quarter, which had been largely destroyed by the Jordanians in 1948, was still being rebuilt; the smell of dust and the sound of drilling were pervasive. Mike emerged from his dorm looking pale and tired from his cold. We walked over to Yeshivat Aish HaTorah, which was on a side street called Misgav Ledach, tucked beside a huge construction site. To the northeast the yeshiva overlooked some of the most spectacular sights in Jerusalem—the Mount of Olives, the Valley of Kidron, and the golden Dome of the Rock. It was a short walk from the Western Wall ("Wailing Wall"), the sacred remnant of King Solomon's Temple.

We found the rabbi in his office. Like his wife, Noach Weinberg has a compelling presence. He is in his mid-forties, but with his white beard, black suit, and air of authority, he seems older. He regarded me with a friendly smile and eyes that suggested he had my number but liked me anyway. I thought he looked like God the Father in His more jovial aspect. After we had been introduced, he told Mike that a kid who had been staying at the yeshiva was about to leave.

"You know why they leave?" he said to me. "They leave because they're scared they'll like it." He shook his head. "Insanity! Do you know how Jews define sin? Sin is temporary insanity."

For instance, he explained, he had a bad habit of wasting time; who in his right mind would want to waste time?

"What about more serious sins?" I said.

Reb Noach raised his eyebrows. "Wasting time," he said, "is very serious. It's a kind of suicide."

For the first few days I stayed with one of Mike's teachers, Shimon Haskel, and his wife Chaya. I began to unwind from my trip and settle in. I was feeling close to Mike, and we talked more openly than ever before about our family, our childhoods, our fears and hang-ups. Mike told me that I seemed so confident he had always been afraid of me; I told him that I'd felt he was Mr. Cool, secretly putting me down. "But now," said Mike, "I'm not afraid of you anymore." I was pleased with the change in him. He was not only more confident but more willing to face his emotional problems—the split between intellect and feeling, the distance from other people, the lack of joy. He was obliged to face them, for they were also religious problems. It was a commandment to be happy; unhappiness in effect denied God's love, dismissed His gifts.

Mike was also absorbed in his work. He found the yeshiva completely different from all the schools he had hated. Both teachers and students were deeply involved in learning; they had no doubt that what they were doing was important. Universities, Mike felt, were dead; Aish HaTorah was alive. For several hours every morning he studied Gemara (the voluminous rabbinical commentaries on the Mishna; Mishna and Gemara together constitute the Talmud). In the afternoon and evening he studied Rambam (Maimonides). Somehow he found the time to talk with new people, listening to their problems, answering questions, and out of this had come another project: he was writing a group of papers arguing various proofs of God's existence and the Torah's divinity. His persuasiveness and intellectual skills had made him something of a star at the yeshiva.

Aish HaTorah is a yeshiva for *ba'al tshuvas*—delinquent Jews who have "returned." It is the fourth such yeshiva that Noach Weinberg has started in the past decade. Recently, others have picked up on Reb Noach's vision and started their own yeshivas in Jerusalem and Tel Aviv.

In America the most conspicuous Jewish evangelizers of Jews have been Hasidim. Hasidism, a tendency within Judaism that stresses joy, prayer, and mystical experience, began in the eighteenth century as a revolt by poor and uneducated Jews against the elitist intellectualism of the yeshivas of Eastern Europe, particularly Lithuania. The *ba'al tshuva* yeshiva movement in Israel comes from the latter tradition, that of the *misnagdim*—rationalist opponents of Hasidism—who emphasize learning Torah as the highest value and chief means of approaching God. A yeshiva like Aish HaTorah operates on the premise that the best weapon against unbelief is rational argument. It follows that the crucial first step is to get people to listen. Boys are urged to come for a day, an hour, a meal, a bed. (No one has to pay unless he can afford to; the school is supported mostly by contributions.) A beginner's program runs for three months and then repeats; a student can start at any point. Those who stay can advance as fast as their ability allows to study of the Talmud and biblical commentaries.

There was a major hitch in my plan to replicate Mike's experience: I could not go to Aish HaTorah. Orthodox education is sexually segregated, and opportunities for women are limited. Learning is a religious obligation only for men; among tradition-minded Jews the issue of whether women should study Torah and Talmud, and if so how much, is controversial. None of the women's schools in Jerusalem offers a comprehensive intellectual and religious experience like Aish HaTorah's. Nor do they cater to transients. Still, I decided to check out a couple of schools and visit a student Mike knew.

Lorie Bernstein was nineteen and the product of a rich Long Island suburb; her divorced parents owned clothing stores. Mike had first met her at the airport on his way back from New York. During the cab ride into Jerusalem she had told him that she had been a Hasid for a while but had reverted to existentialism; Mike had urged her to give Judaism another try. Since then she had become a fervent *ba'al tshuva*. When I introduced myself she hugged me excitedly. She was small and bouncy, with dark hair tucked in a bun; she wore a long-sleeved blouse, a long skirt, and gold-rimmed, blue-tinted glasses.

I had found Lorie just as she was about to do some errands in Mea Shearim, an old, poor, fanatically pious community noted for its anti-Zionists (they believe there cannot be a legitimate Jewish state until the coming of the Messiah), its Hasidim in medieval caftans, and its signs demanding that female tourists conform to Torah standards of modest dress. We walked there together. Lorie stopped several times to give coins to beggars, all the while keeping up a passionate monologue.

"God gives us so much, you just have to do something back. I *love* doing *mitzvos* and helping people. A few agorot mean nothing to you, but you're giving someone food, making him happy. This religion is *so beautiful!*" She was bubbly, breathless; energy rolled off her in waves. "Whether there's a God or not, the Torah helps you live up to your potential. It's like tripping—you get an awareness of everything you do. I really have to *think* about food now—what's milk, what's meat, my mother-love side and beast side? Every day I have to thank God for all kinds of things. Thank God I'm awake. (Think of all the people who aren't awake.) Thank God for commanding me to wash. Whenever I wash, I'm aware of my hands and how wonderful they are. Thank God for clothing the naked. How many people think every day about how they have clothes and other people don't? There's even a prayer for the bathroom—thank God for my ducts and orifices, that they're working properly."

I asked her how she felt about Judaism's view of women.

"I'm *dying* to get married and have children. Right now I'm doing *tshuva*, repentance, for having an abortion. I killed a baby! I'm so upset! What could possibly be more important than having children?"

I mumbled something about wanting to write.

"Writing!" Lorie said scornfully. "I used to write, I used it to get rid of energy. What's writing compared to creating a human being, a soul?"

"It happens to be what I want to do."

"What you *want*! I used to be that way. The most important thing was to be authentic—to do what I *really* wanted to do, even if it hurt someone. My ideal was Meursault in *The Stranger*. Life was meaningless so why pretend it wasn't? Anyway," she said, "most things you think you want to do you don't really want to do. *Other* people want you to do them. The only thing I really miss is getting high. I *love* getting high—I *love* it! If there was one thing that could get me off religion, it would be that."

On the other side of the street—we were now in Mea Shearim—two touristy-looking girls passed by, transgressing the modesty laws by wearing jeans. "If I weren't with you," Lorie said, "I'd go over and yell at them."

"I don't think it does much good to yell at people," I said, feeling resentful about the antiwriting remarks.

"You can't tell," said Lorie. "Sometimes one little thing can change you around. What got me to join the Hasidim was that someone told me how low their divorce rate was. If I just explained about modesty—why it's not good to wear pants—" She stopped. "I'm being too heavy, aren't I? I'm sorry. I get carried away when I meet a new person."

We walked past stalls selling fruits and vegetables, down a narrow, cobbled back street, to visit a friend of Lorie's who might help place some students with families for Shabbos. Leah, a vivacious, middle-aged Hasidic housewife, insisted on serving us vegetable soup, bread, and cream cheese. She supervised the washing ritual, showing me how to pour from the two-handled cup, how to cup my hands, making me do it over until I got it exactly right while Lorie bounced up and down, protesting, "Leah! You'll discourage her! You've got to start out easy!"

I began hanging around Lorie's school, sitting in on classes—which mostly centered on Hebrew texts and made me feel as if I'd stumbled into the middle of a foreign-language movie with inadequate subtitles—and talking with Lorie and her friends. There was Frieda from Brooklyn, strong, blunt, a scrapper, a woman with a vision: she intended to start a *ba'al tshuva* organization in the States. There was Cindy, a blind girl from New Jersey, who had identified with black people so intensely that she still spoke with a trace of a pseudosouthern accent, who had decided to convert to Christianity and had joined a black church, but then—*boruch Hashem!*—praise God!—had realized where she belonged. There was Sarah, who had been born Protestant in Chicago and had converted after investigating every philosophy she'd heard of and deciding that only Judaism made sense.

But at the psychological center of my life in Jerusalem were the rabbi and the *rebbetsen*. Noach Weinberg, the youngest son of a Hasid, grew up on New York's Lower East Side; Denah came from Long Island. They met and married in the late fifties and emigrated to Israel in 1961. Reb Noach was determined to do something to reverse the Jewish drift away from Torah. For six years he studied with his goal in mind and in 1967 he started his first yeshiva. Aish HaTorah has been going since 1973. Reb Noach runs the school, teaches, and makes periodic fund-raising trips to the States. The *rebbetsen* mothers their children, runs their household, studies, teaches, does charity work, and acts as counselor and friend to the yeshiva students and other young people who seek her out. During Aish HaTorah's first year she was also its chief administrator.

On Monday nights a group of women met at Rebbetsen Weinberg's for her class on the 613 *mitzvos*. The *rebbetsen* was currently discussing the *mitzva* to do good. Doing good, in Jewish terms, involves a constant struggle between the two sides of our nature: the *yeitzer tov* (good inclination), which arises from the soul and desires to serve God, and the *yeitzer hara* (evil inclination), which stems from the body and craves unlimited material, sexual, and egotistical satisfactions.

"What's the difference between a war against people and the war against the *yeitzer hara?*" the *rebbetsen* asked. "A people war has an end; there's no end to the *yeitzer hara* war. A people war doesn't go on twenty-four hours a day. In a people war you win something limited. If you win the *yeitzer hara* war, you have everything. And if you lose—"

It was an incongruous image for a Jewish mother of nine, but I couldn't help thinking of Joan of Arc.

"You have to develop a strategy. For instance, suppose you know that when you meet a certain person you're going to talk *loshon hora*."

Loshon hora, slander, is an important sin, the subject of a formidable body of law. It is forbidden to say anything disparaging about someone—whether or not it is true—or to say anything that could be construed as disparaging, or to listen to such talk. It is even forbidden to praise someone in front of an enemy who might be tempted to argue. The Haskels had a sign in their kitchen that said, "Is that *loshon hora?*"

"You should try to avoid the person," said the *rebbetsen*. "But if you can't, then you should think, how can I avoid the bad conversation? Is there some other way I can make her feel good?"

"Why not take the direct approach," one of the women asked, "and just say, 'Let's not talk *loshon hora?*'"

"Not everyone can take that," said the *rebbetsen*. "You might just put her on the defensive."

To be good, Mrs. Weinberg summed up, was to emulate the Almighty, to become as perfect an image of Him as possible. To be infinitely patient, to return insult with kindness—and without self-congratulation. How to do this? "Know the 613 *mitzvos*. There is no other way."

It occurred to me that if Talmudic logic had made Mike realize how Jewish his thinking was, Jewish ethics made me realize how Jewish my feelings were. I was beginning to understand Jewish guilt. Unlike Christian guilt, which assumed one's inherent depravity, it came from the idea that one could and should attain perfection. Jews who took their religion seriously had no need to feel guilty. They knew the 613 *mitzvos* were the way, and if they backslid they could catch themselves and carry on. For Jews like me it was different; secular enlightenment was the brew that provoketh the desire but taketh away the performance. We still craved perfection, and so we pursued utopian politics, utopian sex, utopian innocence. But we had no law to guide or reassure us. With the law, one could have patience with one's shortcomings. Without it, if we were not *there* we were nowhere at all. To live outside the law you must be honest—Bob Dylan, a Jew, said that.

Since the Haskels had three little children and another guest in their crowded apartment, I moved in with Chaya's stepsister, Abby Ginsberg, and her roommate, Sharon Weitz. They shared a large apartment—inherited from Abby's parents, who had gone back to the States—on Shimoni Street in Rasco, an attractive residential neighborhood that was not predominantly religious. Like the Haskels they were from the Midwest. Abby was studying at Hebrew University, Sharon at a seminary. Both women were more religious than their families.

I felt immediately comfortable with Sharon and Abby, in part because their sense of female identity did not seem radically different from my own. They had not grown up isolated from secular life. They had gone to public high school, dated, worn pants; they had not married at eighteen; they were serious about learning; the man Abby was seeing pitched in with the cooking and played blues on his guitar. Unlike Lorie, they were not reacting against their past; because their religious commitment had deepened gradually rather than come through sudden conversion, they had none of the *ba'al tshuva*'s dogmatic intensity.

"Of course I feel a conflict between Judaism and feminism," Sharon said. "It's harder to accept if you've been exposed to Western ideas than if you grew up in Mea Shearim. But if you're committed to Judaism, other principles have to adjust. To me a Jewish life offers so many satisfactions—" She smiled and shrugged. Intellectually she knew where she stood, but emotionally she was still struggling. "The thing I really care about," said Abby, "is being able to learn. If I thought the *halacha* wouldn't allow me to learn—then I *might* have a problem."

Abby was ebullient; Sharon had a quieter warmth. They were ten years younger than I, but I often felt as if our ages were reversed. They projected a balance, an unselfconscious maturity symbolized for me by the way they cooperated in maintaining their cheerful apartment. The Shimoni Street place was just an ordinary middle-class apartment, conventionally furnished by the absent parents, serving as a way station for two young, transient students. But Abby and Sharon made it feel like home. They were, for one thing, enthusiastic cooks. Almost every afternoon I would come back to find them in the kitchen discussing recipes; since Abby was experimenting with vegetarianism, they were always trying new concoctions—cheese-and-spinach soufflés, vegetable pies, fruit salads.

Often Abby's friend Joshua would be there too. He was leaving for the States in a few weeks, right after Passover; in the meantime he and Abby were trying to figure out how they felt about each other. Orthodox Jews do not play sexual games: a man and a woman are either compatible or they aren't, and if they decide they are, they get married. So Josh was at Shimoni Street several nights a week. He and Abby would study and argue points of *halacha*, and then we would all help with the dinner and eat together, talking and joking about the events of the day, what this or that teacher said, my latest argument with Lorie. I would go to bed and read, or write in my notebook, and when I padded to the kitchen or the bathroom at 2 or 3 a.m. I would, as often as not, hear the pacific murmur of one of Josh and Abby's marathon conversations.

TRUTH AND CONSEQUENCES

"The First Commandment," said Reb Noach, "is to know there is a God." We were resuming a conversation we had started a few days earlier. "The disease of Western thought," he had said then, "is: 'There is no absolute truth.' But it's intuitively obvious that either something is true or it isn't. Listen—'There is no absolute truth.' 'Are you sure?' 'Yes.' 'Are you *absolutely* sure?' " I could afford to laugh. I believed something was true or it wasn't; I just didn't think we could know for sure which was which. "They call us fanatics. But a fanatic is someone who won't listen to reason. I say, let's reason together. Let's find a premise on which we can both agree, and reason from there. The purpose of reason," he had concluded, "is to get someone to the point where his intuition will say, 'Yes, you're right.' "

"*Know* there is a God," Reb Noach repeated. "Not 'have faith.' Understand! Reason! But reason can only tell you what you already know. It's a servant, like your hand." He held his hand out. "Hand! Come to my nose!" The hand did not move. "What's this? Revolution? Don't be silly! No, your hand acts on what you really want, not on what you say you want. Reason will tell you what you really know—what are *your* perceptions, not other people's, not society's."

For the next hour or so, Reb Noach tried to persuade my intuition. If my father on his deathbed asked me to say a mourner's prayer for him, would I? Of course. If he asked me to say a bunch of nonsense syllables, would I? Probably not. Why not? What's the difference? Well, I think religious ritual is meaningful, worthy of respect; that doesn't mean it represents absolute truth. If someone ran in front of my car and I hit him, wouldn't I feel guilty, even if I couldn't possibly have stopped in time? Yes, I would. What did that tell me? "Even if it's not technically my fault, someone has suffered because of me. It's irrational, but I'd think, 'If I'd just done something different—taken the bus, stayed home. . . .' "

"The reason you would feel guilty," Reb Noach said, "is that it really *would* be your fault. If you hadn't done something wrong, God wouldn't have chosen you as the instrument of someone's death."

I appreciated Reb Noach's technique. I realized that I had, on occasion, used it myself. (Don't you and your husband both work? Suppose you lived with your sister, and you both worked, and she wanted you to cook dinner every night because she was tired—would you do it? Why not? Well, then, what's different about doing it for a man?) But my intuition was unconvinced. I still couldn't see the ultimate Reality as a being who cared, willed, intervened in our lives, and—might as well bring it up—decreed separate functions for men and women.

"You don't think men and women are basically different?"

"*Basically*, no," I said. "*Basically*, I think we're all human beings."

"One of the craziest ideas in this crazy modern world," said Reb Noach, "is that men and women are the same. Men and women are two different species!"

I insisted that whatever the differences—and who could tell at this point which were inherent, which imposed by a patriarchal culture?—they did not require women to devote themselves to as many babies as chose to make their appearance. Reb Noach shook his head.

"Children are the greatest pleasure," he said, "but people today are so decadent they prefer their material comforts to children."

"It's not just material comfort!" I protested. "People have a right to some freedom—some time for themselves—"

"Decadence, Ellen. I'd have fifty children, a hundred. Every child is a lesson in love!"

"My parents aren't decadent! They've worked hard to bring up three children—to educate us all—"

Suddenly I found myself weeping.

"Ellen!" The rabbi's voice vibrated through me, alarmed, caring, soothing as a touch. "I'm not condemning *people*! Who knows who's better than who? I'm talking about actions. Mistakes, Ellen."

I wasn't sure why I was crying—except that if my middle-class family-centered parents could by any standard be accused of decadent behavior, then I was completely hopeless. My loss of control took me by surprise. I suppose it was my first overt symptom of culture shock.

How long was it since I'd landed at the airport—eight days? nine? It felt much longer. My sense of time had changed, along with my perspective. I was, in crucial ways, an outsider—a reporter, at that—in a strange culture. Yet because I was Jewish, I was also family. Whatever anyone might think of me, whether I was religious or not, so long as I was living in the Orthodox community I was on some basic level accepted as part of it. And so I began, almost imperceptibly at first, to identify with that community and feel weirdly estranged from the secular world. I found myself thinking of nonreligious people as "they." When I had an errand in downtown Jerusalem I felt assaulted by its frenetic, noisy, garish urbanness, by the crowds of Israelis who milled along Jaffa Road without a care for the subtleties of Jewish law.

Even the ever-present political tension began to seem part of that other world. A deep belief that God controls events tends to cool political fervor, and only a minority of Orthodox Israelis fit the stereotype of the militant religious nationalist; Mike and his friends were critical of the rabbinical establishment for what they saw as its readiness to bend the Torah to the demands of the state. I had arrived in Israel at a volatile time: Palestinian students had been demonstrating in the Old City; Israeli Arabs were protesting the expropriation of Arab land in the Galilee. I read about it all in the *Jerusalem Post*, feeling, absurdly, that Israeli politics had been much more vivid to me when I was in New York.

A religious universe enveloped me. I was surrounded by people who believed and, more important, lived that belief every minute. Conversation among Orthodox Jews never strays far from questions of ethics, points of law, one's religious activities; even small talk is inescapably religious: "I'm feeling better, *boruch Hashem!*"; "I ran into so-and-so on Shabbos"; "She's going to have a *milchig* [dairy] wedding." Orthodox life has its own special rhythm. There is the daily rhythm of prayer and the weekly rhythm of preparations for Shabbos: rushing to clean and cook before Friday sundown, when all work must be suspended; setting lights to go on and off automatically; taking turns showering, hoping the hot water won't run out; dressing up; lighting the Sabbath candles. There is Shabbos itself: making *kiddush* (blessing and sharing wine); washing and breaking bread and sitting down to the traditional European-Jewish Friday night chicken dinner; the men going off to *shul* Saturday morning, coming home to a meal of *cholent*, a stew that is made before Shabbos and left simmering on the stove; studying, walking, visiting, or napping in the afternoon; the light supper and finally the *havdalah* ("division") ceremony with which Shabbos ends.

Although the process was less dramatic, my immersion in Jewish life was having a far more potent effect on me than my confrontation with Jewish ideas. I could argue with ideas, but I could not, without being an abrasive nuisance, refuse to adapt, in important respects, to the customs of my hosts. On the most superficial level this meant not washing Abby and Sharon's dairy dishes in the meat sink, but it also meant shifting mental gears to participate in conversations that took a religious outlook for granted. Living with Orthodox Jews was like being straight at a party where everyone else is stoned; after a while, out of sheer social necessity, you find yourself getting a contact high.

There was, for instance, the afternoon I spent talking with Lorie and Frieda. Frieda had recruited Lorie for her *ba'al tshuva* organization; they were planning to go back to New York in July to get the project moving. I started giving advice. If they wanted young, educated women to take Judaism seriously, I argued, their organization would have to engage women's minds the way Aish Ha-Torah had engaged Mike's. That meant . . . and then I heard myself: I was telling them how to seduce *me*.

I had always thought of Orthodox Judaism as a refuge for compulsives: not only did its ubiquitous requirements and prohibitions seem to preclude spontaneity, but since the *halacha*, like any body of law that applies basic principles to specific situations, was open to interpretation, it provided endless opportunities for what outsiders would call hairsplitting. For example, it's Shabbos and Sharon and Abby have a problem: they have, as usual, left a kettle of boiling water on a burner they lit Friday afternoon, and now the flame has gone out. Is it permitted to switch the kettle to another lit burner? If the water has cooled off, heating it up again would violate the rule against cooking on Shabbos. If it's still hot, moving it should be okay. But it must have cooled off slightly. How hot does it have to be? Under the kettle, covering both burners, is a metal sheet, there as a reminder not to turn the flames up or down; does this make both flames one fire, which would mean that switching the kettle is allowed in any case? Abby, Sharon, and Josh debated this issue for half an hour; it remained unresolved, and they did not move the kettle.

I understood now that to call this sort of behavior compulsive was to assume that religious observance was a distraction from life, while for believers it was the whole point; secular concerns were the distraction. If doing *mitzvos*—all of them, not just those you understood or liked—was the way to serve God, to connect with Reality, then it was crucial to do them exactly right. For the people around me, Torah was not a straitjacket but a discipline, shaping and focusing their energies toward the only meaningful end. It was an arduous discipline, but one that was no more inherently compulsive than my own search for the precise adjective or the care with which feminists analyzed the minutiae of sexual relationships.

And what was so sacred, anyway, about the arcane customs of my hyperurban, free-lance existence? For all that I was so attached to it, I had to admit that it was, in the context of human history, more than a little strange. Sociologists liked to talk about how rootless and mobile Americans were, but most Americans at least had families. Despite my reluctance to assume the burdens of motherhood in a sexist society, it disturbed me to think that I would very likely never have children: I felt that child rearing, like working and loving, was one of the activities that defined humanness. Even my work—my excuse for so much of what I did or didn't do—sometimes struck me as ridiculous. What was the point of sitting home scratching symbols on paper, adding my babblings to a world already overloaded with information? And what of my belief in the supreme importance of connecting with Reality? Orthodox Jews acted on their version of that belief; did I? Well, there was my therapy. It occupied all of forty-five minutes of my week—less time than it took me (speaking of compulsive rituals) to read the Sunday *Times*. Did I really have my priorities straight?

If my traumatic talk with Mike had shocked me into realizing that Judaism was a plausible intellectual system, living in Jerusalem was making me realize that Judaism was a plausible way of life. And that realization slid relentlessly into the next: that it was plausible even for me. My rapport with Abby and Sharon weakened my defenses against this frightening idea. I experienced Shimoni Street as a kind of halfway house. Much as I admired the *rebbetsen*, she was too unlike me to be a model. Lorie, in an entirely different way, was also from another world. But Abby and Sharon had the psychology of modern intellectual women. If they found Orthodox life exciting and full of purpose—if they had been exposed to the freedoms I had, yet did not feel deprived— perhaps I did not need those freedoms as much as I thought.

Yet even as I was drawn into the Orthodox subculture, I also resisted it. My resistance took an embarrassing form; it surfaced as a spoiled brat yelling, "I won't!" If I had come to Israel to experience Judaism, it made sense for me to try to observe Jewish law. I had resolved, for instance, to eat only kosher food during my stay. For a month this would scarcely be a major deprivation; I had stuck to reducing diets that required much more discipline. Yet I found that I couldn't keep away from the junk-food stands on Jaffa Road; I stuffed myself with suspect brands of chocolate; under my modest dresses I was puffing out at a disquieting rate. Then there was the synagogue issue. Though communal prayer was not required of women, I felt that I should, at least once, attend services at an Orthodox *shul*. But I was afraid to face what I saw as the total humiliation of sitting upstairs in the women's section. Some journalist, I mocked myself. Lucky no one ever sent you to cover a war.

I began to realize that I was depressed. The weather, still wintry and raw, depressed me. The city itself depressed me, which was a surprise. On my first trip to Israel I had reacted very differently. I was not thinking about religion then; I was preoccupied with politics, war, history, the tragic clash of nationalisms. But I had been awed by the radiance of Jerusalem. Perhaps it was just the combination of natural beauty and antiquity, but whatever holiness was, the city breathed it. Standing before the massive stones of the Western Wall, submerged in a crowd of people praying, I had felt the pain and ecstasy of millions of pilgrims course through me.

A friend had arranged for several members of our group to have Friday night dinner with a religious family, and all evening I felt the way I had at the Wall. Everything had a preternatural clarity and significance. When our host said the blessings over the bread and wine, I marveled that I had been so obtuse as not to *see*. Blessing one's food—appreciating the miracle of food—what could be more fitting? And the whole idea of the Sabbath, one day a week when you were forbidden ordinary distractions and had to be alone with yourself and Reality. . . . I imagined myself back in

New York City, spending a Saturday without writing, eating in a restaurant, taking the subway; a whole day with the phone off the hook and the record player silent. A fantasy, of course, I could never live that way, didn't even want to, and yet I felt a pang: isn't this what it's all about, the acid peace, the connection you say you want, getting rid of all the *noise*?

Now, though I remembered those feelings, I couldn't re-create them. I went to the Wall, saw weathered stone spattered with pigeon droppings, left quickly because of the cold wind. And Shabbos, with all its restrictions, was simply oppressive, like a tight girdle. "Last time," said Mike, "you could be open to it because you weren't seriously thinking about it as a possibility."

It was during Shabbos, the second since I'd arrived, that my depression hit full force. A friend of Mike's had invited us for the weekend. He and his wife were warmly hospitable, and I struggled guiltily against my gloom. I felt suffocated by domesticity, by the children calling for mommy, the men leaving for *shul* and the women staying home, the men sitting at the table and the women carting away the dishes. I wanted to tear off my itchy, constricting stockings. I wanted to write in my notebook, turn on lights, eat without going through half an hour of ritual first.

The next day I went to El Al to confirm my return reservation. The flight I was booked on left April 22, but my excursion ticket was good for two extra weeks if I wanted them, and I figured it was time to decide. I was always superstitious about switching flights; now, looking over the timetable, I felt irrationally certain that if I changed my plans I would end up staying in Israel. *Something* would trap me here. When Lorie first came to Jerusalem, she had dreamed she was in prison, supervised by a mean lady; she had wanted to get out, but by the time they were ready to let her go, a month later, she loved it and wanted to stay. On the strength of that dream Lorie had decided to stay a month and, sure enough, she was still here. . . . This is ridiculous, I lectured myself. If you want to go you'll go; if you want to stay you'll stay; and if God is really controlling your life, it's useless to second-guess Him. I debated staying at least a few extra days, but that would mean going through another Shabbos. I decided to stick with my original flight.

As soon as I left the office, a new wave of paranoia hit: God would punish me for my rotten attitude toward Shabbos. My plane would crash or be attacked by terrorists. *Mida k'neged mida* —measure for measure. Later that day, I realized I couldn't leave on April 22: it was the last day of Passover, and I had been invited to Reb Noach's. The prospect of having to change my reservation after all solidified my conviction that I would never make it back to the States. I had received a sign. There were no coincidences.

When I told Mike about my scheduling mix-up, he looked as if I'd punched him in the jaw. "You're leaving early," he said. "I thought you had six weeks."

"I planned on staying a month. I'm just doing what I was going to do all along."

"It's not just that. You want to leave because you're depressed. You're reacting exactly the same way I did."

My gut contracted.

"Mike, I'm not you. We may be alike in a lot of ways, but we're two different people." Under the panic I had to remember that, hold on to that. "If I want to go home, I'm going home, and I'm not going to feel guilty about it."

"But you can't postpone these questions—" He shook his head. "When you first came, you were really relating to what was going on. Now I feel as if you've withdrawn."

"Do you really have to go back?" the *rebbetsen* asked. I had come over for another talk with Reb Noach.

"Theoretically," I said, "I could throw over my entire life and stay. But I don't want to."

"Do you think it's important to find out if there's a God?"

"Well—" *Leave me alone! Get off my back!*

"If there is, and we don't find out, are we culpable?"

I don't have to listen to this! It's brainwashing, that's what it is!

"I can find out in New York," I said.

"If I offered you a $200,000 business deal," Reb Noach put in, "you wouldn't say, 'I can make the same deal in America.' You'd say, 'Let's talk.' "

"I have a whole life to get back to," I insisted. "I *like* my life."

"Then you *won't* really try to find out," said the *rebbetsen.*

"I didn't say that."

"Well, will you?"

"I don't know," I said, feeling miserable.

I was not in the best mood to face Reb Noach. During our talks he had been going through the proofs of God one by one. His theme this time was: "A design must have a designer." I had by now had this argument with several people. I still didn't buy it. Finally, Reb Noach said, "Ellen, think for a minute: is there a reason you don't want to believe the proofs?"

"Well, I can't deny that," I said. "I don't want to change my whole world view. But—"

"Look at it objectively! If you accept *one proof* it doesn't mean changing your whole world view."

"But I don't accept it. I don't see that the order in the universe has to be created by a personal God."

"There seems to be a wall here," said Reb Noach. "I don't want to pursue this unless you want to."

He started on another tack. "Why was the world created? For our pleasure. What is the one thing we are capable of doing? Seeking pleasure. So how can we go wrong? Insanity! Tell me— what's the opposite of pleasure?"

"Pain," I said.

"No! No! The opposite of pleasure is *comfort*. Pleasure *involves* pain. Decadence is opting for comfort. For example, what's more important, wisdom or money? Ask most people, they'll say 'wisdom.' 'Okay, stay here six months and I'll give you wisdom.' 'I can't—I have a job, a girlfriend, I'm supposed to take a vacation in

the Greek islands.' 'Stay six months and I'll give you $20,000.'
'Fine!' 'What about your job, your girlfriend?' 'They'll wait.'

"The soul wants wisdom; the body wants money. The soul wants
pleasure; the body wants comfort. And what's the highest pleasure? The aim of the soul? God, Ellen. That's real happiness—
ecstasy, Ellen! Find out what you're living for! Take the pain
—pleasure only comes with a lot of pain. I'm your friend—I'm
with you. Give up your life of striving for success, for identity,
your name up there—"

Unfair!

"Do you really think I write just to get my name in print?"

"I think you do it to have an identity. To be 'a writer.' "

"I do like having that. But would you believe that I write mainly
because I enjoy it, and I'm good at it, and"—defiantly—"I think
it's useful work!"

"Shakespeare's okay," said Reb Noach, "but unless you know
the real meaning of life, you're a zombie, a walking dead man. Find
out what you're living for, Ellen. Clarity or death!"

There began to be moments—usually early in the morning, before I forced myself to get up and face the day—when I was more
inclined than not to believe that it was all true, that I was only
resisting because I couldn't stand the pain of admitting how wrong
I was. *What about the prophecies . . .* and the way modern history
seemed almost a conspiracy to drive the Jews back to Israel . . . and
the Bible . . . Mike and I had been going over Genesis, along with
the Rashi commentary, and I had had a sudden vision, like an acid
flash, of a Garden, and a Presence . . . and my personality, my
Sagittarian compulsion to aim straight at the cosmic bull's-eye . . .
"*The blessing and curse of being a Jew,*" said Reb Noach, "*is that
Jews are thirsty for God, for the absolute. A Jew can never have
peace. Whatever he does, he'll be the best at, whether it's being a
radical or being a criminal. It's all misplaced searching for God.
Every Jew is a neurotic. . . .*"

And if I became religious, what would I do? Insanity, decadence, call it what you please, I could never be a traditional Jewish
mother. But maybe I didn't have to be. Actually, only men were
subject to a specific *mitzva* to marry and have children. And not
everyone took the Weinbergs' hard line on procreation—according to one rabbi I'd met, a psychologist, the *halacha* permitted
contraception when necessary to preserve a woman's health, including her emotional health. Nor were the role divisions in the
family absolute; no law actually forbade women to work outside
the home, or men to share housework. Even within the bounds of
Judaism I could be a feminist of sorts, crusading for reforms like
equal education, perhaps contesting the biased *halachic* interpretations of male rabbis. And my experience would put me in a unique
position to reach women like me and bring them back.

In private I could have this fantasy, even take it seriously.
Which would not stop me, an hour or a minute later, from getting
into a furious argument with a man. It was one thing to consider
the abstract possibility that women's role in Judaism was not inherently oppressive, another to live in a culture that made me feel
oppressed. Once when Mike and I were dinner guests of another
of his teachers I complained, "You know, it makes me feel like a
servant when you sit there like a lump while I help serve and clean
up."

"It isn't customary for the men to help," Mike said, "and if I got
up I'd make everybody uncomfortable, including the women." He
had a point—when in Rome and all that—but it was a point he was
not exactly loath to make. The fact was that for Mike, moving
from Western secular society to Orthodox Judaism had meant an
increase in status and privilege; for me it meant a loss.

One night Mike and I got together with Dick Berger, one of his
best friends at the yeshiva. Mike was very high on Dick, who, he
said, was an unusually perceptive person with a gift for sensing
someone's emotional blocks. He had been encouraging Mike to get
more connected to his feelings. I had met Dick once and he had
told me a little about himself. He had been a newspaper reporter in

Pittsburgh, had written an unpublished novel, had been into psychedelics and Transcendental Meditation. Later he had told Mike that he felt I had seen him only as material for my article. I didn't think that was true, but I worried about it anyway. I hated it when people claimed to know my motives better than I did, but I always worried that they were right.

The conversation that night was pleasant enough until Dick and I got into an argument about men sharing child care. Dick suggested that three thousand years of tradition shouldn't be tampered with, and I started getting angry in a way I knew from experience led to no good. Then he really pushed the wrong button.

"You're so emotional! Can't we talk about this objectively?"

"You're hardly being objective. It's in your interest as a man to think what you think."

"I'm feeling detached," Dick insisted. "By that I mean attached to my basic essence. You're reacting out of your conditioning in Western culture."

"You're reacting out of your male-supremacist prejudices, only you have three thousand years of tradition on your side."

"But I'm not being aggressive and hostile—you are!"

"You can afford to be 'objective' and 'detached'! You're happy with the system—I'm the one who's being oppressed by it! Why shouldn't I be hostile—what right do you have to demand that we have this conversation on your terms—" My sentence went hurtling off into the inarticulate reaches of un-God-like rage.

Another time, another friend of Mike's: Harvey, a tall, dark, intense South African. "I'm not here because I want to be," he said. "I want freedom and money and the pleasures of the body. I was happy in my nonreligious life—I miss it. But once you know there's a God—"

We started arguing about design and evolution. "Either there's a God," Harvey said, "or all this harmony and purpose is a coincidence."

"Those aren't the only possibilities—"

"And there are vast odds against coincidence. If you had a dart board that had lots of red and just a little white, where do you think your dart would hit?"

"That's a silly analogy," I said.

"What if you had to lay money on it?"

"I'm not going to play this game! It's ridiculous! It's irrelevant!"

"Answer me," the prosecutor insisted. "Would you bet on white or red?"

"I'm not Pascal!" I yelled. "And I'm not about to change my entire life because of some *abstract intellectual decision* about what the *odds* are on there being a God!"

"The Torah isn't only a carrot, you know. It's a stick, as well. There's punishment—you get cut off—"

And I'm not going to play your guilt game, either! You men are not going to cram your sexist religion down my throat!

There it was: I might be persuaded to return to Judaism—but not by a man. After one of our encounters, Reb Noach had declared, "You are emotionally committed to rebelling against the male sex!" He was right, of course, and in principle I agreed that one ought to be wary of such a priori commitments. But whenever I clashed with a man I seemed to end up with a renewed conviction that my rebellion was a matter of simple sanity. Men with their bullshit head trips! Men with their "objectivity": "Let's discuss this rationally—should I remove my foot from your neck, or shouldn't I?"

EXODUS

And it shall be when thy son asketh thee in time to come, saying, What is this? that thou shalt say unto him, By strength of hand the Lord brought us out from Egypt, from the house of bondage.

—EXODUS XIII:14

You know her life was saved by rock and roll.

—VELVET UNDERGROUND

Mike and I were walking in Mea Shearim, talking about happiness. My revised departure date was nearly two weeks away, time for plenty of changes, but I knew that I would not, at least for the present, become an Orthodox Jew. My decision had involved no epiphany, no cathartic moment of truth; my doubts remained and perhaps always would. But to put it that way was looking at it backward. The fact was that only a compelling, inescapable moment of truth could have made me religious. Nothing less could shake my presumption in favor of a life that made me happy.

From Mike's point of view I was refusing to accept the truth because of a strong emotional resistance; though he too had resisted, his unhappiness with secular life had made it easier to give up. On the other hand, he kept suggesting, I might be a lot less happy than I thought.

"Dick sees you as a very unhappy person," Mike said. "And Reb Noach thinks you're really unhappy."

I felt a twinge of resentment—who were these people, who hardly knew me, to call me unhappy?—mixed with anxiety. Was I fooling myself? I didn't think so. I was not perfectly happy, or as happy as I wanted to be, but in spite of my unresolved problems I was happier than not. Having problems, even serious ones, was not the same as being unhappy. I knew the difference because I had experienced it. For about seven years, beginning the year I started college, I had suffered from a severe depression. At the time I hadn't called it that; I didn't know what to call it. I wasn't especially sad; I just had this puzzling sense that nothing was quite real, that my life was, as I put it to myself, all procedure and no substance. Most of my activities, however theoretically enjoyable, secretly disappointed me. Reading my favorite poets, camping in Yosemite, marching on CORE picket lines, making love, somehow I nearly always felt like a spectator. When I got married I knew I was making a mistake but felt powerless to act on that knowledge; no matter how a movie may horrify you, you don't yell "No!" at it or smash the projector. I was conscious that all was not well, but then, I thought, perhaps everyone felt this way, perhaps this was

just the way life was. In the beginning that thought jibed neatly
with the spirit of the time—the tail end of the silent fifties.

My depression had begun gradually, for no obvious reason, and
ended the same way. But over the years my memories of descent
and recovery had crystallized around a few symbolic events. The
first occurred when I was a Barnard freshman infatuated with a
Columbia sophomore, an old friend from high school. One day I
ran into him on the street and casually suggested—we were
friends, right?—getting together sometime. He looked uncomfortable and mumbled a nonanswer. To my surprise I felt almost no
pain. I noted that fact with detached interest. How sensible, I
thought. Why cry over a situation I have no power to change?
Four years later, when I was living in Berkeley, I heard Bob Dylan
for the first time and was an instant fanatic. Dylan's voice got
straight through to me, and what it said was, No, this is *not* just
the way life is. Then a friend lent me Wilhelm Reich's classic,
Character Analysis. I had never heard of Reich, and the book was a
revelation: among other things, it contained a precise description
of my emotional state. Other people had been in the same condition and been cured! I was not hopeless! It took me a while to pick
up on these messages, but eventually I left my husband, returned
to New York, became a journalist, decided I thought I was really a
radical, and fell in love. Somewhere along the line I noticed that
my strange remoteness was gone.

I had had bouts of depression since then—the worst one had
driven me to my therapist—and in occasional moments of stress I
had reverted to staring at the movie. But I felt certain that I would
never again lose myself in so terrible a way. In retrospect, it was
clear that what had done me in were my conflicts about growing
up female—conflicts I still felt. The difference was that I had
decided to engage and struggle with life rather than withdraw
from it. And making that decision—as often as necessary—was
what happiness was about. I agreed with the Jewish insistence
that happiness was a choice. Yet how I had gained the strength to
choose remained a mystery, part of the larger mystery of how one

connected with Reality. Like the inexplicable, ineffable liberation I'd experienced on acid, my emergence from despair had ultimately depended on what religious people call the grace of God.

Not that external circumstances were irrelevant. Things might have been very different if it had not been for the sixties—and especially for rock-and-roll. Rock had been a major factor in my recovery; it had had the power to move me when almost nothing else did. I had been an ardent rock-and-roll fan in high school. (Sometimes I thought this was why my depression hadn't hit until I arrived at Barnard where—this was 1958—you were still supposed to dance to Lester Lanin.) But by the early sixties I had largely abandoned pop for folk music. Still, when Dylan released his first rock album, I was excited; I felt he had brought it all back home in more ways than one. After my marriage broke up in 1965, I started listening to AM radio again. The sixties renaissance had begun; the pop charts were dominated by the Beatles and Stones and their epigoni, by Motown and folk rock. My new lover was not only obsessed with the music but self-conscious about its cultural significance and its influence on our lives in a way that was new to me. I began to make my own connections. My first serious article was a long essay on Dylan.

Mike had once been a rock fan, but since becoming religious he had come to see rock as a drug, an escapist distraction. He also considered my writing a suspect activity; he and Dick Berger agreed that journalism, like traveling, was a way of observing life rather than participating in it.

"Do you think you would have gotten more out of being here if you had just come and gotten involved instead of having to think about your article?" Mike asked.

"I don't know," I said. "But if I hadn't decided to write an article I probably wouldn't have come."

Without the protection of my writer's role—my license to observe—I might not have had the courage to come. But more important, my overwhelming urge to write about a subject that touched every major issue in my life had routed a powerful impulse to repress, sit tight, let inertia take over; my decision to face up to my spiritual crisis was inseparable from my compulsion to observe and analyze it, to pursue every last connection. Anyway, writing was not just observing—it was sharing one's observations, a social act. It was also hard work. My identity as a writer might, as Reb Noach had suggested, be a prop for my ego, but it also had something to do with taking my work seriously. I had not begun thinking of myself as "a writer" until I had changed my attitude from "Right now I'm writing, maybe next year I'll study psychology" to "I'm going to stop playing games and commit myself to being the best writer I can be." Now, looking back on that change, I saw it as another crucial step toward happiness.

Clarity or death! Reb Noach insisted, and if there was one bit of clarity that emerged from all my confusion, it was the conviction that my happiness was not illusory. As I tried to explain that conviction to Mike, I felt suddenly disgusted with my current funk. No wonder Dick and Reb Noach thought I was unhappy. I was a mess. I had gained ten pounds and developed a cold. I was sleeping later and later. If I had a serious talk with someone it exhausted me so much I would run back to the security of Shimoni Street and take a nap. "When we act out of fear of pain, we're choosing death," Reb Noach was always saying. "The Torah says, 'Choose life!' " I had been running from the pain of uncertainty and conflict, had even thought, "I can't stand any more of this— I'm going to kill myself." How absurdly self-important!

Perhaps it was sheer determination to prove Mike wrong, but my mood slowly began to change. I began, finally, to respond to the beauty of Jerusalem, to the hills and the peculiar atmospheric sparkle I had noticed nowhere else. I felt as if I'd been let out of prison.

Passover was approaching. I had deliberately scheduled my trip so that I would be in Israel for the week-long holiday. The Passover Seder—which was supposed to be celebrated on each of the first two nights—was the one Jewish ritual my family regularly observed. Most years we had our Seders with my mother's sister's family; my uncle, who was observant though not Orthodox, presided at the ceremony. For the rest of us Passover was less a religious occasion than a family party, a spring version of Thanksgiving. Still, it was impossible to retell the Exodus story year after year and be unaffected by it. It was, after all, a story about escaping oppression for freedom, and I was fond of thinking of it in contemporary political and psychological terms; to me, the Seder's concluding invocation—"Next year in Jerusalem!"—expressed hope for both kinds of liberation. To Orthodox Jews, however, Passover meant something very different; as I had learned attending Lorie's classes, the traditional definition of the freedom the Exodus represented was a mirror image of my own.

Passover commemorates a historical event—the deliverance of the Jewish people from slavery in Egypt, the prelude to the revelation of the Torah. But for the religious Jew it is also an ongoing reality. The Haggadah (the account of the Exodus read at the Seder) says, "In every generation each individual is bound to regard himself as if he personally had gone forth from Egypt." According to tradition, Egypt represents materialism, hedonism, amorality. To relive the Exodus is to affirm one's liberation from bondage to the pharaoh within—the *yeitzer hara*—and one's readiness to live in true freedom, that is, under God's law. This theme is made concrete in the central symbol of Passover, the matzo—unleavened bread. Because the fleeing Jews did not have time to let their bread rise, it is forbidden during Passover to eat or possess bread or any food made with leaven; symbolically, leaven represents the expansion of the *yeitzer hara*.

Reb David, a young teacher at Aish HaTorah, and his wife Ruth had invited Mike and me for the first Seder. In the morning we went over to help with last-minute preparations. Ruth put me to work hemming her older son's new holiday pants. Later I played with the kids, who had been sent out on the porch with a bowl of nuts to crack. A week ago, their noise, mess, and bickering would have driven me further into myself; now I was actually having fun.

The Seder began around eight. The idea of the ceremony is to teach everyone—especially the children present—as much about the Exodus and its meaning as possible. Reb David went over each page of the Haggadah, asking questions, discussing various rabbis' interpretations, and by the time we reached the end of the first part—which we had to do before we could eat—it was almost midnight. After dinner we carried on for two more hours. The Seder ended—I had wondered about this beforehand—with the traditional words: "Next year in Jerusalem."

Later in the week, Mike and I were guests at the Weinbergs', along with several vacationing students of both sexes. I was very conscious of the *rebbetsen*, who seemed continually busy—though her admiring female guests competed with each other for jobs, there was always more to do—and continually serene. Occasionally one of the kids gave her a hard time, balking at some little chore. Long after the average parent would have been shrieking with frustration, the *rebbetsen* would calmly repeat her request—or else, with no visible resentment, she would do the task herself.

Feeling guilty about my own lack of patience and selflessness, a lack I was sure was obvious to everyone, I slinked around trying to be inconspicuous. Finally the *rebbetsen* cornered me.

"I think," she began, "that you think you have to hide your femininity to be taken seriously."

For a moment I was speechless. "Why do you think that?"

"Well, for instance, the way you dress. The way you wear your hair."

Oh, if that's all she means, I thought. She doesn't realize, I'm only looking this way because I've been depressed. I knew I had been neglecting my appearance. Most days I stuck my long hair under a scarf so I wouldn't have to bother with it, and I couldn't wear anything with a waistline because I'd gained so much weight.

On the other hand, the baggy dress I had on was actually quite fashionable in New York, and besides, since my normal jeans-and-T-shirt wardrobe was *halachically* unacceptable, what was I supposed to wear, and anyway, wasn't this the same old oppressive business of always judging a woman by her looks. . . . Nice try, but it won't do, I admitted. Face it: she's right.

The big lie of male supremacy is that women are less than fully human; the basic task of feminism is to expose that lie and fight it on every level. Yet for all my feminist militance, I was, it seemed, secretly afraid that the lie was true—that my humanity was hopelessly at odds with my ineluctably female sexuality—while the *rebbetsen*, staunch apostle of traditional femininity, did not appear to doubt for a moment that she could be both a woman and a serious person. Which was only superficially paradoxical, for if you were absolutely convinced that the Jewish woman's role was ordained by God, and that it was every bit as important spiritually as the man's, how could you believe the lie?

I was too much the product of Western libertarian values to travel the *rebbetsen*'s route to self-acceptance, and so far I had not succeeded in finding my own. I did, however, have an idea where to look. For me, the question of women's liberation was bound up with the question of sex itself. And one reason I could not accept Judaism was that I could not swallow the Jewish view of sex. Though Jews regarded sex as a gift of God, to be enjoyed under the proper conditions, the sexual drive, like all physical desires, was seen as destructive unless strictly controlled. Male sexuality was particularly suspect; it was assumed that men naturally sought to gratify a selfish, exploitative, insatiable lust totally divorced from love or social responsibility. I believed—with Wilhelm Reich, who had rejected Freud's contention that the sexual instincts were inherently antisocial—that alienated lust was not natural at all, but the aberration of a culture that viewed women as objects and the penis as an instrument of conquest and possession; I believed that when people were in touch with Reality the boundary between lust and love dissolved. And I believed that since women had not been conquerors, they were more likely to see the truth: that natural sexuality had nothing to do with conquest, that it required, on the contrary, a complete mutual surrender of egos. Sexually, it was men who were more estranged from their humanity; women who were closer to what we all must become. I knew the truth, had always known it—and it scared me to death. Which is why I had not yet been able to make the most important choices of all: to admit that surrender was not necessarily weakness; to stop trying to prove I could be as invulnerable as any man.

On my last night in Jerusalem I went back for a final visit with the Weinbergs. Reb Noach was talking to a young visitor named Ron. Ron was explaining that he had come to Israel to get his head straight, figure out what to do with his life. Did he want to take over his father's diamond-polishing business or what?

"Come to our yeshiva," Reb Noach said. "Find out what Judaism has to say about these questions. For instance, why are we here? What are we here for?"

"To serve God?"

"No. The world was created to give man pleasure. The Torah tells us how to get it. The Almighty didn't want us wandering around like chickens with their heads chopped off."

Ron was obviously interested, and Reb Noach began urging him to come to Aish HaTorah for a week.

"I can't," said Ron. "I've committed myself to work on my kibbutz till the end of July. And my girlfriend is there."

"Don't worry about the kibbutz. They can get someone to take your place. What are you there for? You won't find the answers to your questions on a kibbutz."

"I can't come now," said Ron. "But I promise in three months I'll be back."

"Come now," Reb Noach persisted. "Who knows what could happen in three months? A man should never say, 'When I have time I'll study.' "

"I can't," said Ron, "but my mind is really blown by your concern."

I made my good-byes. Reb Noach gave me some parting advice: "Jews say, whatever else you do, be happy. Even if you're a law-breaker, just fulfill that one commandment."

In the morning Mike went with me to the airport. We stood there awkwardly, unable to say most of what we felt. For the first time since this long trip had begun, I had the old flash that he was my male mirror image.

Judaism teaches the conventional patriarchal idea that men have more of a bent for abstract reasoning, women for intuitive under-standing. I believe that this split is social, not biological—that in a society where men rule and women nurture, it makes sense for men to develop their intellect at the expense of their emotions and for women to do the opposite. Still, I agree that although the difference is probably not innate, and certainly not absolute—I, for one, am more cerebral than most of the men I know—it does exist. And at the moment Mike and I were a study in contrasting male and female sensibilities. I was leaving Israel, with all the intel-lectual questions unresolved, because in the end I trusted my feel-ings and believed in acting on them. Though I might use logic as a weapon against uncertainty, I did not, finally, have Mike's faith that it would lead me to the truth.

Mike had been twenty-four when he became religious. I had been twenty-three when I came out of my deadly depression. It seemed to me that both changes represented the same basic deci-sion to be happy. But mine had been a purely intuitive decision, to allow myself to feel; his had presented itself as an intellectual decision, to go where his logic led. Perhaps our paths were equally valid. Perhaps not. As I kissed my brother good-bye, I still did not know whether my refusal to believe was healthy self-assertion or stubborn egotism; the Jews, the Bible tells us, are a stiff-necked people.

I arrived exhausted at Kennedy, retrieved my baggage, slogged through customs, and went outside to wait for my parents to pick me up. Only then did I allow myself a moment of enormous relief. I had made it after all. No crash, no bomb, no hijacker, no unexplained delay. I was here in New York, body and soul intact. And then I thought, so what? Suddenly I was quite unable to understand what I had been so anxious to come back to. The airport was bleak and sterile. The weather was unseasonably cold, and a freaky windstorm was making everyone run for cover. I huddled in the doorway of the terminal, watching the cars go by like an endless procession of anti-American clichés. When my parents drove up I felt another surge of relief, but on the way back to their house my confusion returned. Where did I belong? What did I want?

The following evening my father drove me home to my apartment in Manhattan. The windstorm had blown away the smog, and from the expressway we had an unusually clear view of the harbor and the skyline. It was dusk, the lights of the city were beginning to blink on, and I was seized with an almost religious tenderness for New York and its special beauty. Yet at the same time, staring at those glittering lights, I saw something else: the temptations of Egypt. My eyes filled, and I thought—groping for irony I could not quite reach—

> *How does it feel*
> *To be on your own*
> *With no direction home*
> *Like a complete unknown?*

1976

Permissions Acknowledgments

319

A NOTE ON THE TYPE

This book was set on the Linotype in Janson, a re-cutting made directly from type cast from matrices long thought to have been made by the Dutchman Anton Janson, who was a practicing type founder in Leipzig during the years 1668–87. However, it has been conclusively demonstrated that these types are actually the work of Nicholas Kis (1650–1702), a Hungarian, who most probably learned his trade from the master Dutch type founder Dirk Voskens. The type is an excellent example of the influential and sturdy Dutch types that prevailed in England up to the time William Caslon developed his own incomparable designs from them.

This book was composed by Maryland Linotype Composition Company, Inc., Baltimore, Maryland, and printed and bound by The Haddon Craftsmen, Inc., Scranton, Pennsylvania.